DISCOVERIES ON THE EARLY MODERN STAGE

This study of the action of discovery as plot device, visual motif and thematic trope on the early modern stage considers an important and popular performance convention in its cultural and religious contexts. Through close examination of a number of "discoveries" taken from a wide range of early modern plays, Leslie Thomson traverses several related disciplines, including theatre history, literary analysis, art history and the history of the religious practices that would have influenced Shakespeare and his contemporaries. Taking as its primary focus the performance of disguise-discoveries and discovery scenes, the analyses include considerations of how this particular device relates to genre, plot structure, language, imagery, themes and the manipulation of playgoer expectations. With strong reference to the visual arts, and an appendix that addresses the problem of how and where discovery scenes were performed, Thomson offers an innovative perspective on the staging and meaning of early modern drama.

LESLIE THOMSON is Professor Emeritus of English at the University of Toronto. She is co-author (with Alan C. Dessen) of *A Dictionary of Stage Directions in English Drama, 1580–1642* (Cambridge, 1999) and editor of *Anything for a Quiet Life* in *Thomas Middleton: The Collected Works* (2010). She has published articles on a range of topics related to early modern stage directions and staging.

DISCOVERIES ON THE EARLY MODERN STAGE

Contexts and Conventions

LESLIE THOMSON

University of Toronto

CAMBRIDGE
UNIVERSITY PRESS

CAMBRIDGE
UNIVERSITY PRESS

University Printing House, Cambridge CB2 8BS, United Kingdom

One Liberty Plaza, 20th Floor, New York, NY 10006, USA

477 Williamstown Road, Port Melbourne, VIC 3207, Australia

314-321, 3rd Floor, Plot 3, Splendor Forum, Jasola District Centre, New Delhi - 110025, India

79 Anson Road, #06-04/06, Singapore 079906

Cambridge University Press is part of the University of Cambridge.

It furthers the University's mission by disseminating knowledge in the pursuit of education, learning and research at the highest international levels of excellence.

www.cambridge.org
Information on this title: www.cambridge.org/9781108454360
DOI: 10.1017/9781108590488

First published 2018
First paperback edition 2020

A catalogue record for this publication is available from the British Library

ISBN 978-1-108-49447-2 Hardback
ISBN 978-1-108-45436-0 Paperback

Additional resources for this publication at http://www.cambridge.org/gb/academic/sub jects/literature/renaissance-and-early-modern-literature/discoveries-early-modern-stage-con texts-and-conventions?format=HB

To *Alan Dessen*

Contents

Figures

Acknowledgements

This book has taken a considerable time to write, and along the way I have had invaluable help in various forms. For always being interested and available with suggestions and support, I am especially grateful to Alan Dessen and to John Astington, who also found several of the pictures of discoveries included in the illustrations. Julian Bowsher, Tim Fitzpatrick, Robert Graves, Roslyn Knutson, Michael Neill, Lena Orlin and Valerie Wayne answered questions and offered encouragement. When Christopher Matusiak was my research assistant, he converted the raw data I had collected into a searchable database, which Rebecca Niles prepared for e-publication. Over the years I contributed papers on aspects of my topic at the Shakespeare Association of America meetings, often in the Theatre History seminars, and always received useful and perceptive comments. This project also benefited from the opportunity to present papers at the Blackfriars Conferences in Staunton, VA, and at the Centre for Reformation and Renaissance Studies at Victoria College, University of Toronto. At Cambridge University Press, Sarah Stanton gave me early encouragement, Emily Hockley was my extremely able and helpful editor, and Tim Mason provided patient advice and assistance. I also gratefully acknowledge the contributions of the Press's anonymous readers. My research was supported by a multi-year grant from the Social Sciences and Humanities Research Council of Canada and by a University of Toronto Research Completion Grant. Last but never least, among the reasons why I am grateful for and to my husband, Peter Blayney, is that he read the entire book and, as always, made suggestions that were too good to ignore.

Introduction

Discoveries on the Early Modern Stage

This is a study of the dramatic use, treatment and staging of performed "discoveries" – actions which the theatre is uniquely able to exploit visually and explore verbally. The motif of discovery – in the now almost obsolete sense of uncovering or disclosing – is prominent in the language and action of Elizabethan, Jacobean and Caroline plays. Visual discoveries are used repeatedly through the period by virtually every playwright, regardless of company or venue. These discoveries are of two different but related kinds: the *disguise-discovery* – the removal of a disguise to uncover identity; and the *discovery scene* – the opening of curtains or doors to reveal a place or the removal of a lid or cover to effect a disclosure. This is the first analysis of staged discoveries as such; in it I show how and why these actions are essential to the way a play dramatizes and explores such interrelated matters as deception, privacy, secrecy and truth; knowledge, justice and renewal. I also consider the symbolic quality of these performed revelations and how this element would have created or added to their meaning for playgoers whose mode of understanding had been at least partly conditioned by emblem books and other didactic art. Similarly, the idea of discovery is central to the language and imagery of Christianity, which would have both helped to determine the uses of dramatic discoveries and influenced playgoer responses to them.

On about 350 occasions in early modern plays a character's disguise is removed on stage; there are also roughly 260 times when a curtain or door is opened to discover a scene; and about thirty instances when a container such as a coffin or casket is opened to reveal the contents or another kind of small discovery occurs. To put it another way, about 330 plays by Shakespeare and his fellow playwrights include upwards of 640 performed discoveries of some kind. If nothing else, these numbers indicate that the business of discovery was popular with both playwrights and playgoers.

I

One reason is obvious: revelations make good theatre; but the kinds of discovery that were used and their effects within the plays suggest more specific reasons for the development and use of a convention with wide-ranging but related formal, thematic and theatrical functions.

The *OED* gives a number of definitions for *discover* and *discovery* that are now obsolete or rare, but are directly relevant here. In particular, early modern usages of *discover* in "Senses relating to the removal of a physical cover or covering" include: "To remove the covering (as a lid, clothing, etc.) from; to uncover; (sometimes) *spec.* to bare (one's head)" and "To unmask oneself, to take off one's disguise; to make oneself plainly visible."[1] And an especially relevant contemporary meaning of *discovery* was "The action of exposing or revealing something hidden or previously unseen or unknown; disclosure, revelation; exposition."[2] Furthermore, in early modern English translations of Aristotle, his concept of *anagnorisis* or *recognition* was defined as "a change from ignorance to knowledge"[3] and rendered as *discovery*, reflecting the idea of revelation. It is important to realize that when *discover* occurs in stage directions or dialogue to signal an action in plays by early modern playwrights, it is being used in one or more of these obsolete or rare senses.[4] At the same time, though, the action of uncovering or opening usually exposes something previously hidden and makes possible new knowledge or understanding: what today we would refer to as *a* discovery. My broad focus in this study is therefore both the physical action of discovery and its consequences in plays written for public performance between 1580 and 1642. But the primary emphasis is on those instances when the event has both formal and thematic significance; that is, when a discovery capitalizes on the inherent potential of the action to create and convey dramatic meaning.

Theatrical discoveries are complex events that use and connect sacred and secular ideas of truth and its revelation in a range of interrelated religious, cultural and political contexts. These contexts apply differently and to a greater or lesser extent depending on the kind of discovery and its location and function in a play, but these ideas can be seen as sources for or

---

[1] The second definition includes the note "Formerly also *intr.* in same sense (chiefly as a stage direction). Now *rare*." ("discover, v." *OED Online*, Oxford University Press, September 2016).

[2] "Discovery, n." *OED Online*, Oxford University Press. September 2016.

[3] Lily B. Campbell, *Scenes and Machines*, 68.

[4] With reference to Robert Greene (but applicable more generally), Reid Barbour notes that "Modern readers need one proviso if they are to understand the patterns of discovery. Greene's term refers to a mode of representation, not (as we might have it) to the act of the audience. For *discover*, the modern reader should substitute, more often than not, something akin to *reveal*, *uncover*, or *represent*" (*Deciphering Elizabethan Fiction*, 44).

concepts in the background of the action of discovery on the early modern stage. For playgoers of the period, these frames of reference helped to create expectations and satisfaction; but for modern readers and audiences they might barely register unless specifically called to their attention. The early modern business of discovery cannot be completely reproduced – or the experience recaptured – today; but the different instances of this explicitly non-realistic performance convention can tell us a lot about how and why it was used to create meaning. Insofar as is possible, therefore, my concerns in this study are the original conceptual and performance contexts in which the device was deployed. Moreover, my analyses are not detailed studies of the plays as wholes but are focused on how actions of discovery in the plays work both structurally and thematically.[5]

In his 1548 commentary on Aristotle's *Poetics*, Franciscus Robortellus observes that "Discovery occurs when we are led from ignorance to knowledge of some matter, out of which springs either grief or joy – nearly always joy, for Discoveries are, with good reason, placed in the last part of a comedy, where the disturbance in affairs begins to subside."[6] Indeed, whereas Aristotle had described *anagnorisis* and its effects in tragedy, by the time the discovery device came to be used on the early modern stage, it was more common in comedy and tragicomedy than in tragedy. In particular, fifth-act discoveries typically initiate the telling of truths crucial to the denouement, and for the most part those revelations make understanding and forgiveness possible.[7] This is especially apparent in tragicomedy when a figure who is revealed in the final act has been thought dead, so the action of discovery is what shifts the play from tragedy to comedy.

Matters to be considered when discussing the formal functions of physical discoveries in drama therefore include where in plots discoveries occur and how they help to determine a play's structure. Particularly significant is how often a discovery initiates a denouement, thereby dramatizing the satisfying idea that truth will be revealed in time. Certainly

---

[5] Many of these plays have of course been extensively analyzed from various different angles; but unless other discussions are directly relevant to points I am making about discoveries, I have generally not included references to them.

[6] Franciscus Robortellus, "On Comedy," 233.

[7] Plots that end with a revelation of truth are common in both Greek and Roman drama, and plots happily resolved by revelations are also a feature of Greek romance, with its formula of lost and found, which was later adopted and adapted by writers of novellas in both Italy and France. These earlier works certainly influenced the use of discoveries in early modern plays, but in classical drama the revelations are typically verbal, not physical, and prose romances might describe a physical discovery but do not – cannot – show it.

the thematic significance of discoveries frequently depends on the action as a revelation of truth, which can lead to further truths. In addition, the element of surprise encourages playgoers to be aware of discoveries as tools of the playwright's art, an aspect often emphasized by dialogue that uses the language of discovery. As explicitly visual events, these staged discoveries are inherently theatrical. Moreover, they are almost necessarily non-realistic, artificial, contrived actions that call attention to themselves as such. The element of "not in real life" is built into their meaning. This quality is often heightened by the presence of observers in the play with whom playgoers share the experience, while also being separate from it. These are moments of truth for both characters and playgoers, but the level and kind of awareness are different for each.

Discoveries in the Pictorial Arts

Discoveries are also a feature of the pictorial arts from the medieval to the early modern periods. Indeed, the discoveries in roughly contemporary works of art indicate a common awareness of how, by its nature, a visual medium invites emblematic representations of such moments of revelation, both sacred and secular. An early and basic trope is the exposure of Truth by Time. Not surprisingly, therefore, many of the discoveries in paintings and other visual media of this period are of events central to Christianity – especially the Annunciation, Nativity and Resurrection – and associated rites. Other works of art depict curtains drawn back to show events or places associated with secrecy, privacy or hidden knowledge, especially beds, studies, tombs and also anatomies.

The trope occurs in paintings, engravings and woodcuts; on title pages and in other book illustrations; in emblems and iconography. In these works of visual art as well as on the stage, discoveries heighten a viewer's awareness not only of the action of revelation, but also of what is discovered and of her- or himself as a viewer analogous to but separate from the figures watching in the play or work of art. The use of a discovery also implicitly creates a relationship between the author or artist and the viewer. Sometimes visual art includes a discovering figure, like a discoverer in a play; and when no such figure is present in a painting, the discoverer is implicitly the artist, and analogous to an invisible playwright who has engineered a revelation.

Because they are essentially visual experiences – for both characters and viewers – discoveries in plays have their full effect only in performance, so they have much in common with those in works of pictorial art. Plays can show both the discovery and responses to it, and although a painting presents only the moment of discovery, these moments can have an imagined "back-story," such as when the subject matter is mythological or Christian. Regardless of the context, moreover, discoveries in plays and visual art are always non-realistic, and usually have an allegorical or symbolic dimension. Whether the effect on the viewer is titillating or satisfying, discoveries in both media encapsulate a moment of revelation, sacred or secular. More particularly, discoveries in the two forms share some common motifs and themes, such as the association of light with both illumination and insight, or the relationship between time and truth.

I have included a number of illustrations, and have also provided links to additional images available online. An internet search will, of course, find one or more examples of all the images on various sites.[8]

Topics and Approaches

A governing premise of – and justification for – this study is that an understanding of how performed discoveries are used in early modern drama is fundamental to an appreciation of the degree to which the plays are artefacts of another era. Discoveries exemplify the essentially non-realistic mode of this drama and, in particular, highlight its medieval-Christian dimensions. One of my chief aims in focussing on the business of discovery, therefore, is to call attention to these pre-modern qualities and to how they relate to playwrights' use of the convention. Simply to list the many uses of disguise-discoveries and discovery scenes would not serve these purposes; only description and analysis can even begin to show how the discoveries *work*. Quotation of stage directions and dialogue is, I believe, the best way to show how discoveries of both kinds are prepared for, cued, performed and reacted to. But I am also very aware that summaries of action can be tedious to read, and I have tried to explain how the contexts I am providing are relevant to the particular aspect of the discovery convention I am discussing. It is perhaps significant, though, that my sometimes lengthy descriptions reflect the complexity of many plays with discovery plots and subplots. Indeed, this complexity might be one reason why many of the most complicated plays are also the most "early" and least "modern," and consequently are rarely read, edited or performed today. This problem is especially acute with disguise-discoveries, partly because what can be easily shown takes a lot of describing, and partly

---

[8] Notably, The Web Gallery of Art and Wikimedia Commons.

because we find it difficult to accept the premises that allowed disguise to flourish on the early modern stage. I nevertheless hope I have been successful more often than not in straddling the line between pertinence and excess.

Moreover, because my purpose is to examine and better understand the uses of a performance convention in plays written four centuries ago, I have concentrated on early modern contexts. I have not included interpretations or analyses that depend on or reflect later ways of seeing, nor, for the same reasons, have I considered how these actions are dealt with in modern productions. Instead I describe the pre-modern beliefs and perceptions that, I contend, influenced both how Shakespeare and his fellow play-wrights used discoveries to dramatize meaning and how playgoers might therefore have responded to those actions. I hope that my focus on the convention and its uses will act as a reminder that the plays in which it was so common are the products of an earlier time.

Chapter 1, "Kinds and Uses," is a survey of the two basic kinds of discovery in early modern drama: disguise-discoveries and discovery scenes,[9] including one-off or unusual examples. After providing statistics about usage, I outline the characteristics of each kind before turning to more detailed discussions with examples, first of disguise-discoveries then of discovery scenes, including what might be called discoveries-in-little. I then provide some examples of plays that include both kinds of discovery. With these contexts established, I then consider the formal, structural and therefore generic uses and effects of staged discoveries. Again, I provide statistics about where in a play discoveries are deployed and examples to illustrate my points.

Chapter 2, "Time and Truth," is the first of two chapters about early modern ideas and beliefs that would have been part of the conceptual framework that (I contend) is reflected in how playwrights used discoveries, and therefore would have influenced how playgoers responded to them. The basic idea that truth will be revealed in time and justice will prevail is central to the use of the device; indeed, a performed discovery is typically a literal manifestation of that belief. In this chapter I provide emblems and other non-dramatic illustrations of the interrelationship between time and truth (including anatomies

---

[9] I use this term in the absence of a better one, but in an early modern context it is anachronistic; the *OED* gives 1781 as the first instance of the phrase, by R. B. Sheridan, "One of the finest discovery-scenes I ever saw" (*The Critic*, iii. i). But he is referring to a scene in a play when the discovery of a relationship occurs, not to a literal, physical discovery. The phrase is not used again until the twentieth century ("discovery, n." *OED Online*, Oxford University Press, September 2016).

with liftable flaps), then turn to instances in plays where the idea underlies both the manner and matter of the action and, especially, the outcome.

In Chapter 3, "Religious Rites and Secular Spectacle," I discuss the Christmas and Easter rituals of the Catholic church – especially their use of curtains for revelations – as early versions of performed discoveries of truth. Again, non-dramatic instances in the pictorial arts and other media are pertinent. The discussion moves from discoveries in religious rites, to discoveries in medieval religious drama, to analogous instances in secular drama that seem to show the influence of the earlier uses. I then turn to the secular world of courtly masques and City pageants, with their more spectacular but not unrelated discoveries, and again consider analogous examples in plays.

In Chapter 4, "Revelation and Belief," I focus on theatrical discoveries that use the same language and imagery as that found in both religious and secular non-dramatic contexts, and which are often a feature of pictorial revelations. In particular, references to seeing on the one hand, and to light on the other, are combined in plays to signal, describe and react to discoveries. Often the result is an experience of surprise and recognition shared by observers both in the play and outside it. I provide a range of examples to show the different ways this imagery is used in dramatic language and action. I also consider how the use of property lights in discovery scenes might have been not only to symbolize illumination but also actually to provide it.

Chapter 5, "Private Places and Hidden Spaces," is concerned specifically with discovery scenes – those occasions when a curtain or door is opened to reveal certain locations, typically a study or other private space, such as a tomb, cave or tent. Shops are also discovered, but with somewhat different implications. My focus in this chapter is thematic: the relation-ships between ideas associated with such places in the real world and their staging as discoveries. Questions and theories about the staging of such discovery scenes are addressed in the Appendix.

In Chapter 6, "Invention and Artifice," I provide examples of some of the more complex and often explicitly metadramatic discoveries in early modern drama. This study does not consist of a continuous argument in which one point or chapter is contingent on the others; but the ideas I advance are interrelated and cumulative, so the examples in this chapter collectively serve as a conclusion. More generally each of the quite different discoveries included in this chapter illustrates how the business of performed revelations was developed and deployed to create or enhance and convey meaning.

At the end of each chapter I turn briefly to the basic fact underlying this study: all the discoveries that constitute my evidence were written for performance on an early modern stage. Both as a reminder of this context and as an encouragement to further studies, I offer some thoughts about how these original circumstances might have influenced or determined a playwright's use of the device; how the action itself could have been emphasized in performance, particularly in relation to the non-dramatic visual contexts that I describe; and how these elements would thus have affected the playgoers' understanding of what they saw and heard.[10]

In the Appendix I turn to the practical matter of how and where discovery scenes were staged. Today, most theatre historians agree that there was a "discovery space" – a term coined in the 1950s to refer to a large curtained opening in the centre of the tiring house wall. But (among other problems) there is no early modern term for such an opening, the Swan drawing does not show one, and the evidence adduced for one is weak. That discoveries were effected by opening a door or drawing a curtain is not the issue. They were, and they were almost certainly placed at or in the tiring house wall. But many of these scenes could have been staged in one of the two doorways (for the existence of which there is an abundance of supporting evidence). Other discoveries could have been staged by opening curtains hung temporarily in front of the tiring house wall.

I address this problem separately because it is largely unrelated to my ideas about the uses of discovery scenes – although if we knew how they were staged they would be easier to discuss, and how we imagine the staging of these discoveries will almost certainly influence how we interpret them. Nevertheless, I do not offer definitive answers because, in the absence of more and better evidence, they are simply not available. What I try to do is to provide a survey of the principal theories of recent years and an evaluation of their merits and demerits. In the context of these theories, I also offer my own speculations about staging possibilities and probabilities.

Quotations from all early modern works are from the earliest edition, with signatures provided in parentheses. Original spelling and punctuation are retained but i/j and v/u are modernized. Stage directions are reproduced in

---

[10] A searchable Excel database of the evidence I gathered and on which I based my analyses and conclusions is available on the CUP website, http://admin.cambridge.org/academic/subjects/litera ture/renaissance-and-early-modern-literature/discoveries-early-modern-stage-contexts-and-conven tions?format=HB.

italics, regardless of how they appear in the original text. Original italics in dialogue and non-dramatic works have been removed unless otherwise indicated. Quotations are from the STC- or Wing-number copy available on Early English Books Online (EEBO) and listed in Primary Works. When quoting from Shakespeare's First Folio, I use Hinman's through-line-numbers (TLN); if a manuscript play exists in a Malone Society edition, I cite its line numbers; so too with other modern editions of manuscript plays. Dates in parentheses after early modern works are of composition (certain or approximate); publication dates are given in the lists of Primary Works.

CHAPTER I

Kinds and Uses

Discoveries were a popular and useful early modern theatrical device, of which the essential element was the inherently visual action, idea and experience of revelation. When *discover* is used in a stage direction by Shakespeare and his contemporaries, it means what it says: something or someone is literally uncovered when either a disguise is removed or a curtain (or other means of concealment or enclosure) is opened to reveal what has been hidden from view. And these discoveries are almost always accompanied by dialogue that calls attention to the action and emphasizes what has been revealed and why it is significant. Despite these common denominators, however, the two kinds of theatrical discovery have essential differences that help to determine both how and where they are used in a plot. That is, although the action and effect of disguise-discoveries are basically similar wherever one occurs in a play, discovery scenes[1] can have various functions: while some are like the removal of a disguise in exposing truth, others show a location or actions that have connotations of privacy or secrecy.

Plays with one discovery often have another; sometimes several and sometimes of both kinds. Of the roughly 330 plays included in this study, 140 have only one discovery of either kind. About fifty-five plays have more than one disguise-discovery; about sixty-five have more than one discovery scene. And although disguise-discoveries and discovery scenes can consist of very different business, and can be put to quite different uses, it is worth noting that seventy-six plays include at least one discovery of each kind. All told, about 100 plays have three discoveries of one kind or the other, while about twenty have at least five.

---

[1] I use "discovery scene" to refer to any kind of staging event that includes the action of opening a curtain or door, or removing a cover or lid, to display or reveal something or someone (but not a disguise) to onstage characters or playgoers, or, as is most common, to both.

Kinds

Disguise-Discovery

By its nature, a literary convention provides writers with a set of implicit rules and practices that can be adapted to their particular purposes. In the case of the theatre, playwrights could draw on both verbal and visual conventions to create and convey meaning and to manipulate playgoer expectations and responses. Over the sixty years from the early 1580s to the closing of the theatres, the onstage discovery of a disguise was a convention that never grew stale because playwrights never stopped exploring and exploiting its possibilities while adhering to the basic elements: the performed removal of a physical disguise. Disguise-discoveries are used by over fifty playwrights between 1580 and 1642. The majority of such discoveries occur in the fifth act, but in some cases a disguise is removed earlier – although perhaps only to one other character who is sworn to secrecy, or perhaps only to the audience. Some plays include not one but several characters whose disguises are removed either serially or simultaneously; other plays have one character who has more than one disguise removed or has the same disguise removed more than once. When playgoers know of a disguise, they will almost automatically expect its removal, so when that happens on stage, it is particularly satisfying. Furthermore, in many cases the playwright uses the soliloquy, aside or other means to remind the audience of the disguise and prepare for its removal, and sometimes the discovery itself is foreshadowed. As noted above, though, sometimes playgoers do not know of a disguise, so its removal is a surprise even to them.

Disguise is a basic and ubiquitous element of early modern drama, which has been studied from various points of view; but disguises that are removed onstage have never been considered as a distinct category.[2] Nevertheless, some disguises are removed off stage and some on stage, to very different effect. In some cases the reasons might be partly practical: more complex costume changes need to be made off stage. But looking only at onstage removals of disguise makes it possible to see how playwrights used the action for reasons to do with structure, meaning and theatrical emphasis. When disguises that culminate in an onstage physical

---

[2] Victor Oscar Freeburg, *Disguise Plots in Elizabethan Drama*, refers only briefly to "undisguisings" and does not discuss them as a separate category. In *Disguise on the Early Modern Stage*, Peter Hyland has a chapter titled "'Tis I': Revelations," but he does not distinguish between disguises removed on and off stage.

discovery are the focus, it becomes apparent that the action is almost always a surprise. As such, it is almost necessarily a theatrical event that emphasizes the visual, even or especially when the action is accompanied by exclamatory and explanatory dialogue. As a theatrical device, the disguise-discovery is a means of highlighting a moment of realization or understanding for the characters and of fostering insights by playgoers. It leads to an awareness of the kind of the disguise, how and by whom it is removed, and the consequences of the act of revelation. Also important is whether or not playgoers know of the disguise and anticipate its removal. Of course, not all disguise-discoveries are exciting theatre or carry thematic weight; but the repeated and continuous use of the device through the period is significant in itself, and often – by Shakespeare and Middleton for example – it is deployed inventively and effectively. In the words of David Bevington:

> Unveiling, unmasking, and removal of disguise are all, on Shakespeare's stage, literal devices of discovery. Structurally they are often reserved for the climactic moment of *anagnorisis*. As such, these gestures serve at once to resolve the complications of the plot and to reveal hidden identity and motive.[3]

Despite the essential difference between disguises that are removed on stage and those that are not, both are of course versions of the same broader convention of character disguise so prevalent in early modern drama.[4] Rosalind Miles summarizes the complex uses to which playwrights of the time put the device:

> disguise has two primary and usually distinct modes in drama. On the one hand it is no more than a piece of plot mechanism, an unsophisticated constructional expedient; on the other, it is a technique whose potential fits it for poetic use, one rich in associations and levels of meaning. That is why what seems to be a rather naive dramaturgic device can rise to effects of surprising subtlety. So far from being imposed on or worked into the structure in a merely mechanical way, it is capable of functioning in ways that are symbolic of the work as a whole.[5]

Among the basic premises of the convention is that characters in disguise cannot be recognized, no matter how simple the new guise. Sometimes the disguise is in effect from a character's first appearance; sometimes the disguise is adopted after he or she has initially appeared *in propria persona*.

---

[3] David Bevington, *Action Is Eloquence*, 62.
[4] Hyland says, "In one form or another, disguise figures in a majority of the extant plays of the early theatre" (*Disguise on the Early Modern Stage*, 8).
[5] Rosalind Miles, *The Problem of "Measure for Measure*," 125.

For the most part, a change in appearance is all that is required to signal a disguise, a fact that emphasizes both the conventional element and the visual dimension. Sometimes stage directions clearly indicate the entrance of a character in disguise or describe the donning of a disguise. More often a stage direction hints that a character is in disguise with the use of "as," "for" or "like," or there is a direction or dialogue reference to a wig, veil, vizard or mask. In some plays, only the dialogue signals that a figure is in disguise. In others, a character appears in disguise from the beginning and even playgoers are kept in the dark. Indeed, while often the list of Dramatis Personae informs a reader of the disguise, in a few cases even the printed play, including speech-headings, keeps it a secret. At the end of a disguise, stage directions are even rarer, and when a disguise is removed on stage – my focus – often the only indications are in the dialogue, as exclamations of surprise and the use of signal-words such as "behold," "look," or "see." But sometimes even those cues are absent, and more oblique dialogue indicates that the character is no longer disguised – something a playgoer can immediately see but a reader cannot.

Searching for the evidence of a disguise and then for the circumstances of its removal made me aware of how frequently little or nothing indicates what a disguise consists of. In the absence of stage directions, this is especially relevant when it comes to the removal of a disguise, because it is difficult or impossible to know exactly what is taken off in the act of discovery. It seems fairly clear, however, that the action was often a grand but simple gesture of removing a cloak or hood, mask or veil, wig or cap, all of which are not just easy to put on and take off but also involve visual business to do so. Some common disguises seem to have required a more elaborate costume, such as a female character disguised as a servant or page, a male as an Amazon, or a nobleman as a shepherd; but the discovery could still have been simply but effectively achieved by removing a covering from the head or face. When a stage direction signals the action of discovery, certain verbs also suggest the nature of the disguise being removed: "plucks off" and "throws off" imply clothing, a head covering, even a moustache; "discover" can mean any of these and more.

When the discovery of a disguise occurs on stage, both the method of revelation and the performer of the action are important. In a visual medium, whether a disguise is removed by the figure wearing it or by another, or whether the exposure is willing or coerced, deliberate or accidental, are instant indications of relative power and agency. These dynamics are often emphasized when the discovery effects a change in gender or social status. When onstage discoveries are the focus, it becomes apparent that certain kinds of disguise are more or less likely to be given this treatment. In particular, whereas the female-to-male disguise is very common overall, often the removal of such a disguise occurs off stage, like Rosalind's in *As You Like It*. Certainly there are performed discoveries that reveal a character disguised as a male to be a female, but they are relatively few, and there are about the same number of instances when a man disguised as a woman is discovered. Not surprisingly, the onstage removal of any disguise is most often performed by a male character, but focusing on the action of discovery highlights how rarely a female character in female disguise performs it herself.

By definition, disguise is deception and involves a false appearance, of which playgoers might or might not be aware. In either case, the removal of a disguise almost necessarily dramatizes an ever-popular early modern theme: Miles observes that disguise is relevant "to any play seeking to dramatise the perennial gulf between outward appearance and inner reality, the eternal paradoxes of immortal aspiration and mortal weakness, of fallible humanity aping divine judgement, or the affirmation of tolerance and love in the face of malice and destructiveness."[6] Further to this, the disguise-discovery convention both relies on and calls attention to the artifice of theatre. Because disguise involves role-playing and costume change, it is implicitly or explicitly metadramatic. More particularly, it capitalizes on and dramatizes the paradox of deception leading to a revelation of truth. Disguises of which they are aware foster playgoers' willingness to believe, on the one hand, and their complicity on the other. When the discovery occurs onstage, therefore, the satisfaction for the playgoer is necessarily greater.

The fact of deception in a fallen world and the idea that truth will be revealed in time (the focus of Chapter 2) are very clearly combined in *Measure for Measure* (1604), and, as always with Shakespeare's use of a physical discovery, the potential of the action to dramatize meaning is capitalized on. The play's teleological structure is established with no small irony near the start, when the Duke tells Friar Thomas that he will adopt a disguise and secretly observe Angelo: "hence shall we see / If power change purpose: what our Seemers be" (TLN 345–6). This visual and verbal focus on deceptive appearance is further highlighted in the middle of the play when the Duke, still in disguise, asks rhetorically, "Oh, what

---

[6] Miles, *The Problem of "Measure for Measure,"* 126. Similarly, Hyland says disguise is "essentially anarchic, inverting systems and relationships, creating a distance between appearance and reality, turning the world upside down" (*Disguise on the Early Modern Stage*, 79).

may Man within him hide, / Though Angel on the outward side?" (TLN 1756–7), and again looks toward the play's conclusion: "So disguise shall by th' disguised / Pay with falsehood, false exacting, / And performe an olde contracting" (TLN 1765–7).[7] As noted above, playgoers' knowledge of a disguise almost inevitably encourages their engagement with the disguiser, and the Duke's Act 4 preparations further this sense of complicity while also creating anticipation of the denouement. When he says he will "keepe [Isabel] ignorant of her good, / To make her heavenly comforts of dispaire, / When it is least expected" (TLN 2195–7), he uses Christian allusions to describe the reversal that will be effected when the truth is revealed. But having hinted at a happy resolution, Shakespeare then complicates the process to suggest just how difficult it is to distinguish reality from appearance. In particular, he paradoxically introduces further deceptions and disguises as means of uncovering the truth. In preparing Isabella for her role in accusing Angelo, the Duke tells her she must dissemble "to vaile full purpose" (TLN 2328). Thus when she refutes Angelo's denial of her accusation with "truth is truth / To th' end of reckning" (TLN 2400–1), and tells the Duke, "let your reason serve / To make the truth appeare, where it seemes hid, / And hide the false seemes true" (TLN 2423–5), playgoers are invited to appreciate the ironic ambiguity. The imagery of both appearance and reality and truth-in-time inflects Isabella's prayer when the Duke rejects her accusation:

> Then oh you blessed Ministers above
> Keepe me in patience, and with ripened time
> Unfold the evill, which is heere wrapt up
> In countenance.   (TLN 2484–7)

This language of covering and uncovering is brought to dramatic life by the use of not just one but three disguises and discoveries at the play's end. Although the audience has known of the Duke's disguise as Friar from the start, when he removes – but then reassumes – it in Act 5, that awareness is emphasized, renewed. When Mariana enters, her face is hidden, probably by a veil, but playgoers know who it is. When a muffled figure is brought on, however, playgoers have only nine lines to wonder who it is before Claudio is revealed.[8] The mini-play that is Act 5 thus incorporates three

---

[7] The groundwork for the play's conclusion is laid several times in the penultimate act: TLN 1851–3, 2040–54, 2165–74, 2308–9.

[8] Susan Baker says that Claudio's disguise "exists only to be discarded. That is, the hiding exists only as a precondition for revelation, and the revelation is explicitly dialogic, explicitly designed to evoke a response" ("Personating Persons," 306).

different disguise conventions: the disguised ruler, disguised bride and the disguise of one thought dead. By 1604 these conventions would almost certainly have been recognized as such, and would have added to the self-conscious metatheatricality that is so much a part of the denouement, effected by a *tour de force* of three disguise-discoveries, each different but all linked in a structural and thematic sequence.

By using three staged discoveries, Shakespeare calls attention to who performs each revelation. Mariana refuses to reveal herself until Angelo "bids" her, "Let's see thy face" and she cues her own action: "now I will unmaske. / This is that face" (TLN 2577–9). Mariana's control over the removal of her disguise is immediately contrasted with what happens to the Duke as friar: Lucio says, "you must be hooded must you? show your knaves visage with a poxe to you: show your sheepe-biting face . . . Will't not off?" (TLN 2733–6) and pulls off the Duke's hood. Reassuming his true role, the Duke replies, "Thou art the first knave, that ere mad'st a Duke" (TLN 2737), which calls attention to how he temporarily lost the initiative. But he regains control and manages the final discovery, asking, "What muffeld fellow's that?" to which the Provost replies, "This is another prisoner that I sav'd, / Who should have di'd when Claudio lost his head, / As like almost to Claudio, as himselfe" (TLN 2885–8), and unmuffles him. Claudio has the least agency of the three, partly because here he is not so much a character as a symbol of the final truth that must be revealed to turn the play from tragedy to comedy.

I earlier noted how the device can be used to encourage playgoer engagement with the figure in disguise, as Shakespeare often does with the Duke in this play. But Shakespeare also prompts playgoers to distance themselves from the Duke with reminders that he – the playwright, not his character – is actually in charge of what happens. This occurs whenever the Duke loses control over the other characters, but it is made especially evident when Barnardine refuses to be executed and the Duke must find another head to disguise as Claudio's in order to save him. By introducing this complication Shakespeare prepares visually and verbally for the discoveries of the three living heads at the end. When planning to use Barnardine's head, the Duke says, "death's a great disguiser" (TLN 2040) and the Provost comments on the resemblance between Claudio and Ragozine. The dead man's head is thus a "seemer" that makes possible the play's final discovery of the truth that Claudio is alive, not dead.[9]

---

[9] Shakespeare seems to go out of his way to emphasize this when he has the Provost bring on the property head just long enough for it to be seen (TLN 2185–90).

Discovery Scenes

Discovery scenes are more various and complex than discoveries of disguises, especially with regard to staging. Probably no kind of scene in early modern drama has raised more questions about staging than those in which a curtain or door is opened to effect a revelation. But in the absence of clear pictorial or descriptive evidence, no amount of research and thought have so far produced definitive answers about how or where these scenes were staged. Indeed, it is often impossible to know even who opens the curtain or door to achieve the discovery. Perhaps another reason why we have not found satisfactory answers to questions about how discovery scenes were staged is that they were deployed in ways that we no longer fully realize or understand, because both the motivations for using a discovery scene and the methods of staging were directly related to their meaning in ways that are more medieval than modern. This is not to dismiss the fact that we cannot be certain how these scenes were staged, and I address the theories and problems in the Appendix; but where staging is concerned, the focus of this study is on how it might have been influenced or determined by ideas behind the action of revelation. To be sure, sometimes a direction to "*discover*" a figure or place (or both) can mean simply or primarily the action of opening a curtain (or door) to another space, but typically there is also the implication of revealing or exposing something hidden; that is, the staging was chosen for its thematic potential. In most cases the action and the characters' responses to it are indicated in some detail, helping to mark its importance. Furthermore, while it is certainly true that what playgoers saw would have been related to how a discovery scene was staged, many plays were performed in more than one type of venue – on the public and private stage, at court, in the provinces – so the staging would necessarily have varied even though, in the context of the play, the meaning of the action was the same.

Uncertainties related to the original staging prompt questions about why discovery scenes were used at all, and why certain kinds of scene are discovered whereas others that might have been similarly staged are not. In broad terms, discovery scenes typically occur when the plot calls for the revelation of figures and properties that are in a fictional location that is secret, private, contained or concealed. Sometimes the fiction also requires the representation of two separate groups, one of which is revealed to the other by the action of discovery. Such stagings would have introduced a kind of literalness that seems at odds with the early modern "unlocalized stage" on which dialogue could, and usually did, designate the main playing area as any place, interior or exterior, that the plot required. Furthermore, using a space that was actually semi-enclosed would have added to the staging requirements and doubtless created sightline problems. On the other hand, perhaps it was more practical to locate scenes that included sizeable properties in a segregated space behind a curtain. But regardless of exactly how or where a particular discovery scene was performed, the visible presence of a curtain in front of an upstage space could have been capitalized on to stimulate playgoer expectation of a discovery; that is, playgoers were probably conditioned by the use of curtains to anticipate a discovery (as a disguise prompted expectations of its removal). By their nature, staged revelations set up multiple levels of viewer, so that playgoers watch the characters who watch the discovery. That discovery scenes were used through the period by at least forty-five different playwrights suggests that there were reasons for doing so that countered any practical difficulties.

The classic and most common discovery scene occurs when a curtain or door is opened to reveal a particular location, usually occupied by pertinent properties and one or more figures. Sometimes the location is designated in the stage directions or dialogue as a study, cave, tomb or shop; but in other cases it is simply an unnamed space, unseen until the moment of revelation. Other discovery scenes involve beds, although often it is difficult to be sure if the bed is revealed behind a tiring house curtain or door, or if it is a curtained bed put out on stage. In either case, when a bed is discovered it is typically a place of privacy. That is, sometimes the discovered location is itself significant, other times not; but in all cases the action itself is important. The discovery and use of the space also ranges from the simple to the complex. Sometimes a figure is exposed by the opening of a curtain or door, those watching are surprised, and he or she comes forward onto the stage. More complex scenes have one or more figures, often with properties, who are revealed in a kind of tableau. In both, the emphasis is on the nature and surprise of the discovery. Some discovery scenes are accompanied by detailed descriptions and explanations, which raises the question of whether the playwright provided the information not only to emphasize the significance of the revelation but also to compensate for what playgoers might not have been able to see well or completely. That is, while the primary purpose of the discoverer's elaboration was determined by the plot, the secondary reason for it was the staging.

Even more than *Measure for Measure*, Chettle's *Hoffman* (1602) is an overtly metatheatrical play, with references to dramatic conventions along with action that embodies those conventions, in this case of revenge tragedy. So perhaps it is not surprising that the play includes several occasions when a discovery is followed by an exposition that seems intended to stop the action and call attention to the device being used, even as it highlights the theatrical artifice. Indeed, the first direction – "*strikes ope a curtaine where appeares a body*" (B1r) – establishes a presentational mode that continues through the play. More particularly, to start a play with a son drawing a curtain to display his dead father seems a deliberate reminder of the father who opens a curtain to display his dead son at the end of *The Spanish Tragedy* (see Chapter 2). If so, the allusion is ironic, because whereas Hieronimo is getting revenge for an innocent son illegally murdered, Hoffman Senior was a pirate, tried and legally executed.[10] In *Hoffman*, this first discovery is actually of the father's "anatomy" in a "cell" or "cave" (B3v, B2r, B3r) and the only onlookers are the playgoers.[11] As the scene progresses Lorrique enters and Hoffman begins a series of descriptive and explanatory speeches that explicate the significant details of the show he has arranged. Lorrique refers to "those bare bones" and Hoffman asks "Seest thou them trembling, slave heere were Armes? / That serv'd the troath lesse state of Luningberge" (B1v). When Hoffman learns that Lorrique is a follower of Otho, the prince of Lunenberg, he forces him to help murder his master. To gain Lorrique's sympathy Hoffman points again to the hanging skeleton: "He was my father" (B2r). Having enlisted Lorrique to join him in "villany" (B2r), Hoffman says, "Forbeare thy Lord is comming ile go in / And royally provide for such a Prince" (B2v), which almost certainly signals his closing of the curtains in front of the space where the skeleton hangs, in preparation for the next discovery. Otho arrives and Hoffman tells him that when his father was executed he vowed to remove the bones from the gallows to a tree, then he opens the curtains again to spring his surprise: "I kept mine oath: looke Luningberg; tis done / Behold a father hang'd up by his sonne" and Otho realizes the truth: "Oh horrible aspect murtherer stand off / I know thou meanst mee wronge" (B3v). Hoffman then gives an emotional description of what Otho, and the playgoer, see:

> My Lord behold these pretious twines of light
> Burnt out by day eclipst when as the sunne
> For shame obscur'd himselfe this deed was done

[10] See Fredson Bowers, *Elizabethan Revenge Tragedy*, 127.
[11] Michael Neill says that in this play, "where the revenger's apocalypse is emblematized in the recurrent 'discovery' of an anatomically displayed skeleton, the transformation of playhouse into anatomy theatre is made ... explicit" (*Issues of Death*, 136).

> Where none but schrich owles sung, thou receptacle
> thou organ of the soule;
> Rest, goe rest, and you most lovely Couplets
> Leggs and armes reside, for ever heere
> This is my last farewell.   (B3v–4r)

After Hoffman and Lorrique have murdered Otho by placing a burning crown on his head (the same way Hoffman Senior was executed), Hoffman again addresses the hanging bones: "This but the prologue to the'nsuing play, / The first step to revenge, this seane is donne / Father I offer thee thy murtherers sonne" (B4r–v). This combination of staging and theatrical references, which seems intended to heighten playgoer awareness of the conventions at work, is repeated at the end of the first act. Hoffman enters with Otho's bones, to which he speaks:

> Come image of bare death, joyne side, to side,
> With my long injur'd fathers naked bones;
> He was the prologue to a Tragedy,
> That if my destinies deny me not,
> Shall passe those of Thyestes, Tereus,
> Jocasta, or Duke Jasons jealous wife.   (C2v)

These references to famous tragic figures remind playgoers that Hoffman too is a part in a play, a fact emphasized when he closes the curtains over the hanging bones and builds anticipation for further shows to come: "So shut our stage up, there is one act done / Ended in Othos death; 'twas somewhat single; / Ile fill the other fuller" (C2v).

At the start of Act 4, "*open a curtaine*" reveals the "tombe" (G1r) where Lodowick and the Duke of Austria are buried. This was probably the same curtained space as the "cave" of Act 1, an ironic staging complemented by Hoffman's disguise as Otho, his first victim. Again acting as director, Hoffman tells the Duke of Prussia, "See Princely uncle the blacke dormitory, / Where Austria and Prince Lodowick are layd / On the cold bed of earth" (G1r). Act 5 returns to Hoffman's cave, where the Duke of Saxony and other searchers find Lucibella, who has been driven mad by the death of her father and husband. Her words imply that here she opens the curtains while describing what she is showing:

> Pray come, see my house
> I have a fine house now, and goodly knacks
> And gay apparrell; looke ye here, this is brave;
> And two leane porters starv'd for lacke of meat,
> Pray let goe mine armes, looke here they bee.   (I1r)

As Act 5 progresses it becomes apparent that the idea of just deserts governing so many dramatic plots in this period has determined this play's structure and confirming dialogue. By the last scene, Hoffman has been tricked by the Duchess, Otho's mother, into bringing her to the cave where her son died and where an ambush awaits. The staging of Hoffman's murder is uncertain because the text is very confused, but the Duchess says, "Looke with thy blood-shed eyes on these bare bones, / And tell me that which dead Lorrique confest / Who ist thou villained that least? who wast?" and Hoffman replies, "Why Otho thy sons, and that's my fathers by him" (L2r). This suggests that in the final moments this play's characteristic method of discovery and exposition is used once more to emphasize the plot's inevitable circularity.

In the category of "discovery scenes" I have also included about thirty occasions when a container is opened or a cover removed to effect a revelation – what I have referred to as *discoveries-in-little*. The container most often opened is a coffin, chest or trunk, almost always for the discovery of a figure who is miraculously alive, not dead. Examples include the "chest" (E3v) in *Pericles* (1608) that contains Thasia, alive, with a scroll telling of who she is and what has happened to her (see Chapter 4). Similarly, Armin's *The Two Maids of Moreclacke* (1606) has: "*They breake the Trunke open, and she sits up*" (G2r). In *The Knight of the Burning Pestle* (1607) Beaumont uses the device twice: first when Luce opens a coffin to find Jasper alive, then later when Jasper opens the same coffin to reveal a living Luce (see Chapter 6). And *The Costly Whore* (1620) has a body enter on a "hearse" and "covered" (G3v), then revealed to be alive (see Chapter 4).

Covers of other kinds are also removed for discoveries. As already noted, sometimes a veil is part of a disguise, but in a few cases one is likened to a curtain over a painting, an analogy made clear in the two examples from Shakespeare. In *Twelfth Night* (1601) Olivia cues her self-revelation to Cesario with "we will draw the Curtain and shew you the picture" (TLN 521); and in *Troilus and Cressida* (1601–2) Pandarus instructs his niece, "Come draw this curtaine, and lets see your picture" (F2r).[12] Fletcher's *Rule a Wife and Have a Wife* (1624) has a woman enter "*vail'd*" and one says, "Her Curtain opens, she is a pretty Gentlewoman" (A4r). An actual curtained picture is uncovered in Hemings's *The Fatal Contract* (1639), initiating a long interpretive description of what it depicts (see Chapter 6).

---

[12] See Chapter 4 for discussions of both the *Twelfth Night* and *Troilus and Cressida* scenes.

Other discoveries involve a variety of smaller properties, such as a casket, basket, dish or box which, like coffins, are opened to show something of importance to the plot. In *The Merchant of Venice* (1596) Shakespeare sets up three double discoveries when curtains are opened to reveal the caskets, which are themselves opened by the three suitors to learn their fates (see Chapter 4). In Middleton's *A Chaste Maid in Cheapside* (1613), when the Promoters lift the cover of the Country Wench's basket, expecting to find lamb, they find a living child (E1r; see Chapter 3). Heywood's *A Maidenhead Well Lost* (1633) provides a particularly telling example of how such discoveries often lead to justice. A serving man enters *"with a child in a covered Dish"* (H4r), which the Duke of Florence discovers, along with a message (see Chapter 3). An especially ironic use of the device involves a small prop in Kyd's *The Spanish Tragedy* (1585–7) when the boy, who has been told by Lorenzo not to look in a box, of course does so, only to find "heeres nothing but the bare emptie box" (F1v), thereby sharing his discovery with playgoers, who watch the ensuing scene knowing that Pedringano's expectation that he will be saved from hanging is equally empty. Near the end of Massinger's *The Renegado* (1624) the imprisoned Vitelli enters above with a *"Bak't-meat"* (M1r), which he breaks open to find instructions and a means of escape (see Chapter 6).

On several occasions a blindfold is removed to effect a kind of reverse discovery. Again, Shakespeare provides an example when, in *All's Well That Ends Well* (1602–3), Parolles's blindfold is removed and he sees the truth of his gulling and about himself (see Chapter 2). In Carlell's *The Fool Would Be a Favourite* (1637) a blindfolded figure has been told he is in a prison, but it is actually a room in a woman's grand house, so when *"they unvail him,"* he exclaims, "Amazement seizes me, is this a loathed Prison?" (D4r). The transition from spiritual blindness to insight is clear in the first dumb show of Dekker's *The Whore of Babylon* (1606) when figures enter *"having scarfes before their eyes"* until *"Trueth suddenly awakens"* and, together with Time, pulls *"the veiles from the Councellers eyes,"* at which *"they woundring a while, and seeming astonished at her brightnes, at length embrace Truth and Time"* (A3v; see Chapter 2).

Combinations

Repetition is one of a playwright's chief methods of creating and conveying meaning; it attunes the playgoer's eye and mind, prompting the perception of similarities and variations. So it is noteworthy that

a number of plays include two or more disguise-discoveries and/or discovery scenes that work structurally with the specific contexts and actions
as a form of dramatic emphasis, creating thematic links and helping to
convey meaning.

In Middleton's *The Family of Love* (1605) the first discovery requires
a trunk, in which Gerardine hides himself and is then brought to
Maria, who has been locked up by Glister, her guardian. Probably
a playgoer would have guessed the ruse and been amused rather than
surprised when "*Gerardine rising out of the Trunke, she seemes fearefull,
and flyes*" (D1r). The accompanying dialogue reassures Maria and the
playgoers:

GERARDINE	Feare not sweet wench! I am no apparition,
	But the firme substance of thy truest friend,
	Knowst thou me now?
MARIA	Gerardine my love?
	What unheard of accident presents
	Thy unexpected selfe, and gives my heart
	Matter of joy, mixt with astonishment. (D1r)

In order to woo Maria, Gerardine then disguises himself as a porter,
and in another discovery signalled by dialogue he reveals himself to
Dryfat:

DRIFAT	What? art thou a welch Carrier, or a Northern Landlord,
	thart so saucy.
GERARDINE	Ist possible sir, my disguise should so much foole your
	knowledge? how, a Northern Landlord? can you thinke I
	get my living by a bell and a Clackdish?
DRIFAT	By a bell and a Clackdish, how's that?
GERARDINE	Why by begging sir, know you me now?
DRIFAT	Ma. Gerardine, disguisd & a shore, nay then I smel a Rat. (F1v–2r)

Gerardine asks for Dryfat's help in freeing Maria from Glister and playgoers hear them plot to disguise themselves and accuse Glister of having got
Maria pregnant. Thus for the final trial scene, playgoers are aware that the
attorney is actually Dryfat and the judge is Gerardine – disguises that create
anticipation for the final revelations. Glister is told that the charges against
him will be dropped if he allows Maria to marry Gerardine. When he
agrees, Dryfat and Gerardine "*discover themselves*" (I3v) and all is well. Each
deception and subsequent discovery is contingent on the next in this play's
comic process.

Multiple discoveries are also essential to the structure and meaning of Jonson's *Volpone* (1606), a play in which different kinds of revelations occur through the plot in a linked sequence. Volpone's and the play's first speech cues the revelation of his treasure: "Open the shrine, that I may see my saint" (2P3v). No stage direction indicates exactly what Mosca opens – a curtain or door? a chest? – to effect this discovery; but whatever he does, Volpone probably repeats the action in the middle of the play, when, attempting to seduce Celia, he tells her, "See, behold, / What thou art queene of" (2S5r). In addition to these discovery scenes, *Volpone* includes the fifth-act removal of several disguises. Indeed, and significantly, the action progresses logically from Volpone's discovery of his gold at the start to his "uncasing" of himself in the final moments of Act 5. Before this happens, however, Jonson introduces the disguise-discoveries of Sir Politic Would-be and Peregrine in 5.4. First Peregrine enters, asking, "Am I enough disguis'd?" (2V4v); he then dupes Sir Politic into believing that his arrest is imminent, prompting Sir Politic to hide under a tortoise shell. The ridiculousness of this disguise is never in doubt, but is especially evident when "*They pul of the shel and discover him*" lying helpless. Having achieved his purpose, Peregrine says, "Now, Sir Poll, we are even" (2V5v), almost certainly cueing his removal of his own disguise. These two actions of discovery can be seen as ironic preparations for that of Volpone himself at the end (see Chapter 2).[13] Sir Politic, who has sunk to imitating an animal, is forcibly exposed; whereas Peregrine, who, like protagonists in other plays has disguised himself to expose folly, controls his own discovery, revealing himself only when the time is right.

Field's considerable experience as a player probably influenced his extensive and adept use of both kinds of discovery in *Amends for Ladies* (1611). As the play begins, Lady Honour, the "Maid," hears Ingen slandering women, so she rejects him and then is told he has married someone else. She next appears "*like an Irish foot-boy*" (D1v), supposedly Lady Honour's servant. Nothing explicitly tells playgoers that this is Lady Honour in disguise, but when she describes her mistress's distress she seems to be speaking for herself, which might have awakened their suspicions. This might have been confirmed when Ingen asks, "wherefore mournes thy Ladie?" and she responds, "Sir, you know, / And would to God I did not know my selfe" (D2r). There is no way to be sure, but since one purpose of Lady Honour's disguise is to investigate Ingen, it seems

---

[13] Jonas Barish refers to the "final unshelling of the tortoise, a parallel to the uncasing of the fox in the last scene" ("The Double Plot," 91).

likely that Field wanted to capitalize on an audience's awareness of the irony when Ingen describes the page as "the prettiest boy" (D1v). Another disguise is introduced when Ingen's brother enters "*like a woman maskt*" (D2v), pretending to be Ingen's wife. No hint, apparent or otherwise, indicates that this is a disguise, and certainly the disguised Lady Honour is completely fooled. The brother's disguise ends abruptly when Proudly blames Ingen for Lady Honour's disappearance and threatens to kill him. Proudly asks Ingen, "art thou not married?" and he answers, "No, behold, it is my yonger brother drest" and "*Plucks off his headtire*" (E1r). If playgoers have not known or guessed before now that Lady Honour is the footboy, her "*aside*" in response to this discovery makes it clear: "Oh doe not burst me joy, that modestie / Would let me show my selfe to finish all" (E1r). Then in Act 4 Proudly, still thinking that Ingen is holding Lady Honour captive, challenges him to a duel. When the footboy is wounded by Proudly, Ingen attacks him and the boy intervenes. This disguise ends when Ingen says, "Kind Boy, stand up, t'is for thy wound he bleeds" and the boy says, "Oh stay, my Lord, behold your sister heere" and "*discovers her selfe*" (G2v).

But although both men are relieved by the revelation, Proudly still insists that Lady Honour marry the old Count, not Ingen, and 5.2 begins with the entrance of the wedding procession, during which Ingen's brother gives Lady Honour a letter, and after reading it she collapses and asks to be taken to her bed. This initiates the next step in a long process of deception and revelation, when Ingen enters "*like a Doctor*" (H2v) to attend to Lady Honour. This final sequence also includes a discovery scene that is particularly noteworthy for how it is set up and performed. Ingen-as-doctor says, "I pray forbeare the chamber, noise does hurt her"; but rather than the others leaving, "*Exit Ingen, Parson shuts the doore*" (H2v), thus shutting out both wedding party and play-goers from Lady Honour's bedchamber. Those left on stage discuss what they saw while the door (or curtain) was closing – "Did you marke how she ey'de the Physition?"; "And when the Parson came to her, she turn'd away, / And still let the Physition hold her by the hand" (H2v) – so although there has been no indication that the doctor is Ingen, playgoers might make that connection now. Soon Proudly asks, "How fares she M[aste]r Doctor" then exclaims, "Z'oons, whats here" when he "*looks in at the window*" (H3r). All the others join him to "look in" and again the playgoer must rely on their comments, which make it clear that a marriage ceremony, and more, is being described. Feesimple says, "Looke, looke, the Parson joynes the Doctors hand & hers; now the

Do[ctor] kisses her by this light," then "Now goes his gowne off, hoy-day, he has read breeches on: Z'oones, the Physition is got o'th top of her, be like it is the mother she has, harke the bed creakes" (H3r). When Proudly realizes what is happening and tries to get in, he says, "S'hart, the doores fast, break 'em open." But Ingen's brother stops him, saying, "When they have done (whats fit) you shall not neede / To breake the doore, thei'l open it them selves," then "*A curtaine drawne, a bed discover'd, Ingen with his sword in his hand, and a Pistoll, the Ladie in a peticoate, the Parson*" (H3r). Faced with this discovery of the true situation, even Proudly finally accepts it, saying to Ingen, "Brother your hand, Lords may have projects still, / But there's a greater Lord, will have his will" (H3v). After this, the last disguise-discovery sequence is anticlimactic, even if it reinforces the idea that marriage is the reward of the clever. Thus the witless Feesimple, who has been tricked into disguising himself as a woman, is offered to the old Count as a replacement for Lady Honour. When the Count tries to kiss the masked Feesimple, he is surprised: "S'foot she has a beard: how now, my sonne?" and Feesimple "*unmasques*" (H4r).

In the much later *Love's Sacrifice* (1632) Ford included three clearly signalled discovery scenes and two disguise-discoveries. The play's main disguise is that of Roseilli, who is sent away from court and returns in 2.2 "*like a foole*" (E2r). In this role he is to serve the Duke's sister Fiormonda, which puts him in a position to overhear the plotting of other characters, report to his friend Fernando and speak to playgoers. He returns periodically in this disguise, each time speaking fool's gibberish to those he is deceiving but courtly language to those in on the deception. The direction that begins 5.3 – "*Enter Fiormonda, and Roseilli discovered*" (L1r) – could mean that he has removed his disguise before entering, but the dialogue suggests otherwise. His first words are "Wonder not, Madam, here behold the man / Whom your disdaine hath metamorphosed: / Thus long I have bin clouded in this shape" and she reacts with surprise: "Strange miracle!" (L1r). The play's other disguise-discovery is quite different, both from this one and from those in other plays. When three women realize that Ferentes has wooed and impregnated them all, they plot revenge. In a masque, with everyone in disguise, the three women "*suddenly fall upon him, and stab him*" (H1r); injured, Ferentes must repeatedly ask to be unmasked: "uncase me," "pull off my visor," "off with my visor," and again, "off with my visor," until the Duke orders, "Take his visor off" and "*They unmaske him*" (H1v). Both Roseilli's and Ferantes's disguise-discoveries show that there was still life in the device.

The three discovery scenes in *Love's Sacrifice* are each significant pieces of theatre that together create a meaningful sequence. Although married to the Duke, Bianca is attracted to Fernando and he to her. In 2.4 she enters and "*drawes a Curtaine, where Fernando is discovered in bed, sleeping*" (F1v). The next use of the device comes at the start of Act 5 when Fiormonda enters above, then "*A Curtaine drawne, below are discovered Biancha in her night attire, leaning on a Cushion at a Table, holding Fernando by the hand*" (I4r). Their love scene is cut short by the entrance of the Duke and others to arrest Fernando and, before the scene is over, to kill Bianca. The third in the sequence of discovery scenes occurs at the end, when "*The Tombe is discovered*" (L1v). A procession of mourners enters and kneels, and "*One goes to open the Tombe, out of which ariseth Fernando in his winding sheet, onely his face discovered*" (L1v).[14] Despite the winding sheet, Fernando is alive, but refuses to leave the tomb. When the Duke tells his guards to "drag him out" (L2r), Fernando drinks poison and dies, after which the Duke stabs himself "Thus on her altar" (i.e., the tomb; L2v) and also dies. I find it difficult to believe that such an important final scene would have been performed upstage in a partly enclosed space, but nothing in the text suggests otherwise. Certainly this third use of a discovery scene for key events in the Duke–Bianca–Fernando triangle obviously and satisfyingly conveys the inevitability of their mutual end.

It might be supposed that by the 1630s the discovery device would have run its course and degenerated to a tired and routine convention, but Massinger's *The Guardian* (1633) also provides clear evidence that such was not the case. This play's disguise-discoveries are performed by Adorio, who "*puls off*" (L7r) a mask worn by Mirtilla, expecting to find Calista. He asks, "How was this / Contriv'd? who help'd thee in the plot? discover" (L7r) and she reveals the truth. The eventual result is that the object of his affections changes from Calista to Mirtilla. Near the end of the play Alphonso, the king, is disguised as an old man until the moment is right and "*He discovers himself*" (N2r) to exclamations of surprise from all but Severino, who says, "Then I am lost," because he has supposedly killed Monteclaro. When the king tells Severino, "My doom's irrevocable," the disguised Monteclaro provides a way out:

---

[14] Together these details suggest that the "tomb" was to resemble "A monument erected to enclose or cover the body and preserve the memory of the dead; a sepulchral structure raised above the earth" ("tomb, n." *OED Online*, Oxford University Press, September 2016). Alan Dessen discusses the staging possibilities, from minimal to maximal (*Recovering Shakespeare's Theatrical Vocabulary*, 178–9).

MONTECLARO	Not dread Sir, if Monteclaro live.	
ALPHONSO	If? good Laval.	
MONTECLARO	He lives in him Sir, that you thought Laval.	
	Three years have not so altered me, but you may	
	Remember Monteclaro.	
DURAZZO	How.	
JOLANTE	My Brother.	
CALISTO	Uncle.	(N2v)

This final comic disguise-discovery helps to counter a mid-play discovery scene that is as bizarre in its action as it is complex in its concept and staging. The episode begins: "*Enter Jolante (with a rich banquet, and tapers) (in a chair, behind a curtain.)*" (K6v). Initially she can be heard speaking behind the curtain, but not seen. When Severino, her banished husband, enters he expects to find her lamenting his absence. Evidently he discovers her, because he asks, "What do I behold?" (K7r) and realizes that she is waiting to entertain another man. This is a classic discovery scene, set up by Massinger for the playgoer to look forward to and enjoy, in which the truth is revealed to the discoverer and a confession follows.

Uses Generic and Formal

Of the roughly 630 actions of discovery of both kinds (in about 335 plays), 299 (47 per cent) are in comedies, 134 (21 per cent) in tragedies, 60 (9 per cent) in histories, and 138 (22 per cent) in tragicomedies.[15] More particularly, comedies and tragicomedies together account for 69 per cent of all discovery actions. And of these uses of the device in comedies and tragicomedies, two-thirds are disguise-discoveries. Playwrights seem to have recognized that the removal of a disguise is essentially "comic" both as a physical action and in what it achieves. As such, the action is well suited to the conclusions of genres characterized by a final note of hope, as in the examples discussed above.

By definition, a performed revelation is the common denominator of all discoveries included in this study. Within this commonality, however, a main difference is determined by the point in a play at which a discovery occurs – in particular, whether or not it occurs in Act 5. Because, while many discoveries are pivotal in helping to determine plot structure,

---

[15] My evidence for the counts here and through this study is in my database, at http://admin.cam bridge.org/academic/subjects/literature/renaissance-and-early-modern-literature/discoveries-early -modern-stage-contexts-and-conventions?format=HB.

fifth-act discoveries usually have a specific function in relation to the denouement, in that what is revealed helps to determine how the play will end. Discoveries that occur in earlier acts, on the other hand, perform a range of different functions even as they share the defining trait of physically exposing someone or something. As I have noted, disguise-discoveries happen most often in the last act, whereas discovery scenes occur more regularly in all five acts, depending on what is being revealed and why. Some statistics convey the difference in where playwrights deployed the two kinds of discovery: of the total disguise-discoveries, 60 per cent are in Act 5, while 5 per cent are in Act 1, 6 per cent in Act 2, 9 per cent in Act 3 and 19 per cent in Act 4. Of the total discovery scenes, 21 per cent are in Act 1, 14 per cent in Act 2, 19 per cent in Act 3, 15 per cent in Act 4 and 31 per cent in Act 5. Note that while the most discovery scenes occur in Act 5 (almost a third of the total), the second highest number are found in Act 1 (21 per cent). To put it another way, whereas only 5 per cent of disguise-discoveries come in a first act, 21 per cent of discovery scenes are in a first act, often at the start of a play. Indeed, discovery scenes account for 77 per cent of all first-act discoveries of both kinds. Similarly, 14 per cent of all discovery scenes are in the second act, but these few are 64 per cent of all second-act discoveries. In act 3, discovery scenes account for 64 per cent of all such scenes, and these are 19 per cent of all discoveries. Act 4 discovery scenes are 15 per cent of that kind, but 41 per cent of all discoveries. As these figures indicate, far more than disguise-discoveries, discovery scenes are of different kinds and serve a variety of functions. Nevertheless, almost half (47 per cent) of *all* performed discoveries of both kinds occur in the final act of these plays.

The organization of almost any early modern play is sequential, but this is especially apparent when the action concludes with a performed, physical discovery. That is, the structure of plays with fifth-act discoveries is either implicitly or explicitly teleological: it is determined by a denouement that reveals truths, answers questions, ties up plot strands, and fulfils playgoer expectations. At the same time, earlier events and dialogue build anticipation for the discovery to come, prompting satisfaction when it occurs – whether the outcome is tragic, comic or tragicomic, justice (however harsh or equivocal) has been achieved. Some examples will help to illustrate these points.

The first words of *The London Prodigal* (1603–5) are from Old Flowerdale: "Brother from Venice, being thus disguisde, / I come to prove the humours of my sonne" (A2r). His disguise is not removed until this City comedy's final moments, toward which the intervening action inexorably leads. Disguised as a "Sayler come from Venice" (A3r), Old Flowerdale is not recognized by his thoroughly selfish prodigal son, whose movement through the play is charted by a series of dastardly deeds, until the end when two discoveries lead him to repent and reform. When Young Flowerdale marries Luce, then rejects her, Old Flowerdale provides her with "some strange disguise" (E3r) – that of "*a Dutch frow*" (F1v), with accent to match. But in an unusual plot twist, she is recognized by Delia: "Sister Luce, tis not your broken language, / Nor this same habit, can disguise your face / From I that know you: pray tell me, what means this?" Luce replies that she will keep her disguise "Untill I see, how time will bring to passe, / The desperate course, of Master Flowerdale" (F2v). These disguises and motives enlist playgoers on the side of Young Flowerdale's father and rejected wife, thereby building anticipation for his comeuppance. But the tone darkens considerably when the disguised Luce asks Young Flowerdale about his wife and he replies that not only has she spent all his money but she is dead. The plot strands finally come together when first Sir Lancelot accuses Luce and calls her a "trull" and she responds (*sans* accent),

> I am no trull, neither outlandish Frowe,
> Nor he, nor I shall to the prison goe:
> Know you me now? nay never stand amazed.
> Father I know I have offended you,
> And tho that dutie wills me bend my knees
> To you in dutie and obedience:
> Yet this wayes doe I turne, and to him yeeld
> My love, my dutie, and my humblenesse.   (G2v–3r)

Luce's self-discovery is accompanied by her choosing to shift her allegiance from her father to her husband, which brings about Young Flowerdale's vow of reform. But one figure is still in disguise, and only when Lancelot accuses Young Flowerdale of murdering his father does Old Flowerdale finally reveal himself: "Looke on me better, now my scarre is off. / Nere muse man at this metamorphosie."[16] In recognition, Lancelot says, "M.[aster] Flowerdale" and Young Flowerdale is finally moved to repentance: "My father, O I shame to looke on him. / Pardon, deare father, the follyes that are past" (G4r).

---

[16] It is unclear what Old Flowerdale means by his "scar" and perhaps it should be "scarf"; several disguises in other plays use a scarf (see Alan C. Dessen and Leslie Thomson, *A Dictionary of Stage Directions*, entry for *scarf*).

Early in Sharpham's comedy *The Fleer* (1606) there is "*Enter Signior Antifront disguised, called Fleire*" (C2v). As the dual names Antifront and Fleer indicate, Marston's Altofronto/Malevole is this figure's direct antecedent in the sub-genre of "disguised ruler" plots. As with the earlier play (discussed in Chapter 2), playgoers know of the disguise from its inception; but unlike Malevole, Fleer takes on two other disguises as the play progresses. His periodic asides also keep playgoers aware of the purpose of these disguises. When the play begins, Antifront has been defeated by Piso and leaves Florence to save himself and find his two daughters. At Fleer's first appearance in disguise, he has fled from Italy to England and is posing as a courtier seeking a place. His daughters have also fled to England, where they have decided to become whores to maintain their standard of living. Fleer, unrecognized by them, becomes a member of his daughters' household. Piso, the son of Antifront's usurper, also arrives in England and woos the elder daughter, who rejects him. Amid a series of interconnected love-intrigues, Piso and the daughters plot to poison two gallants. This initiates Antifront/Fleer's next disguise, as Jacomo, when he briefly takes over an apothecary's shop in order to sell the poison to Piso. In fact, as Fleer/Jacomo tells playgoers, the poison is actually a sleeping potion; but two men seem to be dead and Piso is arrested and brought to trial. At this point just into Act 5, Antifront/Fleer voices a plea for divine help that also reminds playgoers of his purposes: "My intent is good, O let it so succeede" (H1r). He then takes on yet another disguise, as a learned man or "doctor" (H3r), to be the judge at Piso's trial. He also arrests his own daughters and produces a letter written by Fleer as evidence of their guilt; they confess and plead for mercy. Then Piso, having received news that his father has died, also repents: "Let them call backe the banisht Signior Antifront whome they & we, and al have wrong'd: O could I liue but to inquire him out, in satisfaction of his wronges, ide marry his eldest Daughter, and whilst a liu'd a should be restored to his estate, but O hee's——." At this point comes the long-awaited discovery when "*Fleire showes himselfe to be Antifront*" and finishes Piso's sentence: "Heere my Lord" (H4v). These words begin the play's last speech, in which Antifront regains his position, reveals that the men supposedly poisoned are alive, and sets up five marriages in an ending of comic over-determination.

In *King Lear* (Q1608), Shakespeare uses the basic structure of an early disguise leading to a later discovery in such a way as to capitalize on playgoer expectations while also thwarting them to convey an important thematic idea. When Edgar adopts his disguise as Poor Tom in Scene 7, he

does so for self-protection, and his detailed description not only particu-
larizes the disguise but also indicates that it is chosen, deliberate:

> while I may scape,
> I will preserve my selfe, and am bethought
> To take the basest and most poorest shape,
> That ever penury in contempt of man,
> Brought neare to beast, my face ile grime with filth,
> Blanket my loynes, elfe all my haire with knots,
> And with presented nakedness outface,
> The wind, and persecution of the skie . . .
> That's something yet. Edgar I nothing am.[17]   (E3r)

In a play almost obsessed with seeing and blindness, appearance and
reality, a main character takes on a new appearance here and will do so
again when dressed in peasant's clothes,[18] and again when he enters with an
"outside" described by Edmund as "warlike" (L2r). This progression of
disguises is accompanied by soliloquies and asides that, as in other plays,
keep playgoers aware of the disguise and awaiting its discovery. But
Shakespeare uses this aspect of the convention to subvert the expectations
it creates as Edgar repeatedly resists revealing himself to his father. Indeed,
Edgar's asides begin only when he first sees his blind father and continue
only as long as they are together, repeatedly creating expectations about his
self-discovery to his father that playgoers never see and do not hear about
until after the fact. Edgar's desire to "preserve" himself trumps his pity for
his father, it seems. But Edgar's pragmatic disguises also make it possible
for him eventually to regain his identity. Between his pretended swordfight
with Edmund in Scene 6 and their duel in Scene 24, Edgar learns what he
needs to know to be ready to assume his social and familial roles. Still
disguised as a peasant, Edgar brings Albany the letter written by Gonerill to
Edmund that he found in Oswald's pocket; he says, "when time shall serve
let but the Herald cry, and ile appear againe" (K3v). That time soon comes,
and when Edgar enters to fight the duel he is not recognized – the Folio
stage direction says he is "*armed*" (TLN 3067), which must have included
a helmet and visor. After Edmund decides to fight him and is defeated,
Edgar finally discovers himself and in so doing regains, or reasserts, his
identity: "My name is Edgar, and thy fathers sonne" (L2r). Almost immediately Edgar tells how he "Never . . . reveald my selfe unto him, / Untill

---

[17] Note how Edgar's "I will preserve my selfe" anticipates Hermione saying she has "preserved /
My self" in *The Winter's Tale*, TLN 3337–40.
[18] The Old Man tells Edgar he will bring him "the best parrell" that he has (H3r).

some half houre past" (L2v), which did not prevent – and might even have caused – Gloucester's death. By juxtaposing a discovery playgoers see with one they do not see, Shakespeare exploited the conventions of the device to satisfy and to disappoint almost simultaneously.

The Heir (1620) includes a prefatory poem by Thomas Carew praising May's tragicomic plot in terms that highlight its teleological structure of "disclose[ure]":

> The whole plot doth like it selfe disclose
> Through the five Acts, as doth a Locke, that goes
> With letters, for till every one be knowne,
> The Lock's as fast as if you had found none. (A3r)

Indeed, the plot depends on a progressive series of physical discoveries of disguises, each of which reveals one truth – or provides one "letter" – that when combined with the rest makes possible the resolution – or opens the lock. Furthermore, while separately most of these discoveries are conventional in kind, purpose and execution, together they shape the seamless and coherent whole praised by Carew. But invention also finds a place, with one deception and revelation unlike the rest and on which the resolution of one plot element depends.

The play begins with Polymetes having spread the false news that his son, Eugenio, is dead in order to attract a rich suitor for his daughter, Leucothoe, the "heir" of the title. Next comes Franklin, who wants his daughter, Luce, to marry the old but rich Shallow, while she is in love with the young but poor Francisco who wants to marry her. Luce is also visibly pregnant, and although Shallow has never even touched her, Franklin is determined to convince him that the child is his so he will marry Luce. In Act 2, Philocles falls in love with Leucothoe at first sight, but his father, Euphues, and hers, Polymetes, are enemies. Also in the second act, the supposedly dead Eugenio enters disguised as a messenger to bring his father the news that he, Eugenio, is alive. The play's use of dramatic irony begins most obviously here, and is repeatedly deployed so as to make playgoers complicit with the deceptions and to build their anticipation of the revelations to come. Polymetes, of course, does not recognize the messenger as his son and, knowing that the news that his son is alive will effectively disinherit Leucothoe and end her chances of marrying the old, rich and greedy Virro, Polymetes swears the messenger to secrecy. The scene ends with a soliloquy by Eugenio in which his role as observer and potential intervener is established: "Thus in disguise I have discover'd all, / And found the cause of my reported death." He fears that his sister will reject the plan to marry her to Virro, but "how it succeedes / I shall perceive, and whilst unknowne I stay, / I cannot hurt the project, helpe I may" (D2r). In the other plot, Francisco tries to prevent the wedding of Luce and Shallow by getting them arrested for copulation before marriage. But Franklin, Luce's father, decides to pay "some needy Parson" (D3v) to marry Luce and Shallow despite the law.

Plot complications abound in Act 3. Polymetes learns that Leucothoe is in love with Philocles, his enemy's son. Eugenio, still in disguise, and Polymetes overhear Leucothoe and Philocles planning to flee and Polymetes sets up a plan to ambush them and murder Philocles to ensure that Leucothoe will marry Virro. But in another soliloquy Eugenio says he approves of Philocles and that marriage between him and his sister could effect reconciliation of the two families, so he plans to dissuade Virro. Eugenio, disguised as Irus, "a poore Scholler" (E3r), tells Virro that Leucothoe's brother is alive, so she is not Polymetes' heir. This prompts Virro to hire "Irus" to kill Eugenio; Irus agrees but asks Virro for a written contract. As if the dramatic irony were not heavy enough, when the fleeing Leucothoe and Philocles are captured by Polymetes and Philocles is arrested, Eugenio-as-Irus is put in charge of guarding Leucothoe; he contemplates revealing himself to his sister, but decides to wait.

As Act 4 begins, Francisco no sooner learns of Franklin's plan to force Luce to marry Shallow in secret, than Alphonso, Francisco's "old Captaine" (F2v), fortuitously appears and tells Francisco he has returned "that I may now disclose / Thy honourable birth." Francisco learns he is actually "the second sonne / To old Lord Euphues" (F3r) and named Lysandro. Armed with this knowledge, Francisco sets off to find Luce. In the parallel plot, Euphues the father and Philocles his son plead their cases before the king and against each other; when Leucothoe tries to intervene, she is noticed by the king, who is immediately attracted to her. After sending the others away, the king asks Leucothoe what she would do to save Philocles' life: "wilt thou lye with me?" (G1v). When she refuses, the king vows not to pardon Philocles. A further complication is added when the king regrets his vow but cannot escape it. Finally in the lead-up to the last act, Eugenio, still in disguise, gets himself arrested by confessing that he has poisoned Eugenio and that Virro hired him to do it, which he proves with the evidence of the written contract.

Act 5 starts with the entrance of "*Franklin, Shallow, Luce, Francisco in a Parsons habit, and a true Parson otherwise attyred*" (H1v). The marriage of Shallow and Luce by the disguised Francisco occurs offstage, but when the wedding party returns and Shallow claims that he is the father of Luce's child, Francisco "*discovers himselfe*" (H2r), thereby revealing that Luce and Shallow are not actually married. Then comes the play's innovative and unique discovery, cued by Francisco:

> But for the fault that she must answere for, or shame shee should endure in Court, behold her yet an untoucht Virgin, Cushion come forth, here signior Shallow, take your child unto you, make much of it, it may prove as wise as the father.   *He flings the Cushion at him.* (H2v)[19]

The appearance of this cushion is not only a surprise for both characters and playgoers, it also highlights the plot device and its attendant ironies. Indeed, without the cushion, there would have been no plot involving the pregnancy invented by Luce and Francisco so they can marry, a pregnancy that is believed by her father, who then manages to convince Shallow that he is the father, leading Francisco to disguise himself as a parson. For surprised playgoers, the very visibility of Luce's condition creates its seeming authenticity, while the complications of the plot confirm it.

Finally, just as Luce's angry father is telling her to "Take thy fortune, tis thine owne choise," Alphonso enters with Euphues and points to Francisco, saying, "Yonder he is my Lord, that's he in the Parsons / Habit, he is thus disguisd about the businesse I told you of / Lysandro, see your noble father" (H2v–3r).[20] Of course, Franklin now blesses the match and reconciles with Euphues. But one problem remains: the vow of the king to execute Philocles for the murder of Eugenio. A long trial scene ensues, near the end of which Eugenio finally "*discovers himselfe*" (I2r) to reveal that he has not been murdered. One of the judges remarks, "How suddenly this tragicke sceane is chang'd, / And turn'd to Comedy!" (I2r); but in fact, each revelation of truth connects to the next and without all of them occurring in the sequence they do, the "lock" of the prefatory poem would not have been opened.

Almost a decade later in *The Deserving Favourite* (1629) Carlell was still using the disguise-to-discovery formula as the basis for a plot in which deceptions progress to revelations of identity and truth that turn potential tragedy into comedy. In Act 2, Lysander and the Duke, both in love with Clarinda, have a swordfight that ends when the Duke falls, seemingly dead. In 4.1, the Duke enters in an unspecified disguise of which only the audience is aware. In Act 5, as Lysander is about to be executed for killing

---

[19] The only other play in which a cushion is discovered to end a fake pregnancy is Brome's *The Sparagus Garden*, L4r.

[20] This indicates that Francisco is still dressed as a parson, so probably when he discovered himself earlier he removed some kind of head or face covering, such as a hood or beard.

the Duke, the still-disguised Duke tries to intervene, but his insistence that Lysander is innocent is not accepted. Finally, a Hermit "*Discover[s]*" the Duke and the King says, "I am amaz'd; art thou a Conjurer, / And from the quiet grave hath raised / The beloved person of my Kinsman to delude me?" (Mɪv). When asked why he adopted the disguise, the Duke explains that he wanted to test the King's love of him and Clarinda's love of Lysander. Attention then turns to the play's confused romances, with the King giving permission for Lysander to marry Clarinda and the Duke to marry Cleonarda. But in asides these four make it clear that the pairings should now be Clarinda with the Duke and Cleonarda with Lysander. And when the Priest begins the wedding ceremony by asking Lysander if he will take Clarinda for his wife, the Hermit intervenes, telling Lysander to refuse "Because the Marriage is not lawfull" (M3r). When the Duke asks for evidence, the Hermit tells Lysander to send for the "little Cabinet" (M3r) his father left him. In a moment of discovery-within-discovery, the King opens the cabinet to find a paper telling Lysander that he cannot marry Clarinda because she is his sister. The King again asks the Hermit to "prove this to be true" and the Hermit responds, "Then Sir, behold a banisht man" and "*puls off his beard*" (M3v). The King's exclamation – "The Count Orsinio!" – and Lysander's "My Father! your blessing Sir" (M3v) tell playgoers the Hermit's true identity. But the process of revelations is not yet complete, and the Duke asks Orsino to "proceed unto your discovery" (M4r). This initiates an archetypal example of the kind of verbal truth-telling that often follows a physical discovery: Orsino confesses that when his wife could not produce a son, she arranged to steal Lysander, the son of Count Utrante (Clarinda's father), a truth she only told Orsino on her deathbed. This information leads, after a prolonged unwinding of other plot complications, to everyone accepting the marriages of Clarinda to the Duke and Cleonarda to Lysander. The King's concluding speech in praise of love emphasizes that all the pieces required for a comic resolution have fallen into place.

My chief purpose in this chapter has been both to provide an overview of the different kinds of discovery and to show how playwrights used them to shape a play and to serve generic purposes. But the examples I have described are also representative in other ways. In particular, the convo-luted complexity of some discovery plots typifies how the device often seems to have been deployed simply to entertain an audience. Not all discoveries have deeper meaning, nor do they necessarily benefit from close critical analysis. At the same time, however, all are relevant to studies of such topics as the kind of discovery, who makes it, what or who is discovered, how and why. Although I typically do not focus on the implications of these specifics of a discovery, the examples I discuss and the many more discoveries gathered in my online database are available for the detailed study of particulars.

Most discoveries, though, are not only visually effective and structurally necessary, but also thematically significant. As I collected examples and classified the different types of discoveries and their functions, I came to realize the degree to which they exist for reasons and work in ways that we are unlikely to register four centuries later. Indeed, I would argue that only with an awareness of the beliefs and expectations that early modern playgoers brought to the playhouse can we enter their world in our imaginations, and only then might we begin to grasp how Shakespeare and his contemporaries used discoveries to create and dramatize meaning, and to interpret what that meaning is.

CHAPTER 2

Time and Truth

Truth Is the Daughter of Time

In *The Spanish Tragedy* (1587), when Hieronimo and Isabella find Horatio's dead body, she expresses an idea central to the rest of the play: "The heavens are just, murder cannot be hid, / Time is the author both of truth and right, / And time will bring this treacherie to light" (D3v). This idea of "Time the Revealer" is proverbial – Tilley's collection of proverbs includes "Time brings the truth to light" and "Time reveals (discloses) all things."[1] The concept also has some well-known iterations and applications, including, from Shakespeare, "Times glorie is ... / To unmaske falsehood, and bring truth to light" and "Time shal unfould what pleated cunning hides, / Who covers faults, at last shame them derides."[2] Time is literally important when considering the use of discoveries in drama because an audience's experience of almost any play is sequential and chronological: a situation is developed, complicated, then resolved. This playgoer experience is therefore analogous to that of the characters, for whom events also occur in a cause-and-effect sequence until the conclusion. And when, as often happens, the resolution is made possible by a fifth-act discovery of an important truth, the audience shares in the experience of the well-known allegorical motto, *Veritas Filia Temporis* – "Truth Is the Daughter of Time."[3]

Moreover, for early modern playgoers the classical concept of *veritas filia temporis* would have had distinctly New Testament implications since, as Northrop Frye observes:

> The Greek word for revelation, *apocalypsis*, has the metaphorical sense of uncovering or taking a lid off, and similarly the word for truth, *aletheia*, begins with a negative particle which suggests that truth was originally

---

[1] Morris Palmer Tilley, *A Dictionary of the Proverbs in England in the Sixteenth and Seventeenth Centuries*, nos. 324 and 338.

[2] William Shakespeare, *Lucrece* (1594), G3v; *King Lear* (1608), B4v.   [3] Also in Tilley, no. 580.

thought of as also a kind of unveiling, a removal of the curtains of forgetfulness in the mind.[4]

And in Michael Neill's words:

> Apocalyptic thought imagines the End as a grand opening, a laying bare of all that has been hidden. The Gospels repeatedly look forward to such a moment – "For there is nothing covered, that shall not be revealed; neither hid, that shall not be known" (Luke 12: 2); and the New Testament's great book of the End (whose name is simply the latinized form of Apocalypse) takes the form of a visionary unveiling of the Discovery to come.[5]

The belief that in time truth will be revealed and justice achieved is essentially Christian and comic: out of disorder and confusion, order; out of deception and evil, good. This idea therefore also relies on the story of the Biblical Fall and its consequences: human fallibility and especially death.[6] Indeed, it might be said that death gives time its meaning. Although Time the Revealer is the dominant trope in plays with discoveries, it coexists with Time the Destroyer, for, as Shakespeare's Lucrece laments, "Time's glorie" is also "To ruinate proud buildings with thy howres, / And smeare with dust their glitring golden towrs" (G3v). The belief that truth will be revealed in time, set against the knowledge that time is limited, gives especially fifth-act discoveries their particular dramatic effect and significance. That is, while time is necessarily a factor in the structure and experience of all plays, in some the temporal limits are emphasized and capitalized on. In these plays the passing and processes of time are typically called to playgoers' attention before the literal culminating discovery. Such plays, like *The Spanish Tragedy*, are explicitly *about* the discovery of truth in time. They contain repeated reminders of the desire for truth and justice; impatience when plans are inhibited or delayed; early revelations that anticipate those at the conclusion; and signals that foreshadow the final revelations. The effect of such elements is not only to make the eventual discovery of truth the event for which playgoers wait, but also to make the wait itself part of the play's process and meaning.

Much of the creative work produced in the early modern period reflects the concomitant idea that only in the imagination and the art it creates can a return to the prelapsarian state be figured. The tension between the idea

---

[4] Northrop Frye, *The Great Code*, 135; and see Tibor Fabiny, "'Veritas Filia Temporis'," 65.

[5] Neill, *Issues of Death*, 42.

[6] The fact of time – of present and future – is central in the well-known passage from 1 Corinthians, 13.12, "For now we see through a glass, darkly; but then face to face; now I know in part; but then I shall know even as also I am known."

of perfection on the one hand and the fact of imperfection on the other –
between optimism and pessimism – is what gives these allegories of
revelation their special force, even today. Essential to the effect of plays
with culminating discoveries is that patience is rewarded: the wait is worth
it because the truth is finally revealed and justice is possible. Playgoers are
gratified, especially because they can experience vicariously through art
what seldom happens in life. Part of my point is that as a work of art a play
both exists in time and is timeless: the truth is discovered before the
performance time is up and it is discovered each time the play is performed – then, now, always. Furthermore, the use of a staged discovery to
reveal truth is an obvious contrivance that calls attention to its artificiality.
In one sense (*pace* Isabella), Kyd, not Time (or Hieronimo), is the "author"
who engineers the revelation of truth.

An awareness both of the possibilities created by time and of the limitations it places on the fulfilment of those possibilities is, ironically, ever-
present. But the medieval and early modern periods are notable for their
preoccupation with this fact of human life. Writers and especially artists
repeatedly explore both concepts – *veritas filia temporis* and *tempus edax
rerum* – in ways that vividly capture essential characteristics, assign certain
properties and delineate representative behaviours. In particular, the visual
and verbal imagery of Truth revealed by Time would have been familiar to
playgoers from emblem books, paintings and other visual media; thus they
provide an important context for this consideration of theatrical discoveries.
Studies by Fritz Saxl, Samuel Chew and others provide detailed analyses and
numerous examples of the idea and imagery of Time exposing Truth. Here
I shall focus primarily on pictorial representations of "Truth, the Daughter
of Time" that show Time either drawing Truth from a dark cave-like
opening or Time actually uncovering Truth.[7] To consider the performed
discoveries in plays in the context of these concepts and the emblems that
illustrate them is to become aware of analogies and possible influences. In the
emblems Time is an agent, whereas in the plays time is manifested in
a teleological structure, and disguise-to-discovery plots especially revolve
around the inherent and significant paradox that deception makes possible
the revelation of truth. And perhaps Truth's nakedness in many pictorial
representations is analogous to the true identity of a dramatic character,
revealed when a covering disguise is removed. More generally, these similarities between pictorial and performed discoveries are useful reminders of the
symbolic dimension of early modern staging.

---

[7] As in the painting by Charles Dauphin on the cover of this book.

What had begun in classical times as a secular, pagan concept with related images was appropriated first by Christianity and then, in the early modern period, by both Catholic and Protestant propagandists. As a result the versions and images with which playwrights would have been most familiar typically had a providential religious significance which sometimes also became political. But regardless of the particular uses to which the idea of Truth as the Daughter of Time is put, the many versions and wide dissemination of the imagery – both visual and verbal – would have made it well known and easily grasped.

The earliest extant English emblem book is a manuscript of 1566 by Thomas Palmer, "Two Hundred Poosees." In it Palmer gathers emblematic images from several continental sources and supplies English mottos and verses. The image Palmer used for Emblem 67, "Time trieth Truth," originated as the device of the Swiss printer Conrad Badius. Its first recorded use is on the title page of a New Testament in French, printed by Badius in 1554.[8] Badius used the same device on an English New Testament in 1557 (Figure 2.1). In this woodcut, Time with wings, scythe and hourglass draws naked Truth from a dark cave. When used by Badius on the vernacular New Testament, this image had implicit religious significance; but in Palmer's emblem book it is accompanied by a verse that begins by describing the image, then broadens and secularizes its implications:

> Beholde Time drawes his dawghter Truthe
>   oute of the hollowe hill,
> Where nawghtie men had kepte her close,
>   to cloke that they did ill.
> Tyme dothe discover hypocrites:
>   Time heretikes declares:
> Tyme utters sinfull murderers:
>   Time showeth nawghty wares:
> Tyme dothe disclose great robberyes:
>   Time catchethe those that steles:
> Tyme secret thinges dothe make appere:
>   all falshode Tyme reveles.[9]

Together, the woodcut and verse capture basic elements that recur more or less explicitly for a century in pictorial art and drama when discoveries are depicted or performed. The use of "behold" at the start of Palmer's verse draws a reader's attention in much the same way as

---

[8] *Le nouveau testament* (Geneva, 1554).   [9] Thomas Palmer, "Two Hundred Poosees," 72.

THE

NEVVE TESTA-

MENT OF OVR LORD IE-

fus Chrift.

Conferred diligently with the Greke, and beft ap-
proued tranflations.

VVith the arguments, afwel before the chapters, as for euery Boke
& Epiftle, alfo diuerfities of readings, and mofte proffitable
annotations of all harde places: wherunto is added a copi-
ous Table.

GOD BY TYME RESTORETH TRVTH

AND MAKETH HER VICTORIOVS.

AT GENEVA
Printed By Conrad Badius.
M. D. LVII.

Figure 2.1 Title page woodcut, *The Newe Testament*, Conrad Badius, 1557

when the word is used in a play to signal a discovery (see Chapter 4).
"Discover," "showeth" and "disclose" also emphasize the action of revelation. The final two lines express the main idea of uncovering hidden evils.

The "first English emblem book,"[10] and the one that seems to have had the most direct influence on English dramatists, is Geffrey Whitney's *A Choice of Emblemes and Other Devises* (1586). Whitney drew on a number of continental sources, and for many of his emblems he simply reproduced the motto and image and translated the verse; but although the emblems were not new, this was the first time they had been gathered and published in English. Emblem 4, *Veritas temporis filia,*[11] has a rather poor quality woodcut, again depicting Truth being drawn from a cave by Time, but with different additional details, described in Whitney's original verse:

> Three furies fell, which turne the worlde to ruthe,
> Both Envie, Strife, and Slaunder, heare appeare,
> In dungeon darke they longe inclosed truthe,
> But Time at lengthe, did loose his daughter deare,
>   And setts alofte, that sacred ladie brighte,
>   Whoe things longe hidd, reveales, and bringes to lighte.
>
> Thoughe strife make fier, thoughe Envie eate hir harte,
> The innocent though Slaunder rente, and spoile:
> Yet Time will comme, and take this ladies parte,
> And breake her bandes, and bring her foes to foile.
>   Dispaire not then, thoughe truthe be hidden ofte,
>   Bycause at length, shee shall bee sett alofte.   (A2v)

The complexity of the image is partly created by the inclusion of Envy, Strife and Slander, the three figures who, Whitney says, have hidden Truth. Two elements suggested by Palmer are explicit in Whitney's verse: the long time truth has been hidden and the contrast between the darkness of deception and the light of truth – an idea to which I shall return (see Chapter 4).

Badius's use of an image of Time discovering Truth on the title pages of New Testaments in French and English was probably intended to emphasize Protestant reliance on the scriptures that had been made accessible by printing in the vernacular. A similar image had been used earlier in William Marshall's *A Goodly Prymer in Englyshe* (Figure 2.2), first printed in 1535, thus coincident with Henry VIII's break with Rome.[12] The woodcut of Time drawing Truth

---

[10] Donald Gordon, "'Veritas Filia Temporis'," 236.

[11] Gordon notes that Whitney's source for this image is *Hadriani Junii Medici Emblemata* (Antwerp, 1565), emblem 53, page 59 ("'Veritas Filia Temporis'," 236). Whitney's verse is very different from Junius's.

[12] Dawn Massey says that although the motto "had already been associated with the Continental reformers," this is "its first known appearance in England as a political slogan" ("*Veritas filia Temporis,*" 147).

Figure 2.2 Frontispiece woodcut, *A Goodly Prymer in Englyshe*, William Marshall, 1535

out of a dark opening while Hypocrisy hovers overhead spitting venom depicts the liberation of Protestant Truth from Catholic captivity (π1v). The accompanying verse – "There is nothing covered, that shall not be revealed; and hid, that shall not be known" – is a version of Matthew 10.26.[13] The pairing of image and motto conveys how the two kinds of discovery – out of an enclosure and from under a cover – were seen as synonymous.

The obverse of pro-Protestantism was anti-Catholicism, and many contemporary works use *discovery* in their title to advertise exposés of Catholic sedition, treason, cozenage and hypocrisy. Examples include González de Montes's *A Discovery and playne Declaration of the sundry subtill practises of the Holy Inquisition of Spayne* (1569), which provides a step-by-step description of the Inquisition process. The same kind of thorough dissection is advertised by the title of and produced in Reginald Scot's, *The discoverie of witchcraft* (1584). The plot to overthrow Queen Elizabeth and replace her with Mary, Queen of Scots is reported in *A Discoverie of the Treasons Practised and Attempted against the Queenes Majestie and the Realme, by Francis Throckemorton* (1584). At the beginning of *A Briefe Discoverie of Doctor Allens seditious drifts* (1588), William Stanley writes "I thought it a thing verie necessarie, to discover and lay open to the world, the slye & subtile dealings of D. Allen in this pamphlet" (A4r). The continuing worry about the triple threat to England posed by Spain, Catholicism and Jesuits is evident in James Wadsworth's *The English Spanish pilgrime. Or, A new discoverie of Spanish popery, and Jesuiticall stratagems* (1629). The imagery of the dedication is familiar: "the worke is religiously disposed to the discovering of truth, and that all which are any whit inclined to the Sea of Rome, may see the vaile unmaskt wherewith they were hoodwinkt" (A3v).

In 1559, shortly after Elizabeth became queen, she made her official entrance into London in a procession that stopped periodically to view a series of allegorical pageants. At the Little Conduit, the figures of Truth and Time presented "the Bible in English" to the new monarch. The published description makes clear that, as in the two woodcuts discussed above, the Truth being freed is the word of God:

> In the middle between the said hills was made artificially one hollow place or cave, with [a] door and lock enclosed, out of the which, a little before the Queen's highness's coming thither, issued one personage whose name was *Time*, apparelled as an old man with a scythe in his hand, having wings artificially made, leading a personage of lesser stature than himself, which

---

[13] See also Luke 12.2. For discussions of this woodcut see Fritz Saxl, "Veritas Filia Temporis," 203–06 and Massey, "*Veritas filia temporis*," 147.

was finely and well apparelled, all clad in white silk, and directly over her head was set her name and title in Latin and English, *Temporis filia*, the Daughter of Time ... And on her breast was written her proper name, which was *Veritas*, Truth, who held a book in her hand upon the which was written *Verbum veritatis*, The Word of Truth.[14]

This pageant was almost certainly a direct allusion to the fact that Queen Mary, Elizabeth's Catholic predecessor, had used *veritas filia temporis* "for her personal device, for the legend on her crest, on the State seal of her reign, on her coins."[15] The book presented to Queen Elizabeth epitomized the battle between Catholics and Protestants to decide whose method of disseminating the Word would prevail: whether laymen would have direct access to the vernacular Bible or priests would act as intermediaries and interpreters.

Respublica, an allegorical interlude attributed to the Catholic Nicholas Udall, was written in the first year of Queen Mary's reign and performed at court in December 1553. It begins with a Prologue that first refers to vices that have "by cloked collusyon / And by counterfaicte Names, hidden theire abusion" (23–4) under Protestant monarchs, then gives the assurance that "tyme trieth all and tyme bringeth truth to lyght" and "veritee the daughter of sage old Father Tyme / Shewith all as yt ys bee ytt vertue or Cryme" (27, 33–4). In Act 3, Avarice, disguised as Policy, puts a negative slant on the same imagery when he says, "tyme hathe this one Ungracious propertee, / to blab at length and open all that he doothe see" (3.6.86–7). The penultimate scene features the long-expected confrontation between Avarice and Verity that again uses familiar imagery: when Avarice asks where she comes from, Verity responds, "I am sproong owte of the earth" and when Avarice doubts her, she says, "The booke saieth, *Veritas de terra orta est*" (5.9.50, 52; original italics). When Verity accuses her opponent – "Thowe calst thieselfe policie, and arte Averice" (65) – he denies it so she asks him, "what haste thow in thie bosome?" (70). A series of performed discoveries follows, initiated by Verity telling Avarice to "shewe ... foorth openlie ... that bag in thy bosome hid" and "come on, owte with ytt" (73–5). Once the bag has been discovered, she tells him to "Open yt" (81). When Avarice says it is "a bag of rie," Verity responds, "Lett vs see what Rye ytt is, poore it owte in haste" (85, 87, 90). After he has finally complied, Verity describes what has been revealed by using wordplay on "rye" that conveys how language as well as appearances can deceive:

[14] Germaine Warkentin, ed., *The Queen's Majesty's Passage*, 87–8; original italics.
[15] Fritz Saxl, "Veritas Filia Temporis," 207.

VERITEE   Thou saiest even trueth tis a bagg of Rye in dede,
              usiree, periuree, pitcheree, patcherie,
              pilferie, briberee, snatcherie, catcherie,
              Flatterie, Robberie, clowterie, botcherie,
              Troumperye, harlotrie, myserie, tretcherie.   (96–100)

But the dissembling of Avarice and the discoveries of Verity are not finished. When he claims to be "A plaine true deling manne that loveth not to [st]eale" (107), she tells him to "doe of thie gowne, and tourne the inside owtwarde" (109), which exposes the purses he has stolen. Then Verity addresses those with Avarice, saying, "Een suche like counterfaictes shall all the rest appere. / sirs doe of your utmoste robes eche one even heare. / Now what these are yee see plaine demonstration" (130–2), where-upon Authority, Reformation and Honesty reveal their true identities: Insolence, Oppression and Adulation. After all these discoveries Respublica reacts with surprise at how she has been deceived, and Verity, having fulfilled her function, turns the deceivers over to Nemesis for punishment. This mid-sixteenth-century play includes the opening of a container to show evils that have been hidden by deceptive language, as well as disguises effected by clothing that is removed to reveal the truth in time. Together these discoveries make possible a resolution in which Catholic good triumphs over Protestant evil.[16]

By contrast, fifty-three years later in *The Whore of Babylon* (1606), written and performed not long after the discovery of the Gunpowder Plot, Dekker incorporated the imagery and methods of emblems to cele-brate the period of Queen Elizabeth's reign from the death of Mary Tudor to the defeat of the Armada. This work's intertwined religious, political and historical themes are treated in ways reminiscent of the morality play, and its structure is explicitly one in which Time governs the eventual triumph of Truth. The play begins with a Prologue introducing a dumb show that encapsulates the events of the play and anticipates an outcome that playgoers already knew from history. In the show's initial discovery, Dekker reworked *veritas filia temporis* imagery to represent England under Mary:

> *He drawes a Curtaine, discovering Truth in sad abiliments; uncrownd: her haire disheveld, & sleeping on a Rock: Time (her father) attired likewise in black and al his properties (as Sithe, Howreglasse and Wings) of the same Cullor, using*

---

[16] Massey says that the play "locates the historical events of the early years of the English and Catholic Reformation within a providential narrative of religious struggle, culminating in Mary's accession to the throne" ("*Veritas filia Temporis*," 152).

all meanes to waken Truth, but not being able to doe it, he sits by her and mourns. (A3v)

This initial action is a reminder of how the discovery of Truth is often depicted in the visual arts, but a full appreciation of the imagery depends on an awareness of the contrasts between the conventional symbolism and the inversion described.[17] This dumb show also includes the funeral of Queen Mary, represented by a procession of recognizable symbols of Catholicism and its evils: *"Friers, Bishops, Cardinals before the Hearse of a Queen, after it Councellors, Pentioners & Ladies, al these last having scarfes before their eyes, the other singing in Latin"* (A3v). Then the imagery of the show's start returns in conventional form to represent the accession of Elizabeth as the return of Truth:

> *Trueth suddenly awakens, & beholding this sight, shews (with her father) arguments of Joy, and Exeunt, returning presently: Time being shifted into light Cullors, his properties likewise altred into silver, and Truth Crowned, (being cloathed in a robe spotted with Starres) meete the Hearse, and pulling the veiles from the Councellers eyes, they woundring a while, and seeming astonished at her brightnes, at length embrace Truth and Time, & depart with them.* (A3v)

The removal of the veils from the councilors' eyes is a nice use of the discovery device to emphasize the importance of right-seeing, which also helps to convey the "brightness" of Truth, often included in visual and verbal imagery related to the figure or idea (see Chapter 4).

The second and final section of the first dumb show allegorizes Queen Elizabeth as the defender of Truth, defeating the forces of Catholicism. It begins:

> *Enter Titania (the Farie Queene) attended with those Councellors, and other persons fitting her estate: Time and Truth meete her, presenting a Booke to her, which (kissing it) shee receives, and shewing it to those about her, they drawe out their swordes, (embracing Truth,) vowing to defend her and that booke.* (A3v)

This refers specifically to Queen Elizabeth's entry into London, the description of which Dekker evidently knew.[18] But this is only the beginning of Elizabeth's reign, and the last segment of the dumb show initiates the movement into the play proper:

---

[17] The ironies are quite specific since, as noted earlier, Queen Mary's motto was "Truth the daughter of Time." For an analysis of the religious and political implications of this play, see Massey, *"Veritas filia Temporis,"* 156–7.

[18] Dekker was also one of the creators of *The Magnificent Entertainment*, prepared for James's 1604 entry into London (see Marianne Riely, ed., *"The Whore of Babylon" by Thomas Dekker*, 28).

Truth then and Time are sent in, and returne presently, driving before them those Cardinals, Friers &c. (that came in before) with Images, Croziar staves &c. They gon, certaine grave learned men, that had beene banished, are brought in, and presented to Titania, who shewes to them the booke, which they receive with great signes of gladnesse, and Exeunt Omnes. (A3v)

The rest of the play is an always allegorical combination of dialogue interspersed with dumb shows that works to summarize and emblematize important events in Elizabeth's reign, culminating in the one that was the antithesis of the later Gunpowder Plot: the defeat of the Spanish Armada. But as the play also makes clear, the progress toward that earlier triumph was an uneven one, marked, for example, by a series of five attempts on Elizabeth's life. In the dumb show at the start of Act 4, the imagery of Time and Truth, deployed at the beginning of the play to represent the state of England under Catholicism, returns to convey these dangers: "*A cave suddenly breakes open, and out of it comes Falshood, (attir'd as Truth is) her face spotted, shee stickes up her banner on the top of the Cave; then with her foot in severall places strikes the earth*" and figures representing the five potential assassins rise as if from hell. But "*Time, Truth with her banner, and Plain-dealing enter & stand aloofe beholding all*" (G2v). This discovery is explicated in the ensuing dialogue, beginning with Time's words to Truth: "See there's the Cave, where that Hyena lurkes, / That counterfets thy voyce, and calles forth men / To their destruction" (G2v–3r). For part of 4.1, both Falsehood-as-Truth and Truth herself are on stage, providing a visual and emblematized contrast. Plain Dealing finally comments on how attractive false Truth once seemed to be, but "now shee is more ugly then a bawd." Truth responds "Shee look'd so then; fairnes it selfe doth cloth her / In mens eyes, till they see me, and then they loath her" (G3v). At the end of the play, Time is in charge of showing Titania the defeat of Babylon and its Empress – the final truth, as it were. He tells her, "Unseen you shall both see and heare these wonders. / On the greene Mount of Trueth" (K4v). The staging is not clearly described in the quarto, but as Marianne Riely notes, "The 'green mount of Truth' clearly implies the presence of Truth, no doubt holding her banner"; this is compared to the appearance of Falsehood-as-Truth at the start of Act 4.[19] While today this play might seem completely different from the relatively more realistic plays by even Dekker himself, its heightened, emblematic mode would have been easily understood by the playgoers for whom the play was written. Indeed, rather than emphasizing the difference between *The Whore of Babylon* and other

---

[19] Riely, ed., "*The Whore of Babylon*" *by Thomas Dekker*, note to 5.6.96sd.

contemporary plays, it is important to be aware that they all occupy the same spectrum of method and meaning.

An interest in writing about and depicting the "discovery" of truths concerning a range of subjects persisted through the period. Katharine Eisaman Maus notes how in many non-dramatic works:

> The epistemological utility of "discovery" goes far beyond narrowly religious applications. Renaissance philosophical treatises, how-to manuals, miscellanies, jokebooks, accounts of crimes and scandals: all typically create powerful motives for readerly attention by rehearsing distinctions between external falsity and internal truth – and by rehearsing them seeming to promise their erasure. They advertise themselves on their title pages as "brief discoveries," "anatomies," "displayings," and "detections."[20]

Perhaps, indeed, such works helped to cultivate both the fear of hidden threats and the comforting belief that they could be exposed. Certainly an awareness of the discrepancy between appearance and reality is especially acute at times of religious, political and social change, so it is not surprising to find playwrights also capitalizing on or simply reflecting it. The ten-year period from 1600 to 1609 is notable because it includes not only the upheaval caused by the death of Queen Elizabeth and accession of King James, but also a sequence of plots against the state. In 1603 there was the Bye Plot to kidnap James, followed by the Main Plot to replace him with Arabella Stuart. In early 1604 James banished all Jesuits and other Catholic priests and reimposed fines for recusancy. Then on 5 November 1605 the Gunpowder Plot was discovered when explosives were found under the House of Lords. This led to the search for Catholic priests in hidden rooms and secret passages in the houses of sympathizers; some priests were arrested in January 1606 when Hindip Hall was searched and they were found – literally discovered – in a hidden chamber or "priest hole." About eighty of the extant plays written during this ten-year period include ninety-two discovery scenes and eighty-one disguise-discoveries; this is 27 per cent of the seventy-two-year total, higher than for any other decade.[21]

The iconography of Time freeing or discovering Truth in a specifically evangelical context draws attention to how this imagery resembles or is echoed in representations of the Christian concept of Christ as Truth, an especially noteworthy expression of which is understood to be Psalm 85. 10–11: "Mercy and truth are met together; righteousness and peace have

---

[20] Katharine Eisaman Maus, *Inwardness and Theater in the English Renaissance*, 44.
[21] The thirteen years from 1630 to 1642 also have 27 per cent.

kissed each other. / Truth shall spring out of the earth; and righteousness shall look down from heaven."[22] The future tense of the psalm's second verse is a reminder that for Christians the New Testament was the inevitable – providential – completion of the Old. Saint Augustine asks rhetorically, "For what is the 'Old Testament' but a concealed form of the new? And what is the 'New Testament' but the revelation of the old?"[23] Christian typology rests on the idea that events of the New Testament are prefigured in the Old, and on the belief that God's providence will ultimately bring forth truth. Interestingly, the version of the Badius device on the 1557 New Testament title page discussed above is framed by a motto that gives the image this explicitly religious interpretation: "God by Tyme restoreth Truth / And maketh her victorious."

The dark opening from which Time frees Truth presupposes a door or cover that has previously prevented Truth's escape. As such it is analogous to the place revealed by opening a curtain or door in a theatrical discovery scene. Not all images of Time exposing Truth use the symbolism of a dark cave (or tomb?), however. Another iconographic motif depicts Time uncovering Truth, an action more like disguise-discoveries in plays. Examples include a simple drawing by Giulio Mazzoni showing Time and another figure unveiling Truth,[24] and a complex allegorical painting by Jean-François de Troy (Figure 2.3) in which Time, with wings and scythe, unveils Truth, who, in turn, unmasks Fraud; the four Cardinal Virtues kneel before Truth, representing the Christian values she embodies.[25] In the first and earlier of these images, Truth is naked; but in the second and later one, she is partially clothed and the unveiling is quite like the removal of a disguise.

Other artists develop the imagery further by depicting Truth and Time jointly lifting a veil or drawing a curtain. That such discoveries are both by and of truth seems not to have been a problem, and certainly de Troy's version presents Truth as an active participant rather than as passively waiting for release by Time. Moreover, a figure of Truth who has agency is much more like a "good" figure in a play who chooses to both take on a disguise and remove it, or who draws a curtain when the time is right. The title page of Michael Sparke's *The Narrative History of King James, for the*

---

[22] And see the discussion of Figure 3.6 in the next chapter.

[23] Augustine, *City of God*, trans. and ed. by Henry Betteson, Book 16, chapter 26, p. 687. Translations vary, but the basic imagery of concealment and revelation is consistent.

[24] British Museum collection, no. T,11.75.

[25] This description is from the National Gallery website, nationalgallery.org.uk/paintings/jean -francois-detroy-time-unveiling-truth.

Figure 2.3 *Allegory of Time Unveiling Truth*, Jean-François de Troy, 1733

First Fourteen Years, more commonly known as *Truth brought to light and discovered by Time* (π2r; Figure 2.4), shows Time on the right and Truth on the left, each holding open a curtain to discover the dead King James. On the opposite page the first two stanzas of an explanatory verse provide details:

> Triumphant Truth trampling on Errour base,
> With one Hand hidden Secrets doth uncase;
> With t'other drawes the Curtain, shews in King James,
> That Death, Kings, Crowns, Scepters, and all things tames;
> Expressed by this dead Kings posture, right,
> Who Dead, all Regal Ornaments doth flight.
>
> One th'other side All-Conquering Time doth stand,
> A Watchfull Sentinel, and with his Hand
> Draws back the other Curtain, to descrie,

Figure 2.4 Title page, *Truth brought to light and discovered by Time* (Michael
Sparke), engraved by John Droeshout, 1651

That Princes must as well as Pesants die;
And helps t'uncover Secrets covered long,
And under's feet tramples on Death most strong.   (π1v)

The main purpose of this retrospective work is to reveal the secret details of events in James's reign, especially the murder of Thomas Overbury. But these lines also describe how Time and Truth combine to reveal the ultimate truth of time: death.

Middleton's *A Game at Chess* (1624) is *sui generis* even in how it incorporates and uses discoveries. The play's Induction begins with the discovery of Ignatius with Error, asleep.[26] In this initial discovery Ignatius symbolizes Catholicism, and the sleeping Error is Ignorance. As the play progresses, it dramatizes a process in which the evil forces of Catholic deception, represented by the Black House, are defeated by the White House, the good of Protestant Truth. Indeed, as Roussel Sargent notes, "a close look at the play soon reveals that the word *discovery* is used constantly and that a number of 'discoveries' are made during the course of its action; the denouement is merely the most noticeable example of what proves to be a theme."[27] In Act 3 the Black Knight says of the White King's Pawn, "The whitenesse upon him is but the leaprosy / Of pure dissemulation: view him now, / His heart and his intents are of our colour" (F3v).[28] This cues a discovery that emphasizes the black side's control at this point in the game and the play: "*His upper garment being taken off, he appeares blacke under*" (F3v). This revelation prompts the Fat Bishop to comment,

> Is there so much amazement spent on him
> That's but halfe black, there might be hope of that man
> But how will this house wonder, if I stand forth
> And shew a whole one, instantly discover
> One that's all blacke where ther's no hope at all.   (F4r)

When the White King says, "I long for thy discovery," the Fat Bishop replies:

> Looke no farther then,
> Beare witnesse all the house I am the man,
> And turne my self into the blacke house freely,
> I am of this side now.   (F4r)

---

[26] Differently worded directions indicate the same staging: "*Enter Ignatius (discovering Errour sleeping.)*" (STC 17884; A3r); "*Ignatius Loyola appearing, Error at his feete as asleepe*" (STC 17885; B1r). Gary Taylor's gloss for "*appearing*" is "perhaps rising through a trapdoor, as if coming from hell" (*A Game at Chess: A Later Form*, Induction.0.2 note); but no other other stage directions for a figure to "appear" indicate rising from the trap, whereas a number of directions use the term to indicate a discovery (see Dessen and Thomson, *A Dictionary of Stage Directions*, entry for *appear*).

[27] Roussel Sargent, "Theme and Structure in Middleton's *A Game at Chess*," 726. Sargent summarizes the play's discoveries, including those made by dialogue only.

[28] Quotations are from STC 17885.

To my knowledge, no editor even speculates about whether those words cue a physical discovery in which the Fat Bishop also removes his white robes to show the black underneath;[29] but the language certainly invites that inference and a performed discovery would more effectively make the thematic point about deceptive appearances. To put it another way, why would or should it *not* be a physical discovery?

The game is over when the Black House essentially defeats itself: the Black Knight brags that "What we have done, has bin dissemblance ever" and the White Knight replies, "There you lye then: / And the Games ours, wee give the checke mate / By discovery, King the noblest mate of all" (K3r–v). But then the White King says, "Tis their best course that so hath lost their fame, / To put their heads into the bag for shame; / And there behold the bags mouth (like hell) opens" (K3v). Possibly this "bag" is the trap; but this reference to a "mouth" like "hell" in a theatrical context recalls morality-play imagery of a hell-mouth devouring sinners.[30] Furthermore, given the discoveries of the Catholic Black House figures at the start of the play and in the altar scene, it would be thematically and dramatically fitting for the action to end with a kind of reverse discovery that uses the same location – probably an upstage curtained opening. As the play is ending with the triumph of the good, the White King cues a reversal of the conventional action, so that rather than truth being discovered, duplicity is consigned to oblivion in the "bag":

> So let the Bagge close now (the fittest wombe
> For Treachery, Pride and Falshoold, whilst we, winner like)
> Destroying through Heavens power, what would destroy;
> Welcome our white Knight with loud peales of Joy.   (K4r)

The appropriation of the discovery motif for anti-Catholic propaganda is also evident in two engravings of Queen Elizabeth that depend for their effect on the viewers' awareness of what they allude to. A knowledge of Titian's *Diana and Callisto* is necessary to appreciate fully its parody by Pieter van der Heyden in *Queen Elizabeth and Pope*

---

[29] Gary Taylor adds a direction: "*Fat Bishop of Spalato crosses to the Black House*" (*A Game at Chess: A Later Form*, 3.1.291.1 note).

[30] Both T. H. Howard-Hill (*A Game at Chess*, 5.3.179 note) and Taylor (*A Game at Chess: A Later Form*, 5.1.178.1 note) suggest that the trap is used for the bag. But a Spaniard who saw a performance reported that "he who acted the Prince of Wales heartily beat and kicked the 'Count of Gondomar' into Hell, which consisted of a great hole and hideous figures" (Howard-Hill, ed., *A Game at Chess*, App. I, 195); this playgoer's ability to see these figures indicates that they were in a "bag" or opening on the stage, not below stage in the trap.

Figure 2.5 *Queen Elizabeth as Diana with Time and Truth disclosing the pregnancy of Pope Gregory XIII as Callisto*, Pieter van der Heyden, c. 1584

Gregory XIII as Diana and Callisto (Figure 2.5). In this "Anti-Catholic satire with Queen Elizabeth as Diana, seated in judgment upon the Pope as Calisto":

> Elizabeth, naked, is seated to [the] right holding a shield with the coat of arms of England and surrounded by nymphs representing the pro-testant powers of Europe; to [the] left, Pope Gregory XIII is stripped by [the] allegorical figures of Time and Truth. Beneath the pope are large eggs, one of which has an inscription referring to the assassination of William the Silent by Baltasar Gérard in 1584, another carries the name of Chiappino Vitelli, the general in the service of Spain who came to England in 1569 in an attempt to negotiate peace; from others hatch creatures including a cockatrice labelled "Inquisition."[31]

[31] This description is from the British Museum Collection online (item 1850,1109.7) www .britishmuseum.org/research/collection_online/collection_object_details.aspx?objectId=1450180& partId=1&searchText=queen+elizabeth+and+pope+gregory&page=1; see also Saxl, "Veritas Filia

In more generally applicable terms, "The Pope's shame is being revealed by the Reformation allegories of Time and Truth" in "a gesture of exposure, an act of discovery, which lifts the robes of propriety to reveal the obscenity beneath."[32]

The Time–Truth relationship is also a feature of Thomas Cecil's engraving, labelled *Elizabetha Angliae et Hiberniae Reginae &c* (1625). It shows Queen Elizabeth as Saint George, on horseback and trampling a seven-headed hydra as, just in time, she is handed a lance by the figure who comes from a cave holding a book inscribed "Truth." In the background is the Armada and army at Tilbury.[33] Both engravings involve complex allusions and require sophisticated viewers, but at the heart of each is that old idea: *Veritas filia Temporis.*

In *The Spanish Tragedy*, Kyd used both the verbal and visual to prepare for the play's famous final discovery. Indeed, this play is probably more explicitly about the discovery of truth in time than any other discussed in this study. Not only does Kyd have Isabella set out the principle that "truth" and "right" will be brought to "light" by "time," but he also uses it as the basis for the teleological structure of both the "Andrea" and "Horatio" plots, most explicitly the latter. By combining Hieronimo's repeatedly articulated impatience to learn the truth and then get justice, with staging that charts the progress from murder to revenge, Kyd encouraged playgoers both to look forward to the final discovery and to be satisfied by its completeness. When Horatio's murderers "*hang him in the Arbor*" (D2v), the sequence is set in motion, because whatever property represented the arbour reappears in the next scene when Hieronimo finds the body and cuts it down, and then again in 4.2 when Isabella tears the arbour apart before killing herself. As editors and critics have suggested, the same structure, possibly located in the same place, could also have been used for the scaffold on which Pedringano is hanged in 3.6 and, finally, the structure on which Horatio's body is hanging when Hieronimo discovers it at the play's climax.[34] Indeed, although the staging of Horatio's murder is unclear, if the arbour were discovered by opening a curtain, both it and the hanging body could be hidden by the murderers closing the curtain as they exit. When Hieronimo enters, thinking a woman is in danger and saying,

---

Temporis," 209–10; Margaret Aston, *The King's Bedpost*, 146; and David Howarth, *Images of Rule*, 111–14.

[32] Louis Montrose, "Idols of the Queen," 122–3.

[33] See Aston, *King's Bedpost*, 147; Saxl, "Veritas Filia Temporis," 210; and Massey, "*Veritas filia Temporis*," 158–9. For the engraving, see the British Museum Collection online (item 1849,0315.2).

[34] See, for example, *The Spanish Tragedy*, ed. Clara Calvo and Jesús Tronch, 4.4.87 SD note.

"heere within this garden did she crie. / And in this garden must I rescue her" (D3r), that would be the location to which he refers. He would then reopen the curtain as he exclaims, "But stay, what murdrous spectacle is this? / A man hangd up and all the murderers gone, / And in my bower to lay the guilt on me" (D3r). There is no way of knowing if Hieronimo did physically discover his son's body in this way, but certainly his final revelation is a discovery, which is set up with the direction *Enter Hieronimo, he knocks up the curtaine* (K2v); and his words in 2.4 clearly anticipate his speech at the end, when he "*Shewes his dead sonne*":

> Behold the reason urging me to this,
> See heere my shew, look on this spectacle:
> Heere lay my hope, and heere my hope hath end:
> Heere lay my hart, and heere my hart was slaine:
> Heere lay my treasure, heere my treasure lost:
> Heere lay my blisse, and heere my blisse bereft.   (K4r)

In his study of *veritas filia temporis* imagery in art, Saxl refers to artists who "fell involuntarily into the mother-tongue of Christian iconography, even when their subject was unrelated to the teaching of the Church" (212). While he means pictorial artists, the same could be said of dramatists. Certainly Isabella's belief that "The heavens are just" is essentially Christian, based as it is on the idea of a benevolent Providence. And this belief is central not only to *The Spanish Tragedy*[35] but also to many of the plays in which a fifth-act discovery of truth makes possible the achievement of justice.[36]

A straightforward progression from deception to truth is found in *A Knack to Know an Honest Man* (1594). Near its start, Sempronio and Lelio fight a duel because Sempronio has tried to seduce his friend's wife. When Lelio injures Sempronio, seemingly fatally, he runs away and Sempronio is saved by Philip, a hermit. The now remorseful Sempronio asks Philip to disguise him as a hermit and to keep his identity secret. Sempronio vows "Never to disclose my name, / Untill such time as thou

---

[35] Ronald Broude notes how "the revenge of Horatio's murder could be read by Elizabethans as the work of God" and cites a contemporary ballad, also titled "The Spanish Tragedy," in which "The last stanza sums up the moral": "For murther God will bring to light, / Though long it be hid from man's sight" ("Time, Truth, and Right in *The Spanish Tragedy*," 141, note 24).

[36] Broude quotes Thomas Beard's *The Theatre of Gods Judgements* (1612), 305: "When the justice of man is either too blinde, that it cannot search out the truth, or too blunt, that it doth not strike with severitie the man appointed unto death, then the justice of God riseth up, and with his owne arme hee discovereth and punisheth the murderer" ("Time, Truth, and Right in *The Spanish Tragedy*," 140).

releasest me" (B4r). Playgoers are therefore aware of this disguise and inhibiting vow from this point as they watch Sempronio search for the honest man of the title. In his roles as either an observer and commentator on what he sees or a participant in the action, Sempronio is on stage for much of the play. At the same time, Lelio tries to escape capture and trial for murder by disguising himself. But he is quickly found out by Servio: "How now, who walkes heere in this disguise? / Let's see thy face?" (G2r). As Lelio is being taken away to trial, his daughter assures him, "Father time shall discover all, till then farewell" (G2r).

This metatheatrical note of hope is echoed when, after Lelio is sentenced to death, the disguised Sempronio reminds playgoers that he has the power to save him. Referring to the vow he made to Philip, he wishes, "O were there one could find Sempronio out, / How might we make a famous comedie" (H2r). When just as Philip arrives the duke says, "except Sempronio live, Lelio must die," the comic discovery is signalled and the denouement initiated:

PHILIP	Sempronio lives, my Lord, see where he stands.
DUKE	Hermit why dalliest thou?
	Sempronio was yong, but this is olde,
	Sempronio was dead, but he doth live:
HERMIT	Old Sempronio now is young againe,
	And dead Sempronio now doth live,
	Beholde him Lelio, dost thou know him now?
LELIO	Sempronio. (H2v)

Like many plays in which discoveries of truth come in the final moments, this one concludes with a series of trial-like confrontations that have various figures confessing their crimes. This includes Sempronio, who admits that it was indeed his "loose unbridled love" (H3r) for Lelio's wife that caused the duel that started it all. Servio also confesses his misdeeds and is sentenced by the Duke. Comic justice prevails, as forecast.

In a number of plays Shakespeare initiates the conclusion with a literal discovery of a crucial truth.[37] Not surprisingly, as he did with any

---

[37] Besides the two discussed here, Shakespeare's other fifth-act performed discoveries are: *The Two Gentlemen of Verona*, of Julia, by herself; *Romeo and Juliet*, of Juliet in the tomb, by Romeo; *Much Ado About Nothing*, of Hero, by herself; *All's Well That Ends Well*, almost certainly of Helen, by Diana; *Othello*, of Desdemona on the bed, by Emilia; *King Lear*, of Edgar, by himself, raising his helmet; *Macbeth*, of the soldiers, by themselves, lowering the branches of Birnam Wood. Possibly also *The Comedy of Errors* when the Abbess produces Antipholis and Dromio of Syracuse from the abbey. I discuss each in the course of this study.

convention, each time he used a discovery as part of a denouement, he inventively reworked the device to make the business integral to the concerns of the particular play. I shall focus here on *The Winter's Tale* and *The Tempest* because not only do they both end with a discovery of truth, but they also do so after repeatedly calling explicit attention to time structurally, thematically and metatheatrically. As a consequence, playgoers are likely to be affected (however subliminally) by the step-by-step progression of events in each play from the initial deception to the final revelation of truth, thereby participating in an experience that only (paradoxically timeless) art can achieve. Given that the two plays share these fundamental similarities, it is instructive to realize how differently time is presented and used in each, and how much the individual treatment helps to explore and dramatize each play's distinct thematic concerns.

For example, although the idea of *veritas filia temporis* is prominent in the discoveries that initiate the resolutions of both plays, whereas in *The Winter's Tale* time is a matter of years, in *The Tempest* time is a matter of hours. Time in *Winter's Tale* is long, vague and fluid, and Apollo's oracle determines when the truth will be revealed. Time in *Tempest* is short, specific and immediate, and Prospero controls the process leading to the revelation of a truth he has made possible. In both plays, the final discovery of truth is beheld by an audience within the play, so that playgoers observe both the event and the watchers. But in one play the truth revealed is a surprise for both sets of observers, while in the other it is more or less expected by playgoers but not by those watching on stage. Within these broader contexts, both plays include specific references to and anticipations of the discovery of truth in time, and these signals are related to the particular nature of the truths revealed.

Shakespeare's main source for *The Winter's Tale*, Robert Greene's novella *Pandosto*, is subtitled "The Triumph of Time, Wherein is discovered by a pleasant Historie, that although by the meanes of sinister fortune Truth may be concealed, yet by Time in spite of fortune it is most manifestly revealed" (A1r).[38] The appearance and speech of the emblematic figure of Time at the start of Act 4 to mark the passage of sixteen years not

---

[38] Inga-Stina Ewbank observes that "The *Pandosto* story itself fails to work out its motto – *Temporis filia veritas* – for it puts all the emphasis on Fortune, with her wheel, as the ruling agent of human affairs. Shakespeare, on the other hand, makes the Triumph of Time into a controlling theme of his tale; and in doing so he transforms what the conventional motto suggests – a simple victory of Time, the Father of Truth – into a dramatic exploration of the manifold meanings of Time" ("The Triumph of Time in *The Winter's Tale*," 84).

only calls attention to the artifice, but also underlines the duality of Time as both destroyer and revealer.[39] Furthermore, when Time turns his hourglass at the mid-point of his speech, he marks the shift from past to future events. But the preparation for and anticipation of the final discoveries of truth in Act 5 actually begin immediately after Leontes loses faith in Hermione. Paulina warns him "how [this will] grieve you, / When you shall come to clearer knowledge" (TLN 701–2), and Antigonus says that everyone would be moved "To laughter ... / If the good truth, were knowne" (TLN 817–18). Leontes comments that "good speed" has brought the oracle, and sees it as an indication that Apollo "suddenly will have / The truth of this appeare" (TLN 1135–6). Ironically, and significantly, Dion here uses language that will be echoed at the play's conclusion:

> when the Oracle
> (Thus by Apollo's great Divine seal'd up)
> Shall the Contents discover: something rare
> Even then will rush to knowledge. (TLN 1168–71)

In fact, the opening of the oracle is one of several actions of discovery that prepare both literally and symbolically for those in the last act. Leontes's command requires that the officer "Breake up the Seales, and read" the "truth" of the oracle (TLN 1312, 1319), and what he reads are truths that will be confirmed in Act 5. In addition, although playgoers might already believe that "Hermione is chaste, Polixenes blamelesse, Camillo a true Subject, Leontes a jealous Tyrant, his innocent Babe truly begotten," they will not at this point understand the full meaning of "and the King shall live without an Heire, if that which is lost, be not found" (TLN 1313–16). When the shepherds find the abandoned Perdita, they also find what is later called a "farthell" (TLN 2591); again, the dialogue cues the action of discovery: "looke thee heere, take up, take up (Boy:) open't ... what's within, boy?" (TLN 1555–8). What they discover, of course, is the evidence of Perdita's true origins and some gold, which they decide to keep secret. Playgoers must wait through the long festival scene (4.2) and the two-hundred-plus lines of 5.1 before they finally hear the description of what happens when the fardel is opened again by Leontes in 5.2. As we will soon be reminded, Time "makes, and unfolds error" (TLN 1581), but it can be a long process and part of a playgoer's experience of the play is of that truth.

---

[39] For discussions of these two aspects of Time, see Samuel Chew, *The Pilgrimage of Life*, 12–22; Frederick Kiefer, *Shakespeare's Visual Theatre*, 159–68; and Erwin Panofsky, *Studies in Iconology*, 69–93.

From the narrow point of Time's soliloquy, the play opens out again (creating a structure not unlike that of an hourglass, one might note).[40] The second half of his speech echoes the idea of Greene's subtitle:

> let Times newes
> Be knowne when 'tis brought forth. A shepherds daughter,
> And what to her adheres, which followes after,
> Is th' argument of Time.　　　　　　　　　　　　(TLN 1605–8)

Indeed, the focus on Perdita emphasizes the crucial importance of the Truth about this lost daughter that will be revealed by Time – the emblem motto *veritas filia temporis* is made literal in this work of art. This thematic thread is picked up in the relationship between Perdita and Florizel/Doricles, with its potential for a comic resolution in marriage. The old shepherd comments, "If yong Doricles / Do light upon her, she shall bring him that / Which he not dreames of" (TLN 2003–5) – a reminder of the fardel and what it contains. Later in the scene when Perdita and Florizel decide to flee in disguise, he tells her to "muffle your face, / Dis-mantle you, and (as you can) disliken / The truth of your owne seeming" (TLN 2528–30). Then Autolycus meets the two shepherds, who are taking the fardel to Polixenes to prove that Perdita is worthy of his son. The old shepherd tells Autolycus, "there lyes such Secrets in this Farthell and Box" (TLN 2638–9) and his son concurs: "We must to the King, and shew our strange sights" (TLN 2699–700).

Near the start of 5.1 when the question is raised of Leontes remarrying and having children, Paulina reminds the courtiers of the oracle's condition "That King Leontes shall not have an Heire, / Till his lost child be found" (39–40). That this should happen, she says, is "monstrous to our humane reason" (TLN 2772–4), although playgoers, knowing that Perdita is on her way to Sicilia, will expect the oracle's fulfilment. But Shakespeare also starts preparing for the revelation of a truth of which the playgoer is not aware: that Hermione is alive. When Leontes tells Paulina that he will remarry only if she permits it, she replies, "That shall be when your first Queen's againe in breath: / Never till then" (TLN 2827–9). The conditional tense that governs much of the second part of this play is especially apparent once Florizel and Perdita arrive in Sicilia. Leontes says, "What might I have been, / Might I a Sonne and Daughter now have look'd on, / Such goodly things as you!" (TLN 2937–9). By repeatedly capitalizing on the playgoer's knowledge of the truth about Perdita, Shakespeare again builds expectations for the moment

---

[40] For a summary of other critics on Time and the play's structure see Kiefer, *Shakespeare's Visual Theatre*, 162.

of revelation. But that event is reported, not shown, perhaps partly because despite what Paulina has said, more that was "lost" needs to be "found" than just Hermione's daughter – as Paulina will later tell Leontes, "It is requir'd / You doe awake your Faith" (TLN 3300–1). The play's culminating discovery, the one playgoers are not prepared for and will actually see, is initiated in the penultimate scene by a description of "the opening of the Farthell" (TLN 3013) and the reunion of father and daughter. One of those listening to this report says, "This Newes (which is call'd true) is so like an old Tale, that the veritie of it is in strong suspition"; but one of those who were present insists it is "Most true, if ever Truth were pregnant by Circumstance: That which you heare, you'le sweare you see, there is such unitie in the proofes" (TLN 3037–9, 3040–2) – among which are that fardel's contents.

This play's concern with Time is a context for its treatment of Art and Nature, and vice versa. The first mention of the "statue" of Hermione is that it was made by the artist Julio Romano, "who (had he himselfe Eternitie, and could put Breath into his Worke) would beguile Nature of her Custome, so perfectly he is her Ape" (TLN 3105–7). Moreover, the improbability that Hermione has been "preserv'd" (TLN 3339) alive for sixteen years is more easily accepted by the playgoer because it happens not in our world of time and nature but in art, where almost anything is possible. The revelation of truth begins when Paulina says, "prepare / To see the Life as lively mock'd as ever / Still Sleep mock'd Death: behold, and say 'tis well" (TLN 3206–8). Her later threats to "draw the Curtaine" closed (TLN 3267, 3285) indicate that she draws one open here, to effect a literal discovery. In a microcosm of the idea that time (aided by Paulina) governs the revelation of truth, Leontes is brought to believe it in a gradual process that reverses his self-deception and loss of faith in Act 1. Finally, Paulina says to Hermione, "'Tis time: descend: be Stone no more" (TLN 3307). When she tells her that "Our Perdita is found" (TLN 3332), Hermione responds with a final reminder of the contingency of the two discoveries: "I / Knowing by Paulina, that the Oracle / Gave hope thou wast in being, have preserv'd / My selfe, to see the yssue" (TLN 3337–40). But Hermione is also sixteen years older, and her son Mamillius is still dead: Time the revealer and Time the destroyer – the comic and the tragic – exist together in this overtly artificial discovery and tragicomic conclusion.[41]

[41] For a similar treatment of the duality of Time in the play's conclusion see Kiefer, *Shakespeare's Visual Theatre*, 166–7. According to Susan Snyder and Deborah Curren-Aquino, Time here "has the telic design of Fate, the moral rigour of Justice, and the regenerative mercy of Providence" (*The Winter's Tale*, Introduction, 68).

In *The Winter's Tale* the appearance of Time to effect the instant passage of sixteen years, together with the prophecy of Apollo's oracle, creates the impression that Time itself, not any of the characters, controls the revelation of Truth. In *The Tempest*, by contrast, one character – Prospero – is explicitly in charge of how and when the final discoveries occur. Indeed, because the time during which the play was performed is virtually the same as the time it takes for Prospero's "project" (TLN 1002, 1947) to succeed, playgoers might feel he controls their time too.[42] Similarly, despite the longer period of twelve years during which the events occurred that led to this three hours, the repeated references to the time, together with the many uses of *now*, create an immediacy that fosters a playgoer's sense of inclusion.

Twelve years had to pass before circumstances were right for Prospero to begin the three-hour process that would culminate with the union of Miranda and Ferdinand; but because Prospero knows what he wants from the start, and playgoers will have a good idea what that is, the action and dialogue focus on the carefully timed process by which he achieves it. When Prospero begins to tell Miranda of their past, he says, "'Tis time / I should informe thee farther" and "The howr's now come / The very minute byds thee ope thine eare" (TLN 108–9, 124–5). Significantly, Prospero acknowledges both that he can engineer events only on the island and for a limited time, and the cooperation of a greater power:

> By accident most strange, bountifull Fortune
> (Now my deere Lady) hath mine enemies
> Brought to this shore: And by my prescience
> I finde my Zenith doth depend upon
> A most auspitious starre, whose influence
> If now I court not, but omit; my fortunes
> Will ever after droope.   (TLN 289–95)[43]

Ariel's role as Prospero's timekeeper is one of the more telling aspects of the immortal sprite's captivity by a mortal with time-sensitive plans. The clock starts ticking, as it were, when Prospero asks Ariel the time and the latter offers a nicely vague, "Past the mid season"; Prospero is more specific: "At least two Glasses: the time 'twixt six & now / Must by us both

---

[42] Early in the play, Prospero tells Ariel it is "at least" two o'clock and that they have until six (TLN 361–2), which is four hours; but at the end of the play Alonso remarks that it is "three howres since" (TLN 2101–2) their ship was wrecked.

[43] This is, of course, a manifestation of Time as Opportunity, which Prospero here seizes firmly by the forelock.

be spent most preciously" (TLN 360–2). Until that time, Ariel is Prospero's agent, engineering the process necessary to prepare both Miranda and Ferdinand on the one hand and Alonzo on the other, for the final revelations. In addition, the audience is given verbal signals to mark the progress to the final discoveries. When Miranda and Ferdinand immediately fall in love in 1.2, Prospero's control is clear: "this swift busines / I must uneasie make, least too light winning / Make the prize light" (TLN 604–6). After Ariel frightens Alonso, Sebastian and Antonio with the disappearing banquet, Gonzalo observes: "All three of them are desperate: their great guilt / (Like poyson given to work a great time after) / Now gins to bite the spirits" (TLN 1643–5). As Caliban, Stephano and Trinculo run off pursued by the "*diverse Spirits in shape of Dogs and Hounds*" (TLN 1929–30) Ariel has set on them, Prospero comments:

> At this houre
> Lies at my mercy all mine enemies:
> Shortly shall all my labours end, and thou
> Shalt have the ayre at freedome: for a little
> Follow, and doe me service. (TLN 1940–4)

The last act begins with a clear reminder of Prospero's schedule:

> Now do's my Project gather to a head:
> My charmes cracke not: my Spirits obey, and Time
> Goes upright with his carriage: how's the day?
> ARIEL On the sixt hower, at which time, my Lord
> You said our worke should cease. (TLN 1947–51)

When Prospero asks Ariel for his Duke's hat and rapier, he says, "Thou shalt ere long be free" (TLN 2043); and as he sends Ariel to awaken the mariners and bring them to him, Prospero again promises, "but yet thou shalt have freedome" (TLN 2053).

When Prospero releases Alonso and the others from his charmed circle, the resulting confrontations, confessions and reunions achieve the conditions necessary for the moment when he "*discovers Ferdinand and Miranda, playing at Chesse*" (TLN 2141–2). Indeed, given the emblematic quality of especially this last scene and the emphasis through the play on Prospero's timing of events, it seems likely that as he performs this action Prospero *is* Father Time, freeing his daughter from a cave. Moreover, for both Alonso and those with him on one side of the curtain, and for Ferdinand and Miranda on the other side, this is a discovery of truths that produce important moments of overtly comic resolution (before reminders of the fallen context return). Father and son learn that each is alive and Miranda finds a "brave new world" (TLN 2159). Language linked to revelation is used by both Sebastian: "A most high miracle!" (TLN 2151), and Miranda: "O wonder! / How many goodly creatures are there heere? / How beauteous mankinde is?" (TLN 2157–9). In this context, the use of *now* three times in the Epilogue (TLN 2322, 2324, 2334) helps to signal the shift from the three hours during which Prospero was in control of time, to the real world of the player and playgoer who were, are, and always will be controlled by it.

If we are to come close to appreciating these two highly artificial romances as the playgoers for whom they were written could have done, it is necessary to consider both the emblematic tradition within which images of Time releasing Truth existed and the dramatic convention of staging literal fifth-act "dis-coveries" that enacted the idea. An early modern playgoer's satisfaction with such efficacious discoveries of truth – possible in art if not in life – should not be underestimated.

A similar but less obviously contrived teleology governs most plays with a sequential structure that charts the process toward a final revelation by a disguised protagonist. Both of the following examples demonstrate how playgoers are kept aware of a disguise being used to seek justice and then see justice being achieved. But while one is straightforward, the other is a parody of the conventions.

In a number of early seventeenth-century plays a ruler adopts a disguise near the start of the action, speaks of his purposes in soliloquies and asides through the play, and discovers himself at the end.[44] In Marston's *The Malcontent* (1602–4) Altofronto takes on the disguise of Malevole because he has been deposed and banished by Mendoza. He first appears as Malevole, but playgoers are soon let in on the disguise, along with Celso in whom he confides: "constant Lord, / (Thou to whose faith I onely rest discovered, / ...) / Behold for ever banisht Altofront / This Genoas last yeares Duke" (B3v–4r). The "behold" suggests a physical discovery of himself here, which anticipates several more that occur nearer the end of the play but before his culminating revelation. These repeated self-discoveries also create a kind of coexistence of Malevole and Altofronto, so that the contrast between surface appearance and interior nature is emphasized – Altofronto's disguise does not change his essential self.

---

[44] In *The Disguised Ruler in Shakespeare and His Contemporaries*, Kevin Quarmby discusses examples of this disguise convention, but mentions the discoveries only in passing and does not distinguish between onstage and offstage revelations of identity.

In addition, his soliloquies and conversations with Celso through the play remind playgoers that Malevole is a disguise assumed for a purpose: revenge on his usurper. Malevole ingratiates himself with Mendoza, who enlists him to murder Pietro, the current duke, so that Mendoza can seize power and marry Maria, Altofronto's wife. Malevole reveals this plot to Pietro, who then repents and agrees to work with him against Mendoza, at which point Malevole *"undisguiseth himselfe"* (G4r) to Pietro. As this indicates, Marston's plot piles intrigue upon betrayal upon deception, dramatizing the main idea that nothing is what it seems in a fallen world, until virtually every character is involved as either deceiver or deceived. The last stage of this process begins when Mendoza asks Celso to organize a celebratory masque and those who have been his victims seize the opportunity for revenge: *"the maske enters. Malevole, Pietro, Ferneze, and Celso in white robes, with Dukes Crownes upon lawrell, wreathes, pistolets and short swords under their robes"* (I2v). As Malevole dances unrecognized with his wife Maria, he tells her to "Keepe your face constant, let no suddaine passion speake in your eies" and she exclaims "O my Altofront!" (I3r). Clearly he has discovered himself to her – probably by lifting his mask – but not to anyone else except the playgoers. Finally, after a second measure, all four disguised figures not only *"unmaske"* (I3r) but also expose the hidden pistols, which they turn on Mendoza. Then, in keeping with the idea that truth will be revealed in time and justice achieved, Marston has Altofronto confront Mendoza with his crimes; he also has the restored duke voice a truth about appearances:

> th' inconstant people,
> Love many men meerely for their faces,
> And outward shewes: and they do covet more
> To have a sight of these then of their vertues. (I3v)

As in *The Malcontent*, the plots of disguised-ruler plays typically let the audience in on the secret disguise from the start. Playgoers are then kept aware of the reasons for the disguise and the benevolent trickery it makes possible; they are also often prepared by the protagonist for the moment of his discovery and his consequent achievement of justice. All these elements are both present and parodied in Jonson's *Bartholomew Fair* (1613), which uses the recognizable and expected plot devices themselves to comment ironically on both the convention and the kinds of message it is often used to convey. The underlying premise of virtually every play of this kind is that in disguise a ruler can both see his world for the fallen place it is and establish ways to reform it. The treatment of Justice Overdo in *Bartholomew Fair* depends especially on the playgoers' familiarity with how such plots lead to the moment when the disguise has served its purpose and the time for discovery has arrived. Jonson's comic exaggeration of the device begins with Overdo's first entrance, happily praising himself for his disguise as "mad Arthur" – he thinks no one will recognize him because "they may have seene many a foole in the habite of a Justice; but never till now, a Justice in the habit of a foole" (C4v). In this disguise he spies on the "enormities" (D1r) of the Fair and congratulates himself for his success in asides and soliloquies: "My disguise takes to the very wish, and reach of it. I shall by the benefit of this, discover enough, and more: and yet get off with the reputation of what I would be. A certain midling thing, betweene a foole and a madman" (D2v). At the end of a long mid-play soliloquy Overdo gives an exaggerated version of the kinds of vows to persist that are spoken by disguised figures in other plays:

> These are certaine knocking conclusions; out of which, I am resolv'd, come what come can, come beating, come imprisonment, come infamy, come banishment, nay, come the rack, come the hurdle, (welcome all) I will not discover who I am, till my due time; and yet still, all shall be, as I said ever, in Justice name, and the King's, and for the Common-wealth. (F2v)

Overdo appears periodically in his disguise as mad Arthur to comment on the sins he thinks he has discovered. Then at the start of 5.2 he enters "*like a Porter*," saying, "This later disguise, I have borrow'd of a Porter, shall carry me out to all my great and good ends," but "neither is the houre of my severity yet come, to reveale my selfe, wherein cloud-like, I will break out in raine, and haile, lightning, and thunder, upon the head of enormity" (K3v). Here again Jonson seems to be explicitly parodying disguised figures in other plays who repeatedly remind playgoers of their purposes and create expectations for the revelation of truth when the time is right. Almost immediately after Overdo speaks these words, however, he naively reveals himself to a figure he thinks is Trouble-all the madman but is actually Quarlous in disguise. Overdo tells him, "I am the man, friend Trouble-all, though thus disguis'd (as the carefull Magistrate ought) for the good of the Republique, in the Fayre, and the weeding out of enormity" (K4v). The action then turns to the others at the Fair. When Overdo, still disguised as a porter, sees Grace his ward with Winwife, he says, "in the company of a stranger? I doubt I shall be compell'd to discover my selfe, before my time!" (L2v); but hearing of the puppet play, Overdo changes his mind, saying, "this will proove my chiefest enormity: I will follow this" (L3r). Finally, when he sees that everyone has been seduced by the puppet play, "*The Justice discovers himselfe*," saying, "It is time, to take Enormity by the fore head, and brand it; for I have discover'd enough" (M3r–v).[45] But Jonson is not done playing with the convention. Proud of himself, Overdo brags, "looke upon mee, O London! and see mee, O Smithfield; The example of Justice and Mirror of Magistrates: the true top of formality, and scourge of enormity. Hearken unto my labours, and but observe my discoveries" (M3v–4r). He triumphantly announces what he has discovered about some of the fairgoers, only to be confronted with the truths that Quarlous has been disguised as Trouble-all and that his own wife is drunk and ill. As the play ends, Quarlous tells Overdo,

> remember you are but Adam, Flesh, and blood! you have your frailty, forget your other name of Overdoo, and invite us all to supper. There you and I will compare our discoveries; and drowne the memory of all enormity in your bigg'st bowle at home. (M4v)

In using Overdo's disguise and discovery to show the truth that justice can be blind and imperfect, Jonson might also have been calling into question the neatness of the disguised-ruler convention as used by Marston and others.

Know Thyself

John Droeshout's use of a discovery to depict the dead King James on the title page of *Truth brought to light and discovered by Time* (Figure 2.4) is reminiscent of how time and truth are often linked in *memento mori* images, as if to surprise the viewer into an awareness of time's inevitable effects in a postlapsarian world. One unnerving example is a sculpted tomb (c. 1697) in a churchyard in the Suffolk town of Brent Eleigh (Figure 2.6), with its image of parted curtains revealing a skeleton with spade and hourglass.[46] Very different but conveying a similar message are a series of four engravings, two of a female, two of a male; in the first of each the figure is elaborately clothed, but the second of each has a flap that lifts to show part of a skeleton – the upper half of the female, the lower half of the male. The engravings of the male include several other relevant iconographic elements: he holds a clock in one hand and his other hand is wrapped around a tree entwined by a snake-like scroll and with a crucifix at the top (Figures 2.7a and 2.7b).

---

[45] Miles observes that this moment "derives its humour entirely from the well-established convention that the unmasking of the disguiser is an effective, important, and climactic dramatic episode" (*The Problem of "Measure for Measure*," 250).

[46] I am grateful to John Astington for bringing this tomb to my attention.

Figure 2.6 Sculpted tomb in a churchyard, Brent Eleigh, Suffolk, c. 1697

Early moderns' acute awareness of living in a fallen world of false appearances fostered a desire to see below the surface of people and things. One
manifestation of this concern was the interest in "anatomy," a word that
meant both the dissection of a body and a skeleton.[47] Of particular relevance
to my concerns in this study is the relatively new use of dissection as
a scientific method, which was demonstrated in "anatomy theatres" and
spoken of using the language of discovery. Neill cites *The historie of man
sucked from the sappe of the most approved anathomistes* (1578) by John
Banister, an Elizabethan surgeon and anatomist who tells his readers,
"I have earnestly, though rudely, endevoured to set wyde open the closet

---

[47] "Anatomy, n." I. The process, subjects, and products of dissection of the body.
    1. a. The artificial separation of the different parts of a human body or animal (or more generally
    of any organized body), in order to discover their position, structure, and economy; dissection.
    4.a. *pop.* A skeleton. [In this and the allied senses the word was often reduced to "atomy" *arch.*
    (*OED Online*, Oxford University Press, September 2016).

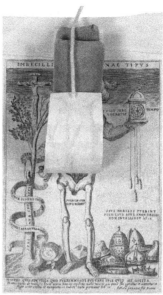

Figure 2.7a *Memento mori* male with flap closed, Battista Parmensis, c. 1585
2.7b *Memento mori* male with flap raised, Battista Parmensis, c. 1585

doore of natures secretes, whereinto every Godly Artist may safely enter, to see clearly all the partes, and notable devices of nature in the body of man" (B1v). Banister again uses the discovery metaphor when referring to the accomplishments of Hippocrates and Galen: "what secret so daintie, that they have not uncovered? yea what misterie so covert, the doore wherof they have not opened?" (B2r). Anatomy also acquired metaphoric implications. Jonathan Sawday notes the "numerous 'anatomies' which began to appear after the 1570s. Religion, death, women, time, war, sin, the soul, the individual, and, especially in England, catholicism, all could be, in some way, 'anatomized'."[48] And Neill observes that for the physician and anatomist Andreas Vesalius "anatomy involved moral as well as biological discovery, and that this science was to be esteemed partly for its ability to lay bare truths about human beings that were to be found deep within the fabric of the body." More, particularly, Neill says that "The idea of discovery is inscribed in the theatrical form of Vesalian anatomy."[49] Devon Hodges also

[48] Jonathan Sawday, *The Body Emblazoned*, 44.   [49] Neill, *Issues of Death*, 125.

notes the existence of both physical and "spiritual anatomies," with the latter being "ostensibly moral works designed simply to cut away sins that hide the truth from sight."[50] An example is Augustino Mainardi's *An Anatomi: that is to say A Parting in peeces of the Mass. Which discovereth the horrible errors, and the infinite abuses unknown to the people, aswel of the Mass as of the Mass book* (1557), described by Hodges as the earliest such work in English.[51] To achieve "ecclesiastical reform" Mainardi "employs the anatomy as an aggressive critical method for studying vice and attacking it. By cutting apart vice, the anatomist cleanses a diseased body and discovers the cause of its sickness for our edification."[52] The idea of an anatomy as a discovery of truth is also explicit in the title and accompanying illustration for a later work, *The anatomie of the English nunnery at Lisbon in Portugall dissected and laid open by one that was sometime a yonger brother of the covent* (1623; Figure 2.8). Small letters on the title page engraving (A2r) refer to an explanatory verse on the facing page, which emphasizes what readers "see" and repeatedly uses the language of discovery. It begins with "Behold" and describes each image, including the friars and nuns going from bed to banquet:

> Till Robinson doth fret to see the guile,
> How such dissemblers at the world can smile:
> So in a fury hee the Curtaine takes,
> And open wide, with either hand it shakes;
> Bidding all men (behold) how they collude,
> And doe poore silly Novices delude.

The duplicity is emphasized in the final verse, which begins "For though they doe pretend the Worlds brave scorne, / Yet to their secret Vaults treasure is borne" and ends:

> They doe indeed faire chastity professe,
> Obedience, povertie, and seeme no lesse:
> But God doth know, and Robinson can tell,
> All is a beastly falshood in this Cell.   (A1v)

Even more literal discoveries are essential to the anatomical illustrations with flaps that the viewer must lift to see into the body. The most famous of these are the intricate "engraved, etched, and letter-press printed anatomical broadsheets"[53] of *Catoptri Microcosmici* (*Mirrors of the Microcosm*), first published in 1613, that were engraved by Lucas Kilian to illustrate the findings of the anatomist Johann

---

[50] Devon Hodges, *Renaissance Fictions of Anatomy*, 6.   [51] Ibid.   [52] Ibid.
[53] Suzanne Karr Schmidt, with Kimberly Nichols, *Altered and Adorned*, 82.

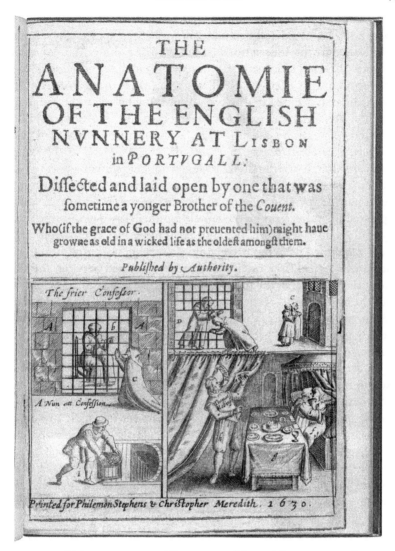

THE

ANATOMIE

OF THE ENGLISH

NVNNERY AT Lisbon

in PORTVGALL.

Diffected and laid open by one that was
fometime a yonger Brother of the *Couent.*

Who(if the grace of God had not preuented him)might haue
growae as old in a wicked life as the oldeft amongft them.

Publifhed by Authority.

The frier Confeffor.

A Nun att Confeffion.

Printed for Philemon Stephens & Chriftopher Meredith. 1 6 3 0.

Figure 2.8 Title page engraving, *The anatomie of the English nunnery at Lisbon in Portugall*, Thomas Robinson, 1623

Remmelin.[54] These sheets have "over a hundred super-imposed organ flaps allowing the viewer to dissect male and female corpses."[55] The first

[54] See the Folger Shakespeare Library Digital Image Collection (LUNA), DI209024.
[55] Schmidt, *Altered and Adorned*, 82.

sheet "shows a male and a female figure after Dürer's 1504 engraving of
Adam and Eve,"[56] a detail that adds allegorical and specifically Christian
significance to the illustrations by emphasizing the causal connection
between the Fall and death. Commenting on the synonymous use of
"anatomy" and "skeleton," Neill says that "what the science of dissection ultimately seemed to disclose was nothing less than the 'original of
Death' – the death that is always already inside us."[57] Another similarly
inflected "interactive" flap image is found in a fragment titled
Interiorum corporis humani partium, or *The Anatomie of the inwarde
Partes of man* (1559). It includes several woodcuts showing a seated male
and female each with flaps over the torso that the reader must lift to see
the organs below (Figure 2.9).[58] The link between body and spirit is
expressed on a sign held by the female figure: "Nosce te ipsum / Knowe
thyself." Neill points out that for early moderns "the mysteries [the
body] contained were not merely physiological, but moral-ontological,
and psychological. In a fashion ambiguously poised between the metaphoric and the literal, the interior of the body was imagined as inscribed
with the occult truths of the inner self."[59] He also notes that "The idea of
the human body as a cabinet of physical secrets awaiting discovery by
the surgeon's probe – spectacularly embodied in Vesalian 'flap anatomy'
illustrations which invited the viewer to peel back successive layers of
a cadaver until the skeleton lay revealed in all its bareness – easily lent
itself to moralizing inflection."[60]

Sawday also considers the relationship between anatomy and self-
knowledge with specific reference to illustrations in which a figure discovers its own interior: "The core of the self-reflexive gesture, which
allowed the anatomized subject delicately to lift and peel back its own
skin, lies in the doctrine . . . – 'Nosce te Ipsum'. What the device of self-
demonstration guaranteed was a literal interpretation of the searching,
inward gaze recommended by philosophical self-examination."[61] Many
of the images that illustrate Sawday's points are notably theatrical, with
the figure looking directly at the viewer as he or she performs a self-
discovery. One example, from Berengarius's *Carpi commentaria cům
amplissimis additionibus super Anatomia Mūndini* (1521), shows a female
figure with the skin of her abdomen opened, removing a cloak as she
steps down from a pedestal "in the familiar gesture of art becoming

[56] Ibid.   [57] Neill, *Issues of Death*, 133.
[58] Figure 2.9 shows only the female's flap raised. An interactive version of the engraving is available at
    https://anatomia.library.utoronto.ca/application/092–0001.html.
[59] Neill, *Issues of Death*, 123.   [60] Ibid., 122–3.   [61] Sawday, *The Body Emblazoned*, 117.

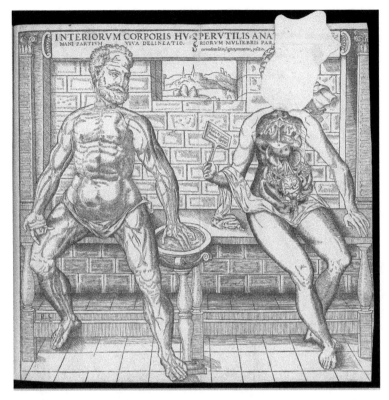

Figure 2.9 Engraved anatomical plate with one flap raised, *Interiorvm corporis humani partium*, 1559

life"[62] (Figure 2.10). Other examples from Berengarius include a male figure holding open the skin of his abdomen to expose organs.[63]

The imagery of discovery in some book titles of the period could readily describe the action in a play when a disguise is removed, something particularly evident in two works focused on revealing the secrets of the human heart and mind. Samuel Hieron's purpose is explicitly religious: *The discoverie of hypocrisie in two sermons, upon Mathew. 3. verse. 10. And three other, called the perfect patterne of true conversion, upon Matth. 13. ver. 44.* (1607). Hieron reminds his readers that "by [Christ's] comming, the thoughts of many harts should be discovered." He continues, "As it was in the person of Christ, so in the word of Christ, it doth as it were

---

[62] Ibid., 214. [63] Wellcome Collection online, image L0001202.

Figure 2.10 Engraved anatomical plate, female figure, *Carpi commentaria cūm amplissimis additionibus super Anatomia Mūndini vna cum textu eiusdēm in pristinūm et verum nitorèm redacto,* Jacopo Berengarius, 1521

anatomize the hearts of men, and plucks off the vizard from the hypocrite, laieth forth the poison that lurked before, and displaieth the gall that lay hidden in the heart" (B6r). A more secular example is Daniel Dyke's *The mystery of selfe-deceiving. Or A discourse and discovery of the deceitfull-lnesse of mans heart* (1614). The Dedication says it is about "the art of knowing a mans selfe; it discovers unto us, the infinitely intricate windings, & turnings of the darke Labyrinths of mans heart. Indeed oftentimes the discoveries of cousenages, and deceits in the worlde make many, before honestly ignorant, to turn couseners and deceivers" (A3r). In addition, readers are told they will "find that dangerous Art of selfe-Sophistry displayed, by which millions of soules are enwrapped in the snares of Satan. And so by seeing their selfe-deceit, shall come to their self-knowledge" (A3v). The first chapter begins with an image of discovery: "The Text opened; A preparation to the treatise following, shewing the originall of the hearts deceitfulnesse, the difficultie, and yet the meanes of knowing it" (B1r). The second chapter begins with a reference to "the anatomizing knife of the word" (B6v) and deals with exposing the deceit of others, such as "the uncasing of the hypocrite." In particular, Dyke asks "How many covers and curtaines hath every ones heart drawne before it to hide it selfe?" (D2r).

In *All's Well That Ends Well* (1604–05) the blindfolding of Parolles is a unique action that reworks the discovery convention to explore the play's central theme of self-knowledge. By including a blindfolding in a visual medium, Shakespeare prompts the playgoer to be conscious of seeing what Parolles literally cannot, thereby emphasizing the important relationship between seeing and knowing the truth. More particularly, one of his abductors uses language alluding to one kind of discovery when he says they will "case" (TLN 1837) – uncase or strip – Parolles, and to another kind when he promises that Bertram will see Parolles "anathomiz'd, that hee might take a measure of his own judgements, wherein so curiously he had set this counterfeit" (TNL 2138–40). In the event, Shakespeare adapted the "discovery of truth" action of revelation when, like a curtain or disguise, the blindfold is removed and Parolles sees the truth of his gulling – and about himself. Appropriately, therefore, one of Parolles's flamboyant scarves almost certainly serves as the blindfold – after it has been removed the erstwhile Interpreter comments: "You are undone Captaine all but your scarfe, that has a knot on't yet" (TLN 2421–2).

Much evidence supports the idea that this scene is paradigmatic of the play's concern with knowing or finding the truth about oneself or others. Indeed, there can be few if any plays with as many repetitions of versions of

to know and, especially, *to find* – in senses related to discovery – as occur in
All's Well. As the ambush of Parolles is being planned, one of the captains
tells Bertram "You do not know him my Lord as we doe, . . . he will steale
himselfe into a mans favour, and for a weeke escape a great deal of
discoveries, but when you finde him out, you have him ever after" (TLN
1823–7). He adds, "when his disguise and he is parted, tell me what a sprat
you shall finde him" (TLN 1838–9). Having removed the blindfold, the
Interpreter taunts Parolles, "So, looke about you, know you any heere?"
(TLN 2411). Parolles's self-recognition is couched in the same language:
"Captaine Ile be no more" (TLN 2429),

> Simply the thing I am
> Shall make me live: who knowes himselfe a braggart
> Let him feare this; for it will come to passe,
> That every braggart shall be found an Asse.   (TLN 2431–34)

In a further acknowledgement of this truth, when next he meets
Lafeu, Parolles tells him, "you were the first that found mee" (TLN
2683–4).

We have every reason to think that in *Volpone* (1606) Jonson was deliberately reworking the conventions of a particular discovery-play format to
foster an audience's amusement and awareness.[64] In many plays a principal
character assumes a disguise to achieve justice for himself and others. In this
case, however, Volpone's motives are greed and power, and the calls for
justice by others are ironically undercut. Often in plays with a final discovery
that brings justice, its eventual achievement is prepared for in earlier acts, as
we have seen. Jonson seems to acknowledge that practice in the middle of
this play when Bonario, having saved Celia from Volpone's clutches, tells
Volpone he is "loth to snatch thy punishment / Out of the hand of justice"
and reassures Celia that Volpone "ere long shall meet his just reward."
Volpone's immediate response, "I am un-masked, un-spirited, un-done"
(2S6r) might be said by an antagonist at the end of another play, but here it
only marks a pause in the protagonist's career of deception. His exposure and
defeat will come, but as this scene suggests, it will be in a knowing and
allusive parody of the fifth-act discovery convention. In the final courtroom
scene, Volpone, supposedly dead but disguised as a commendatore, realizes
he has been tricked by Mosca, who is about to gain his master's gold. With
nothing more to lose, Volpone announces, "The Foxe shall, here, uncase"

---

[64] As he would do again later in *Bartholomew Fair*, discussed above.

and "*puts off his disguise*" (2X3r). Then, as often happens at the end of a play when a disguised figure has discovered himself, the revelations of truth continue verbally: "I am Volpone, and this is my knave; / This, his owne knave; this, avarices foole, / This, a Chimera of wittall, foole, and knave." The first avocatore's exclamation – "The knot is now undone, by miracle!" (2X3v) – would be an appropriate response to more straightforward discoveries, but here it is an ironic indication of how this play parodies the convention. In particular, unlike those protagonists who choose when to reveal themselves, thereby effecting a comic resolution, Volpone is trapped by his own duplicity. Any playgoer familiar with the convention (and many would have been) would have recognized how Jonson had manipulated it to make a point: corrupted by greed, the court is blind to the truth and therefore unable to effect justice; Volpone, the chief deceiver, is forced by self-interest into discovering and thereby condemning himself.

Middleton's *Michaelmas Term* (1606) has an ending not unlike that of *Volpone* in how the disguise convention of self-discovery is used ironically to dramatize the self-defeat of the protagonist.[65] By Act 4 the plotting of the merchant Quomodo to acquire Easy's land has been successful, but Quomodo cannot resist knowing the response of his wife Thomasine and son to his achievements, so he feigns death and, disguised as a beadle, attends his own funeral. When he hears himself criticized and maligned by all, especially his son, he decides to disinherit him. What Quomodo does not know but playgoers do is that his wife is also glad to have him gone so she can marry Easy. In the fifth act Quomodo, still in disguise, comes to Thomasine to be paid for the funeral functions he performed (as a beadle). While a receipt for the payment is being prepared, Quomodo decides to sign his own name as a way of telling his wife he is alive. But unknown to him, Thomasine has married Easy and the receipt is made out to him, so Quomodo signs away any claims on Easy's property. When Quomodo realizes this, he discovers himself, saying, "will it please you knowe mee now, mistirs Harlot, and master Horner, who am I now?" In an amusing reworking of the usual response of recognition to a disguise-discovery, Thomasine comments, "Oh, hee's as like my tother husband as can be" (I1r). To recoup his losses, Quomodo takes Thomasine and Easy to court, but before the trial they tell the judge they are not sure if he is Quomodo or "some false spirit that assumes his shape" (I1v). In an ironic version of an identity test, Quomodo is asked by the judge if he is "the famous cousner" who tricked Easy and "laid Nets oer his land" (I1v–I2r); when Quomodo

---

[65] Both plays are thought to have been written in 1605–6, so we cannot know which came first.

denies it, the judge responds, "Then y'are not Quomodo but a counterfet."
Seeing no alternative, Quomodo then confesses that he "cousned him
indeed." When his identity is accepted by the judge, Quomodo's comment – "I am found what I am" (I2r) – goes to the heart of the self-
discovery he has unintentionally brought about.

Because of how they use the just deserts formula, these and other
disguise-discoveries are still entertaining and satisfying – audiences
always enjoy seeing a deceiver get his comeuppance. But, I contend, the
various non-dramatic uses of the discovery-of-truth trope – both pictorial
and verbal – that I have discussed in this chapter would have influenced
both how playwrights used discoveries and how playgoers perceived
them. For example, the many vivid images of moral and physical truths
being literally discovered in emblems and other contemporary visual art
would have created contexts that added nuance and significance to the
action of discovery in the playhouse. Playgoers used to interpreting
emblems would probably have registered the same moralizing conventions at work in similar moments on stage. Indeed, in many instances
the combination of a visual discovery and accompanying dialogue is
a performed version of the emblem trio of image, motto and verse.
More generally, on the page a discovery occurs in a moment or two,
but on the stage it can be emphasized by grand gestures accompanying
the dialogue announcements of the event and exclamatory responses to it.
The cause-and-effect structure that often culminates in a discovery could
have been emphasized if the action paused long enough to highlight
visual echoes and emphases. When a disguise was removed, for example,
the action and process of announcement and recognition could have been
prolonged to exploit the appearance–reality dichotomy. The performance of all these discoveries was therefore a necessary element of their
intended effect and meaning.

CHAPTER 3

Religious Rites and Secular Spectacle

Christian Rituals and Images

The pervasive influence of Christianity on early modern ways of thinking and seeing cannot be overestimated or even fully appreciated today. In particular, the central, framing events of the Nativity and Resurrection were fundamental to Christian worship and art, both of which used actions and images of discovery to represent and celebrate these "miracles." These religious practices had their origins in the Catholic liturgy, but centuries of repetition would have created a legacy of images and ceremonies not eradicated by the Reformation. Indeed, even in the post-Reformation English church the practices and iconography of Catholicism did not completely disappear, and between 1553 and 1558 the old religion had returned under Queen Mary.[1] And as David Cressy and Lori Anne Ferrell remark:

> Catholics had not disappeared from the Elizabethan scene. Some of the clergy were wistful for the old religion, while many of the laity, perhaps more than is generally credited, remained deeply attached to traditional beliefs. Catholicism survived in England in an attenuated, underground form despite the institutional overlay of the Church of England.[2]

It therefore seems significant that the imagery and performance of discoveries in the drama of the period often echo the language and rituals associated with the revelations at the heart of Christianity.

Historians of medieval drama have long theorized about how the "*quem quaeritis*" trope evolved into early modern drama; here I will focus first on

---

[1] Eamon Duffy says that among the items to be returned to churches under Mary were "altar frontals and hangings, three linen cloths, two for covering the altar," also "a great veil to hang across the chancel before the altar in Lent." Duffy adds that in "hundreds ... of parishes up and down the country ... concealed or rescued images, vestments, and books had been restored at Mary's accession" (*The Stripping of the Altars*, 545, 569).

[2] David Cressy and Lori Anne Ferrell, eds., *Religion and Society in Early Modern England*, 7.

some specifics of that ritual and their visual representation in pictorial art before turning to discoveries in plays. In the mid-tenth century Ethelwold, Bishop of Winchester oversaw the preparation of the *Regularis Concordia*.[3] This was a set of rules for the governance of English monasteries that provided instructions on how Divine Office was to be practised. It includes "one of the earliest descriptions of a play in medieval Europe"[4] – the *Visitatio Sepulchro* by the three Marys, or Easter *Quem quaeritis* trope. In it, three priests come to the "sepulchre" (altar) and are asked by an angel, "*Quem quaeritis in sepulchro?*" They say they have come to anoint Christ's body and the angel tells them, "He is not here; he has risen as he foretold"; then the angel asks them to "Come and see the place where the Lord was laid" and "Singing these words he rises and lifts the curtain, and shows them the place with the cross gone but with the linen cloths in which the cross was wrapped lying there."[5]

In the late thirteenth century a French bishop, Guillaume Durand of Mende, or William Durandus, wrote the *Rationale divinorum officiorum*, or *The Symbolism of Churches and Church Ornaments*. In a section titled "Of Pictures and Images" three items deal with why and how curtains were used for the Easter liturgy:

> 34. Now all things which pertain to the ornament of a church, must be removed or covered over in the season of Lent: which according to some taketh place on Passion Sunday, because after that time the Divinity of Christ was hidden and concealed in Him . . . Then therefore the crosses are covered, that is, the virtue of His divinity is hidden . . . according to the use of some places, two coverings or curtains are then only retained: of which the one is hung all round the choir, the other is suspended between the altar and the choir: that those things which be within the Holy of Holies may not appear. In that the Sanctuary and Cross are then veiled, we be taught the letter of the Law, that is, its carnal observance, or that the understanding of Holy Scriptures before the Passion of Christ was veiled, hidden, and obscure: and that in that time there was a veil: that is men had an obscurity before their eyes. It signifieth also the sword which was set before the gate of Paradise: because the carnal observance we have spoken of, and this obscurity, and the sword at the gate of Paradise, were removed by the Passion of Christ. Therefore the curtains and veils of this kind are removed on good Friday . . .

---

[3] For details see E. K. Chambers, *Medieval Stage*, vol. 2, p. 14 and William Tydeman, *Theatre in the Middle Ages*, 35–6.

[4] Peter Meredith and John E. Tailby, eds., *Staging of Religious Drama*, 3.

[5] Tydeman's translation (*Theatre in the Middle Ages*, 36); see also Chambers, *Medieval Stage*, vol. 2, pp. 14, 306.

35. [There are] three kinds of veils which be hung in churches: that which concealeth the mysteries: that which divideth the sanctuary from the clergy: that which divideth the clergy from the laity ... The second, namely the curtain that in the office of the Mass during Lent is suspended before the altar, was set forth by the veil which was hung up in the tabernacle, and divided the Holy of Holies from the holy place ...

36. But on Holy Saturday all the curtains are taken away, because on the Passion of the Lord the veil of the temple was rent: and by that thing the spiritual intelligence of the Law was revealed unto us, which till that time lay hid, as is said afore: and the door of the kingdom of heaven is opened, and power was given unto us, that cannot be overcome of our carnal concupis-cence, unless we ourselves do yield.[6]

The continued use and significance of these rituals is described by art historian Barbara Lane:

Curtains that hung from rods on either side of the altar are documented in many inventories of cathedrals and parish churches in France, Flanders, and Germany in the fourteenth and fifteenth centuries, and appear in many Northern miniatures of this period; they often accompany praying devo-tional figures to indicate the sanctity of the space, as in many of the portraits of the Duke of Berry.[7] The purpose of such curtains, to conceal the mysteries of the transubstantiation, is described by Durandus in his *Rationale divinorum officiorum* (1286). At the moment of the elevation, the curtains were opened to reveal the transformed Host, as illustrated in the *Mass of St. Giles* of ca. 1500 by the French master named from this painting [Figure 3.1].[8]

According to Dunbar Ogden the Easter *Visitatio Sepulchro* ceremony described by Ethelwold in the *Regularis Concordia* was "our first medieval play." He says that the action

embodies a quest which comes to a successful conclusion in discovery. Lack of knowledge serves as the impetus for verbal exchange followed by a discovery, a jubilant reaction, and a public proclamation of the new knowledge. The structure we may call comic in that the play moves from complication to happy resolution, turning climactically on the two-phase revelation: the angel says "He is risen," the women reacting with an *Alleluia*, and then the angel calls the women back to give them physical proof.[9]

---

[6] *The Symbolism of Churches and Church Ornaments*, 56–7, 57–8, 60.
[7] See, for example, "Elevation of the Host," *Petite Heures of Duke de Berry*, Bibliothèque nationale de France, reference ms. lat. 18014, p. 139, gallica.bnf.fr/ark:/12148/btv1b8449684q/f287.image.r= Horae+ad+usum+Parisiensem+ou+Petites+heures+de+Jean+de+Berry.langEN.
[8] Barbara Lane, "*Ecce Panis Angelorum*," 480.
[9] Dunbar Ogden, *The Staging of Drama in the Medieval Church*, 24.

Figure 3.1 *The Mass of Saint Giles*, c. 1500

Ogden continues, "All of the elements of theatrical production exist in this performance. The playing space is a part of the church itself, here at the high altar, where a sepulchre has been set up with a veil in front."[10]

[10] Ibid.

Ogden's summary of the action and its meaning could be applied to many of the secular early modern plays included in this study.

We also have evidence that curtains were used as part of the Christmas *Officium Pastorum*. Karl Young's analyses of thirteenth-century manuscripts from Rouen Cathedral describes how the *Quem quaeritis in praesepe* trope developed into a dramatic performance. He says that in the "*Officium Pastorum* as it comes to us from Rouen, all our demands of impersonation and *mise en scène* are finally satisfied."[11] In particular, "the action of this dramatic office centers in a specially constructed *Præsepe*, or crib."[12] He notes that "during the period from the twelfth to the fourteenth centuries a structural Crib was used for dramatic performances [of the Nativity]. The Crib contained figures, and was closely associated with the altar."[13] He continues:

> In information as to the actual nature of the *Præsepe* these dramatic texts are not generous. From the *Officium Pastorum* of Rouen we learn that the structure, erected behind the altar, was large enough for the two *Obstetrices* [midwives, played by priests] to stand in it. It was provided with figures representing Mary and the Child, which were hidden, until the fitting moment, by a curtain.[14]

Furthermore, Young notes that the Rouen texts of the *Officium Stellae* (Adoration of the Magi) "seem to indicate that the *Præsepe* was placed upon the altar, or was perhaps, the altar itself. The statuette of the Mother and Child seems to have been set upon the altar-table and surrounded by a curtain that was opened at the suitable dramatic moment."[15] Whether curtains were also used elsewhere for these offices is impossible to say, but religious practices tended to be widespread and, at least from this distance, given the readily apparent symbolism, it seems more likely than not that this action of revelation was a common practice.

Interestingly, Young comments that "since the trope *Quem quaeritis in præsepe* is itself modeled upon the Easter trope *Quem quaeritis in sepulchro*, one is tempted toward the inference that the *mise en scène* before us is merely an imitation of the similar *mise en scène* shown in . . . texts of the Easter trope."[16] But he then offers "a second consideration" that "may serve to absolve the authors of the Christmas trope from the stigma of mere blind imitation in this detail of *mise en scène*, for it may be that the altar was actually regarded not only as *sepulchrum*, but also, independently, as *Præsepe*." Young adds, "The same possibility arises also from

---

[11] Karl Young, "*Officium Pastorum*," 323.   [12] Ibid., 334.   [13] Ibid., 338.   [14] Ibid., 339.
[15] Ibid., 340.   [16] Ibid., 307.

the fact that, according to certain texts of the *Officium Pastorum*, the *præsepe* is found behind the altar, or near it."[17] Given the concept and practice of biblical prefiguring, that the altar could represent both the crib of the Nativity and the tomb of the Resurrection as Young suggests seems entirely probable. Furthermore, the symbolic action of opening a curtain to reveal Truth – both birth and rebirth, in the form of an occupied manger and empty tomb – was central to the performance and meaning of both liturgical tropes.

Although we unfortunately have no pictorial or textual evidence directly linking the medieval church ceremonies described by Ethelwold, Durandus and Young to the performance and meaning of discoveries on the early modern English stage, we do have both medieval and early modern works of visual art that include curtains, and numerous others that use curtains in discoveries representing or linked to the essential events of Christianity. In the words of art historian Martha Hollander:

> The curtain had been a feature of liturgical architecture since the late Middle Ages. Curtains suspended on a rod around an altar would be pulled back at the climax of the Mass to reveal the body and blood of Christ, miraculously transformed into the Eucharist. Accordingly the curtain was featured in fourteenth- and fifteenth-century religious art as an instrument of divine revelation, at once hiding and, at an important moment, disclosing a sacred object.[18]

In a consideration of the relationship between the laity and the "most sacred and central of the rites of Christendom" before the English Reformation, Eamon Duffy discusses the presence and function of the veil that hid the altar, noting that during Lent "a huge veil was suspended within the sanctuary area, to within a foot or so of the ground, on weekdays completely blocking the laity's view of the celebrant and the sacring" (consecration of the Eucharist). He says the veil marked a "boundar[y] between the people's part of the church and the holy of holies":

> The veil was there precisely to function as a temporary ritual deprivation of the sight of the sacring. Its symbolic effectiveness derived from the fact that it obscured for a time something which was normally accessible; in the process it heightened the value of the spectacle it temporarily concealed.[19]

---

[17] Ibid., 309–10.   [18] Martha Hollander, *An Entrance for the Eyes*, 69.
[19] Duffy, *The Stripping of the Altars*, 111.

As Old Testament analogies to the Eucharistic sacrifice developed in the third and fourth centuries, the *ciborium* – a canopy on four columns over the altar – began to symbolize, along with the chancel area in general, the Holy of Holies of the Old Testament temple. Curtains were hung between the columns of the ciborium and kept closed except during Mass, when they were opened to symbolize the rending of the temple's curtain and subsequent, unobstructed accessibility to God. The doctrine of transubstantiation contributed yet another layer of meaning to the ciborium: designating the presence of the body and blood of Christ upon the altar.[20] A mosaic in the Byzantine basilica of Saint Appolinaris in Classe, in Ravenna, shows a bishop inside what appears to be a ciborium, with the curtains drawn open and a crown hanging above. Another mosaic in this basilica depicts a curtained altar, with Melchizedek as the high priest in the temple administering bread and wine. On the left Abel offers a lamb to be sacrificed, and on the right Abraham offers Isaac, both prefigurations of Christ's sacrifice.[21] Altar curtains survived the decline of the ciborium in both East and West. An Elevation of the Host during Mass, when the curtains were opened, is illustrated in Figure 3.1. The related practice of veiling religious statues is depicted in *The War between Carnival and Lent* by Pieter Bruegel the Elder: "Just inside the entrance [of the church on the right] a veiled statue can be seen, hanging on one of the pillars of the nave. It was customary to cover up all the works of art in church at Lent until Easter Sunday – when, in celebration of Christ's resurrection, the carved and painted figures of saints and prophets would be triumphantly unveiled, brought back to life like the Saviour himself."[22]

Open curtains, implying a revelation, are also sometimes used in depictions of the Nativity and Adoration of Christ, as in a psalter of Ingeborg of Denmark (Figure 3.2), which makes the symbolism clear. But far more complex, and perhaps the best example of this kind of discovery, is the late-fifteenth-century Nativity-Adoration by Hugo van der Goes (Figure 3.3). In her study of this painting, Barbara Lane argues that the two figures at the forefront (generally thought to be the prophets Jeremiah on the right and Isaiah on the left) and the curtains "can be explained in relation to the

[20] See G. van Hemeldonck, "Ciborium (ii)," *Grove Art Online, Oxford Art Online* (Oxford University Press).

[21] William J. Hamblin and David Rolph Seely, *Solomon's Temple*, 111.

[22] Andrew Graham-Dixon, "In the Picture," *The Sunday Telegraph*, 2 March 2003; Andrew Graham-Dixon Archive, www.andrewgrahamdixon.com/archive/itp-150-the-fight-between-carnival-and-lent-by-pieter-bruegel-the-elder.html.

Figure 3.2 *Nativity*, Copenhagen Psalter, twelfth century

eucharistic nature of the Nativity theme."[23] Noting the sheaf of grain in the foreground, lying below the crib, Lane quotes John 6.51: "I am the living bread which came down from heaven: if any man eat of this bread, he shall

[23] Lane, "*Ecce Panis Angelorum*," 476.

Figure 3.3 *Nativity*, Hugo van der Goes, c. 1480

live for ever: and the bread that I will give for the life of the world is my flesh."[24] Her detailed analysis of the painting's "altar-manger motif" concludes:

> The parted curtains reveal the Child just as altar curtains disclosed the transformed Host to the congregation. Opening these curtains, Isaiah and Jeremiah introduce the scene as did the prophets of the liturgical Christmas plays performed around the altar; their identities relate, respectively, to the interpretation of the altar as both manger and tomb. Finally, the very shape of the painting, suggesting a sarcophagus, points to the ultimate purpose of the Nativity: the death of Christ and consequent redemption of mankind.[25]

More particularly, Lane notes how "Hugo has clearly identified his curtains as belonging to an altar by his emphasis on the curtain rod, for it is actually a piece of wood attached to the panel, over which the rings have been painted" and that "by implying that the curtains are opened in the viewer's space, it also intensifies the dramatic revelation for the worshipper."[26] For Erwin Panofsky, the two prophets opening the semi-transparent curtains constitute a "boldly literal illustration of their function 'to reveal,' that is, 'to unveil,' the New Dispensation."[27] The overt artifice of the curtains makes viewers conscious of the act of revelation, of themselves as observers, and of what is being revealed. In this it functions much like the staging of discoveries in plays.[28]

With such uses of curtains in mind, one becomes more aware of their presence and analogous implications in other religious art. The Virgin is frequently framed by curtains held open by angels or other figures, as in Rogier van der Weyden's *Medici Madonna* (Figure 3.4) and in Sandro Botticelli's *Virgin and Child with Four Angels and Six Saints*, both of which are noteworthy for their "staged" quality.[29] In the Botticelli, the angels on

---

[24] Ibid., 479.   [25] Ibid., 486.

[26] Ibid., 480. Lane provides examples to illustrate her point that "Altar curtains are often included with the manger-altar motif in Gothic Nativity scenes, where their presence suggests the miraculous transformation that they so often concealed" ("*Ecce Panis Angelorum*," 480).

[27] Erwin Panofsky, *Early Netherlandish Painting*, 337.

[28] Referring to this and other paintings with curtains, Hollander comments that "the drawn curtain and drape have obvious theatrical associations. Both imitate the curtains over the central archway of the Renaissance stage, which are suddenly pulled back at key moments in the drama to reveal important scenes and characters. Dutch painters often used the curtain to suggest dramatic revelations without actually reproducing a theater" (*An Entrance for the Eyes*, 74). Hollander does not indicate that she is referring specifically to Dutch theatres, but it is worth noting that she is an art historian, not a theatre historian, and while there are a number of reliable illustrations of early modern Dutch theatres, the same is unfortunately not the case for English theatres of the period. Indeed, as I emphasize in the Appendix there is no unequivocal evidence that early modern London playhouses were equipped with a central opening in the tiring house wall.

[29] See also Raphael's *Sistine Madonna*, with curtains suspended from a visible rod, at http://skd-online -collection.skd.museum/de/contents/show?id=372144.

Figure 3.4 *Medici Madonna*, Rogier van der Weyden, 1460–4

each side of the throne carry the crown of thorns and the nails of the cross, creating a conflation of the Annunciation, Nativity and Crucifixion.[30] About the van der Weyden, Lane says, "It can hardly be coincidental

---

[30] See the Web Gallery of Art or Wikimedia Commons.

Figure 3.5 *Madonna del Parto*, Piero della Francesca, *c.* 1460

that this tent echoes the appearance of cloth coverings of the Host in
hanging tabernacles. The word *tabernaculum*, in fact, originally signified
the 'veil or small tent of cloth' that covered Host containers suspended over
the altar."[31] In Piero della Francesca's *Madonna del Parto* (Figure 3.5) the
pregnant Madonna stands between two angels holding back curtains and
looking out at the viewer. Her outer gown is also slightly opened, perhaps
by her left hand, which anyway calls our attention to the opening, as if
anticipating or signalling the birth of Christ, who is symbolized by the

---

[31] Barbara Lane, *The Altar and the Altarpiece*, 32.

pomegranates on the canopy. The sacred and ritualistic – and highly contrived – nature of this image is further emphasized by the fact that the angels are mirror images of each other.[32]

The belief that the Fall of Man brought with it death and therefore time, on the one hand, and that the Nativity anticipates the Resurrection, on the other, are brought together in two paintings with iconography that combines a discovery with an hourglass in ways reminiscent of the *memento mori* examples I discussed in Chapter 2. The first of these is Lorenzo Lotto's very complex *Recanati Annunciation*.[33] Among its many symbolic details, in the background lower centre is a stool on which sits an hourglass with what appears to be a small curtain or cover that has been opened and hangs at both sides. A *Holy Family* attributed to Marcello Venusti shows Mary with an infant Christ lying Pieta-like on her lap (Figure 3.6). As Fritz Saxl describes it,

> the Madonna . . . uncovers the Child with her left hand, while in her right hand she holds an open book inscribed with the words of the Psalm, *Veritas de terra orta est, et justitia de coelo prospexit.* The symbolic significance of this seemingly idyllic act of unveiling becomes clear: Truth has appeared on earth through the birth of Christ, and Truth is uncovered in the same gesture as the Child to all who recognize Him as the Saviour.[34]

There is an hourglass in the lower right. The idea that "Truth shall spring out of the earth; and righteousness shall look down from heaven" (discussed in Chapter 2) is a paradigm for the dramatic structure that builds to a literal discovery of truth, in which the act of revelation is a manifestation of the belief in an eventual, miraculous discovery of truth that leads to the recognition of error, deception and evil, and permits understanding, reconciliation and a just resolution. The influence of this Christian version of the idea that Truth is the daughter of Time is especially apparent in secular drama when a fifth-act discovery is used, but it might be said to be present every time a discovery leads to these effects and outcomes in early modern plays.

Early Christian Drama

In addition to the religious ceremonies in Latin performed in churches by the clergy, which came to be dramatized over time, the pre-history of early

---

[32] These details are from the Web Gallery of Art.
[33] See www.lorenzolottomarche.it/en/annunciazione-15271529/.
[34] Saxl, "Veritas Filia Temporis," 217.

Figure 3.6 *Holy Family with Young Saint John the Baptist*, attributed to Marcello
Venusti, nd

modern drama includes medieval mystery cycles based on biblical texts and
morality plays with a Christian message, which were performed outside the
church in the vernacular by laymen. As with the evolution of liturgical
performances, the relationships between the explicitly Christian medieval

works and the drama that followed are difficult to chart. To be sure, both disguises and curtains are found in medieval performance contexts, so the potential for physical revelations existed; however, the surviving texts include only a few examples of performed discoveries of disguises or scenes.

Evidence for the use of curtains in mystery plays is mostly continental and their presence does not necessarily indicate that a discovery was part of the action; but a few of the extant examples seem to include one. The records for a Passion play at Mons in 1501 include payment for "one iron upright supporting two cross pieces and a ring used for hanging a curtain to enclose God the Father on his throne in Paradise"; and for a Passion play at Semur in 1488, "God the Father is in Paradise on a throne and angels on each side ... and they shall draw back some curtain which was before him so that he is clearly seen by the people."[35] Perhaps to permit a similar divine revelation, the preparations for a performance at Lucerne in 1583 stipulate that "Heaven should be fitted with a roof and curtains which can be pulled round in front." Two other records from Lucerne in 1597 (and therefore probably with earlier origins) relate to the Crucifixion: "when the Savior reaches the cross he is to draw up the curtain and draw it quickly apart when he dies" and "When the Savior is put on the cross, the youngest of the Jews in the Temple is to pull the curtain round the Temple and, when he has died, is to pull it quickly apart."[36] Probably this action was intended to represent the tearing of the veil at the moment of Christ's death, described by Durandus (quoted above). An undated record of a Saint Francis play on Majorca provides considerable detail about how a curtain will be used to both hide and expose:

> Now [St. Francis] is to be raised and, after he has been raised a little, they shall cover him with the curtain, and he shall stand up and walk towards the Christ which is also to be behind the curtain; and when the curtain is opened, St. Francis shall be revealed with the stigmata on his hands, feet, and side. And after he has stood like that for a little while, they shall close the curtain again, and St. Francis shall return to his little platform from which he was raised.[37]

For an undated Nativity play in Siena, "When [Mary] has reached the scaffold and everything is ready, two angels shall come and lift the canvas, and Jesus shall be born." The instructions for an early fifteenth-century Assumption play in Valencia (probably performed in the cathedral) include: "When Mary has gone up onto the scaffold she shall go to her

---

[35] Meredith and Tailby, eds., *The Staging of Religious Drama*, 123.   [36] Ibid., 130, 85, 137.
[37] Ibid., 110.

chamber, which is to be prepared and enclosed with curtains ... And the handmaidens shall pull back all the curtains so that Mary can be seen by the people."[38] And an ambassador in Florence who was impressed by an Annunciation and an Ascension play in 1439, left this detailed description:

> When the time comes to begin the great and marvelous spectacle, many people gather silently in the church, their eyes fixed on the scaffold in the middle of the church. After a short while the curtains and hangings are drawn back and one can see, seated on the magnificent seat by the small bed, the man who represented the Virgin.[39]

Evidence for the use of curtains in early English staging, whether or not for a discovery, is even patchier.[40] Said to be the "earliest of the surviving morality plays,"[41] *The Pride of Life* exists in a manuscript fragment from about 1400. At one point the King says, "Draw the cord, Sire Streynth, / Rest I wol now take" and the accompanying stage direction notes: "*Et tunc clauso tentorio dicet Regina secrete nuncio* [*Then, having closed the curtain, the Queen speaks privately with the messenger*]" (303–6 and note). David Klausner says that "The king asks Strength to draw the cord which pulls a curtain across a space on the stage, likely an inner room or booth. In its simplest form, this would have been the back part of the stage, separated from the front by the curtain and cord to which he refers. It might well have contained a couch or bed on which the king can take his rest."[42] This is not a discovery, but it does call for curtains. A section of text is missing, so it is impossible to know, but perhaps the curtain was opened again later when the king returns to the action. In any case, this text indicates the presence of curtains and the ability to effect a discovery by opening them.[43]

The *Ludus Coventriae* (c. 1463–75) plays include several directions that call for a curtain to both hide and reveal figures: "The Last Supper" has "Here Chryst enteryth into the hous with his disciplis and ete the Paschal lomb; and in the mene tyme the cownsel-hous beforn-seyd xal sodeynly onclose, schewyng the buschopys, prestys, and jewgys syttyng in here astat, lyche as it were a convocacyon" (p. 261). A little later in the same play, "than xal the place ther Cryst is in xal sodeynly unclose rownd abowt, showing Cryst syttyng at the table and hese dyscypules eche in ere degré'

[38] Ibid., 165, 230.   [39] Ibid., 244.
[40] A search in Records of Early English Drama volumes produced no references to curtains (or hangings) in a context of performance.
[41] David Klausner, ed., *The Pride of Life*, Introduction, 2.   [42] Ibid., 26, note to line 303.
[43] See Janette Dillon, "From scaffold to discovery-space," 193–4. Dillon refers to "the special quality of secrecy" highlighted by the use of curtains in this play (195).

(p. 270). "The Trial of Christ" has "Herowdys scafald xal unclose, shewyng Herowdes in astat" (p. 303). Glynne Wickham describes a large open space or acting area with stages, some small, others larger: "The latter are equipped with curtains which can be swiftly drawn open to present a startling 'discovery', or closed to obliterate that area from significance to the action."[44]

In the fifth act of John Foxe's *Christus Triumphans* (1551?) Ecclesia calls on Christ to "break through the heavens" and exclaims, "what new light, what wondrous fragrance of perfume suddenly breathes upon my senses?" This is accompanied by a stage direction: *"(Here from the upper part of the theater, when the curtains open, are shown as if from heaven thrones with books placed upon them)."*[45] Andreas Höfele comments:

> It is symptomatic that this stage direction, the only one in the whole text specifying the use of machinery and props, serves the purposes of allegory rather than localization. Its function is not to create an imaginary place elsewhere, but to incorporate a transcendent "elsewhere" into the here and now of the performance. A veritable *coup de théâtre*, this spectacle corroborates the Prologue's claim to the Church-like sanctity of the show. It could even be argued that at this climactic moment the theatre surpasses the possibilities of the Church, offering a miracle that becomes almost real in its affective impact on the onlookers.[46]

The removal of a cover rather than the opening of curtains is the means of a discovery in the Townley cycle *Second Shepherds' Play* (1400–50), in which Mak steals a sheep and his wife Gill disguises it by "wrap[ping]" it like a baby, putting it in a cradle and pretending it is her child. When the shepherds from whom Mak has taken the sheep arrive with sixpence for the "baby," the third shepherd wants to see it. Mak tries to stop him, but the shepherd says, "Give me leave him to kiss, and lift up the clout. / What the devil is this? He has a long snout!" (583–5). With this discovery the shepherds realize it is their sheep, and when Mak and Gill continue to dissemble, the third Shepherd says, "I know him by the ear-mark; that is a good token" (611). It seems probable that the shepherds' discovery of the sheep in the cradle was intended and seen as a parody of the liturgical Christmas play, in which

---

[44] Glynne Wickham, *Early English Stages*, vol. I, 155.
[45] Andreas Höfele, "John Foxe, *Christus Triumphans*," 136.
[46] Ibid. Höfele notes that "The opening (and closing) of the 'heavens', i.e. of curtains installed in 'the upper part of the theatre', is a common feature of mid-sixteenth-century continental stagecraft" (note 29).

the Christ-child – the Lamb of God – is discovered on the altar.[47] More generally, John McGavin and Greg Walker argue:

> This is drama interested in the artifice of its own medium, playing with, and thematizing its fundamental resources of pretence, disguise, and disclosure. It seems to be part of a phase in drama during which plays were generally fascinated with or anxious about their own status as a medium based on the contrary forces of falsehood and revelation.[48]

The Cradle of Security was a play that has survived only in the memoirs of one Richard Willis, who in 1639 described a performance he saw in Gloucester when he was a boy in the mid-1570s. The play was evidently a morality, in which a prince is lulled into a false sense of "security" by worldly pleasures.[49] Despite justifiable doubts about the anecdote's provenance and accuracy,[50] the degree of detail Willis provides suggests that he really did see something like what he remembered. The piece of business that would have been the most complex to stage – at least as Willis describes it – is certainly memorable:

> in the end they got [the Prince] to lye downe in a cradle upon the stage, where these three Ladies joyning in a sweet song rocked him asleepe, that he snorted againe, and in the meane time closely conveyed under the cloaths where withall he was covered, a vizard like a swines snout upon his face, with three wire chaines fastned thereunto, the other end whereof being holden severally by those three Ladies, who fall to singing againe, and then discovered his face, that the spectators might see how they had transformed him. (F8r)

This summary provides details about the engineering of a special effect, and the business it describes is impressively sophisticated in how it both creates dramatic irony and anticipates action to come. That a young boy would have perceived and understood how the mask was smuggled under the covers and how the wire chains were controlled is surprising – although perhaps the players called attention to these actions with elaborate miming. Indeed, the moment when the three Circean Ladies "discovered his face, that the spectators might see how they had transformed him" is, to my knowledge, unique. Nothing like this intricately contrived discovery exists in any other extant play. As Willis notes, this discovery was for the

---

[47] John McGavin and Greg Walker note that "The staged revelation of the sheep is then supplanted by the staged revelation of the Christ child as Lamb of God in the final scene" (*Imagining Spectatorship*, 130).

[48] Ibid.   [49] See *Macbeth*: "Security / Is Mortals cheefest Enemie" (TLN 1462–3).

[50] See E. Pearlman, "*R. Willis and* The Cradle of Security," 357–73.

spectators' benefit, not for the Prince asleep in his "cradle of security." The Ladies remove the "cloaths," thereby literally discovering the Prince's transformed "face" – actually the "vizard" – to reveal the truth of which he is as yet unaware. As with any such revelation, the resulting dramatic irony creates a distance between the ignorant character(s) and knowledgeable playgoers. Only when the audience is aware of not just the Prince's sinful state but also his lack of self-knowledge do two old men enter and awake the Prince, who starts up "barefaced" (F8v) – realizing too late that he is condemned.

In Thomas Garter's *The Most Virtuous and Godly Susanna* (1578) the heroine is falsely accused and at her trial her face is modestly covered. As McGavin and Walker note, "The culmination of the play's action is a moment of staged revelation."[51] Pretending not to recognize Susanna, the aptly named Sensua says, "what she is that standeth there, we can do nought but muse. / She is so muffled about the face, we thinke it is not she, / A crafty Dame may compasse so to have us go awry" and insists, "I meane to see her face, / And know if it be she or no, before I speake in place." When the judge orders the bailiff to "Discover her face," Susanna stops him – "I pray thee Gayler holde thee still my selfe wil do it to" (B4v) – and removes her own veil. This is not a disguise, nor is the discovery a surprise, but it is a discovery nevertheless. In particular, "the unveiling . . . offers at once a contradictory image of female agency and powerlessness."[52]

Based on these few extant English examples, covers were probably opened or removed to effect "dis-coveries" in many other medieval plays, concerned as they were with demonstrations of power and revelations of truth.

Later Echoes, Allusions and Inversions

Admittedly, a long time and a religious revolution separate the practices prescribed in the *Regularis Concordia* or those described by Durandus, from the world of Shakespeare and his contemporaries; but it is most unlikely that the entrenched rituals of Catholicism would have disappeared completely from the imaginations of playwrights and playgoers. Indeed, a familiarity with the use of curtains to hide the altar is indicated by a reference in Henry Glapthorne's 1635 play *The Hollander*: "That sacred night which spred its starry wings, / (Like Curtaines shadowing the Altar) ore / Our Hymeneall couch" (F4v). The casual way this comparison is

---

[51] McGavin and Walker, *Imagining Spectatorship*, 116.   [52] Ibid.

made suggests that it would have been generally understood well into the seventeenth century. So while I would not argue for a direct or deliberate link between the revelations performed in the medieval Catholic liturgies of the Nativity and Resurrection and discoveries in early modern drama, having those earlier ceremonies in mind has heightened my awareness of possible echoes and allusions that add an important dimension to later uses of the device. Unlike the medieval examples just discussed, the discoveries in post-Reformation plays are allusive rather than explicit in their references to Christian symbolism. But some of the most apparent secular instances are those in which the treatment of a discovery seems to rely on playgoer knowledge of the earlier liturgical rituals for an awareness of irony or parody that acts as a kind of commentary.

Perhaps the most obvious of these is the discovery that begins *Volpone*. Jonson – who was Catholic – has Volpone allude to specific religious and philosophical images, rituals and ideas that make it clear his worship of gold is intentionally blasphemous: "Open the shrine that I may see my saint. / Hail the world's soul, and mine" (2P3v). Furthermore, Volpone's religious imagery seems intended to convey how this action and what it reveals constitute a diabolic inversion of the ceremony of opening altar curtains during the Nativity rituals of the church or in the revelation depicted by van der Goes (Figure 3.3). In Act 3 Volpone probably performs another discovery when he tells Celia, "See, behold / What thou art queen of; not in expectation, / As I feed others, but possessed and crowned" (2S5r). Here too the circumstances and language suggest a perverted and distorted version of a revelation at the heart of Christianity, in this case the Annunciation.[53]

These kinds of inverted revelation, in which the discovery is of the antithesis of the events and values embedded in the Catholic Mass celebrating the Nativity and Resurrection, might also add meaning to scenes in which the discovery is explicitly of evil or sin. Near the end of Barnes's *The Devil's Charter* (1607), for example, Alexander, who has sold his soul to the devil to become pope, "*draweth the Curtaine of his studie where hee discovereth the divill sitting in his pontificals*" (L3v). Having Alexander reveal the devil dressed as himself and sitting in his study encapsulates the play's pervasive anti-Catholicism. Similar revelations of satanic figures occur at the start of *The Merry Devil of Edmonton* (1601–3), when the Prologue gives

---

[53] When Bonario rescues Celia he refers to Volpone's treasure as "this altar, and this drosse, thy idoll" (2S6r).

a short biography of Peter Fabell, the "merry Fiend of Edmonton," before he "*Draw[s] the curtaines*" (A3r–v), saying:

> Behold him heere laide on his restlesse couch,
> His fatall chime prepared at his head,
> His chamber guarded with these sable slights,
> And by him stands that Necromanticke chaire,
> In which he makes his direfull invocations,
> And binds the fiends that shall obey his will,
> Sit with a pleased eye untill you know
> The Commicke end of our sad Tragique show. (A3v)

Note the reference to "these sable slights" – presumably black curtains that the Prologue has opened to discover this tableau. And a scene in Middleton's *A Trick to Catch the Old One* (1605) begins with "*Dampit the Usurer in his bed, Audry spinning by*" and Dampit saying, "drawe the Curtaine" (G3r) to reveal him. When Lamprey and Spitchcock then enter, Lamprey's description emphasizes the emblematic quality of the scene: "Looke you, did not I tell you he lay like the devill in chaines, when he was bound for a thousand yeare." And Spitchcock's response continues to develop the idea and the picture: "But I thinke the devill had no steele Bedstaffes, he goes beyond him for that" (G3v). In another Middleton play, the anti-Spanish *A Game at Chess* (1624), there is "*An Altar is discovered with Tapers, and Images standing on each side*" (I2v).[54] This is a show by the Black Knight to impress the White Knight, although the latter's aside – "Ther's a taste of the old vessell still" (I2v) – indicates how this spectacle resembles aspects of Catholic worship.

Middleton – a Puritan – included discoveries in other plays that also seem intended as ironic allusions to the central rituals of Catholicism. In *The Second Maiden's Tragedy/Lady's Tragedy* (1611) the Lady's "*Toombe*" is "*discovered ritchly set forthe*" (1726–7) and the Lady's body is removed by the Tyrant. At the end of the scene, the "stone" (1870) in front of the tomb is replaced and a soldier comments that they "cover emptines" (1872). In the next scene when Govianus comes to the tomb and addresses it as if it contained the body, a voice "*With in*" says, "I am not here" (1923), then:

> *On a sodayne in a kinde of Noyse like a Wynde, the dores clattering, the Toombstone flies open, and a great light appeares in the midst of the Toombe; His Lady as went owt, standing just before hym all in white, Stuck with jewells and a great crucifex on her brest.* (1926–31)

---

[54] STC 17885; different editions have slightly different wording.

This figure tells Govianus, "the monument is robd, behold I'me gon / my bodie taken up" and Govianus confirms "tis gon indeed" (1950–2). Both verbally and visually these episodes seem to rework the post-Resurrection visit of the two Marys to Christ's tomb that is the basis of the *Quem quaeritis* trope: "And, behold, there was a great earthquake: for the angel of the lord descended from heaven, and came and rolled back the stone from the door ... the angel answered and said unto the women ... He is not here; for he is risen ... Come, see the place where the Lord lay" (Matthew 28, 2, 5–6).[55] Middleton's *A Chaste Maid in Cheapside* (1613) includes a brief scene in which a Wench enters "*with a Basket, and a Child in it under a Loyne of Mutton*" (D4v), then departs after making two Promoters swear to keep the basket until she returns. When their curiosity leads them to look in the basket, they make two discoveries. They find the expected loin of mutton, but instead of what they think is "a Lambes Head" (E1r), under the mutton they find the Wench's baby. The similarities between this discovery and the shepherds' discovery of the stolen sheep in *The Second Shepherds' Play*, discussed above, are noteworthy – although in the earlier play the context is the Nativity and in *A Chaste Maid in Cheapside* it is Lent, and the allusion is therefore to the Crucifixion and Resurrection of the "Lamb of God."

The use of one or more discoveries to shift the mood of a play from dark to light is common enough that it can often seem little more than formulaic. But the idea that such revelations are possible and that they can initiate a happy conclusion can be seen as a version, however reductive, of the governing Christian belief in the "divine comedy" of human existence. A case in point is *The Honest Lawyer* (1615) in which the two plots, both concerned with the suspicion, deception and litigation of City life, are resolved by disguise-discoveries that lead to reformation and renewal. In the main plot, Vaster, having mortgaged his estate to Old Gripe and suspecting his wife of infidelity, sells her to a bawd. He then fights with Benjamin Gripe (the honest lawyer of the title), is injured, and pretends to be dying, which leads Benjamin to promise he will look after Vaster's children. This goodness causes an abrupt change in Vaster, who when left alone says, "Now for some strange disguise, till time I find, / To pleasure him that was to me thus kind" (B2v). When next Vaster appears, he is disguised in the "russet-shape of a plaine-dealing yeoman" (C3v); but after two thieves try to rob him, he joins them.

---

[55] This probable allusion is noted by Anne Lancashire in her edition of the play (4.4.42.1–48 note).

The middle of the play deals with the avariciousness of lawyers such as Old Gripe and usurers such as Bromley, who persecute Vaster's children and wife; and with the good figures, such as Benjamin Gripe and Sager, who offer to help the children despite, in Sager's case, having little money of his own. The multiple interrelated deceptions, robberies, seductions and betrayals are geared to hold the interest of playgoers, while also depicting an exaggerated version of the London they lived in. When Sager wins a judgement against Bromley, for example, his life is in danger, so he too adopts a disguise. And when the disguised Vaster encounters the wife he has sold, he tries to seduce her. Not recognizing him, she says she has the pox, whereupon he erupts: "Politick whore! / What, do you ken me now?" and "*discovers himselfe*" (H4v). His wife responds, "My husband? O, / Into your armes I flie," but he rejects her: "Infection, no. / Y'are dangerous by your owne confession," so she explains "Alas! I forg'd that answere, to avoid / Sinfull embracings" (H4v). But he does not believe her and makes new plans to implicate her in a robbery.

This brings the action to the trial scene of Act 5, with a number of disguised figures on stage including Vaster, now "*in a Priests habit*" (I3r), and Sager. In the course of a trial too complicated to summarize fully here, Old Gripe is accused of murdering the Widow Sorrow (the name adopted by Vaster's wife) and Bromley is accused of murdering Sager. Both plead guilty to what they think is the truth. But the junior Gripe tricks his father into signing over Vaster's mortgages to him, then reveals that the "widow" is alive. Next Vaster, still in disguise, accuses Benjamin Gripe of killing Vaster and describes how he found him dying and "bury'd him" (K2r). Since Benjamin did fight with Vaster, he believes this and pleads guilty to killing his wife's father. Knowing the truth because her husband has revealed himself to her earlier, Vaster's wife asks, "Can nature so degenerate, that a man should live, stand by, and see another suffer for murdering him?" and Vaster intervenes, "Once againe off disguise. / My lord, thus I prevent this fear'd disaster / My second case pull'd off, I am plaine Vaster" (K2r). Moreover, as if aware of the tragicomic conventions within which he exists, Vaster says, "I am new borne" and "I am now / New marry'd to my love and to my life" (K2v). But the play is not over and one disguise remains to be discovered. Benjamin Gripe asks Bromley to give Sager's widow and children the disputed lease and when Bromley agrees, Sager cues his self-discovery: "Sager lives, / And hartie thankes for your forc'd kindnesse gives" (K2v). Recognizing how multiple deceptions have led to these final revelations of truth, the Abbot says, "Happy delusions! in such waies of ill, / I wish men may be thus mistaken still" (K2v).

Whoever wrote *The Faithful Friends* (1621?) seems to have appreciated and capitalized on the visual and thematic potential offered by disguise-discoveries. Indeed, although otherwise unremarkable theatrically, this play includes a sequence of linked self-revelations by three main representatives of the good in a world of duplicity and danger. In Act 1 Lelia, sister of Tullius and in love with Marius, enters disguised as Janus, page to Philadelphia, the new wife of Tullius. When Marius returns to Rome, he learns that Lelia has disappeared; but thanks to her asides playgoers know that Janus is Lelia. When she hears that Marius is going to war, she decides to accompany him. On the battlefield in Act 3 Tullius receives a letter saying that the king, Titus Martius, is trying to seduce Philadelphia, so he decides to return secretly to Rome to see for himself. He asks Marius to

> weare my Coate Armor, that disguise alone
> will make us undistinguisht, but with all,
> take this rich Scarffe, which for her sake that gave it
> has bin my individiall ornament
> and cheefest marke of note.   (2000–4)

When Sabinus, the enemy, pretends to offer a truce, the disguised Marius meets with him and, taken for Tullius, is (it seems) stabbed to death. To keep the body with her, Lelia (Janus in speech-headings) falsely discovers herself to Sabinus as Philadelphia, Tullius's wife: "Sabinus see, behold the wretched wife of Tullius, / looke what a Wofull Widdowe you have made" (2180–1). Then after Sabinus has left, Lelia speaks to the body, revealing her true identity:

> Oh Marius I have wrongd thy blessed spiritt
> to mourne thy death by a contrarie name
> but twas a sisters love, then pardon mee
> if any life remaine, fix but thyne eye
> uppon thy Lelia's sorrowe, crying now.   (2216–20)

Hearing this, Marius realizes who she is and reveals he is not dead but is

> transported into paradice
> wrapt above apprehension to behould
> my dearest Lelia's sight, hast thou bin dead
> to all mens knowledge since I first left Roome
> and dost survive to be my lives preserver.   (2231–5)

So in a nice double use of the device, Lelia's false discovery seems to save Tullius, and her true discovery actually saves Marius.

The sequence that picks up and completes these discoveries-of-the-good begins when Tullius enters Philadelphia's bedchamber and "*stepps behinde ye Arras*" to watch and listen to the King seducing her – "Arras thou / shalt hide my body, but light myne understanding" (2622–3). After hearing enough, "*Tullius stepps out*" (2706) from behind the arras and the King exclaims, "Howe's this? surpry'zd? o me tis Tullius" (2709). The King pretends he was merely testing Philadelphia, but Tullius is (rightly) sceptical and when he and Philadelphia are alone he tells her,

> yet since things
> lye but at halfe discoverd, for a time
> in some strange shape ile shrowde mee, free from
> the knowledge of the Kinge, or any
> untill these tares bee weeded, when there ripe
> Ile be my selfe and shine unlymitted.   (2807–12)

This sets up Tullius's appearance at court "*in disguise amongst other Peticoners*" (2930–1). In an aside he says, "I hope this habitts undiscoverable, / in wch as in a perspicle[56] I shall see / these hidden furies tread the divells maze" (2932–4). As always with this play, playgoers are aware of the disguise and prompted to await a satisfying discovery. When a Captain "discover[s the] black Trecherie" (3068) that Tullius's ostensible murder on the battlefield was arranged by the King, no one believes him, so Tullius finally discovers himself and confronts the actual perpetrators. His father calls it a "blessed metamorphosis" (3154) and the King tells Tullius, "Thou still transcendst in goodnes" (3167). This is typical of the overwrought language that characterizes *The Faithful Friends*, but it also evokes descriptions of Christian revelations, and certainly Tullius is portrayed as a heroic figure who forgives his enemies, even the duplicitous King.

The quarto of Heywood's *A Maidenhead Well Lost* (1633) illustrates the play's unusual discovery on its title page, and this woodcut reappears in the text near where the event occurs (Figure 3.7). In the plot, Julia is to marry the Prince of Parma, but tricks by others have made him suspect her of having another relationship and he rejects her. But she is pregnant with Parma's child which, when it is born, is taken to the woods and left to die until found and saved by Parma. In Act 5 the direction "*Enter a Serving-man with a child in a covered Dish*" (H4r) provides information to readers that is not available to playgoers for whom, as for the

---

[56] "Perspicil, n." A lens; an optical instrument, as a telescope or microscope. (*OED Online*, Oxford University Press, June 2017).

Figure 3.7 Woodcut illustration, *A Maidenhead Well Lost*, Thomas Heywood, 1634

characters, the discovery is a surprise. The Duke of Florence must open the dish because he exclaims "What's here, a Child?" and Julia cries, "Oh my perplexed heart!" Then the Prince of Florence sees that "Upon his brest ther's something writ, Ile read it" and does so: "'Tis fit, if Justice bee not quite exil'd / That he that wedds the mother, keepe the child" (H4r). The crude accompanying woodcut (H3r) shows a table on which sits the "dish" (it looks more like a box); figures on either side hold open half of the cover to expose the child (it looks more like a miniature adult). The dish is ostensibly a wedding present to the Duke of Florence and Julia from the Prince of Parma, who then enters. Not surprisingly, this double discovery of child and message resolves all confusions and conflicts, permitting a comic ending. Indeed, the woodcut not only illustrates the discovery but also, in a side panel, an embracing couple – probably the child's parents, Julia and the Prince of Parma, whose reunion the revelation and resulting confessions have made possible.

Masques, Pageants and Shows

Royal entries, Lord Mayor's shows and court masques also used the device of discovery – although such works were fundamentally different from stage plays, being one-off events for which no expense was spared that were performed in a variety of venues. But because discoveries, especially of tableaux, are common in these works, their relevance to discoveries in plays merits consideration. In these occasional events, discoveries of scenes generally occur earlier than in plays; indeed, they often initiate the performance. In other instances discoveries recur as a series of visual surprises. Furthermore, these *coups de théâtre* were crafted primarily to flatter and amuse a ruler or leader. Not surprisingly, therefore, the emphasis on elaborate spectacle, together with the staging made possible by large sums of money, gave primacy to the visual dimension. This does not mean, however, that in these one-off spectacles "theatre" always or necessarily trumped "theme." Indeed, discoveries in masques and civic pageants are governed more overtly than in plays by the conventions of allegory, in which image and word are combined to convey meaning. This might partly explain why in plays discoveries of disguises are more common than discovery scenes, while the reverse is true in the occasional shows. Another reason for this difference was probably that disguises in plays are part of a plot, whereas in shows they are typically part of a spectacle and have primarily local significance. And while in masques royal figures and courtiers often donned costumes or masks that they removed at the end of the performance in a kind of pseudo-discovery, these pretended disguises are essentially different from those adopted by characters in plays. Worth noting, though, is that masques in plays sometimes appropriate this court practice and have courtier-characters in disguise who discover themselves as part of the plot.

A sequence of commands in *Albion's Triumph*, a Caroline masque by Aurelian Townshend – "Behold! ... Observe! ... Admire!"[57] – succinctly conveys the emphasis on the visual impact and message that characterized discoveries in masques and other elaborate shows through the period. From at least the late fifteenth century such revelations were made possible by the availability of curtains sizeable enough to cover a wide opening. For example, the York record of Henry VII's first progress, in 1486, includes a pageant in which "*shall appeir a citie with citisyns.*"[58] John Meagher says

---

[57] Aurelian Townshend, *Albion's Triumph*, A3v.
[58] John Meagher, "The First Progress of Henry VII," 53.

that "The appearance was probably by sudden disclosure, the movement of a curtain, revealing a stylized city ... with its mythical founder and its citizen-representatives."[59] In a second York pageant, *"on the hight of Ouse brigge a rioall troyne and therein sodanely appering set togidder in counsail sex kinges crouned betokining the sex Henries."* Meagher notes that "'sodanely appering' suggests again the use of a curtain of some sort controlling a discovery space on the huge throne which seems to have served as a stage for the scene."[60] And records of courtly entertainments in Henry VIII's reign seem to describe fairly spectacular discoveries by "letting down" a curtain on at least four occasions.[61]

While the early use of discoveries to surprise and impress the audiences of masques and pageants might have established a convention, the device began to occur regularly only in the Jacobean era; but by the end of Charles I's reign it had become a predictable element. The staging conditions at court – indoors and with somewhere to suspend a curtain – would always have made it easier to execute discovery scenes than did conditions in the streets of London, but there are nevertheless several instances of discoveries in street shows, particularly in *The King's Entertainment through the City of London* of March 1604. This consisted of a series of extravagant triumphal arches designed by John Harrison for the staging of emphatically allegorical tableaux, composed largely by Dekker and Jonson. Jonson's description of the first arch at Fenchurch Street includes a discovery that anticipates his later use of the device in masques:

> the whole frame, was covered with a curtaine of silke, painted like a thicke cloude, and at the approach of the K. was instantly to bee drawne. The Allegory being, that those cloudes were gathered upon the face of the Citty, through their long want of his most wished sight: but now, as at the rising of the Sunne, all mistes were dispersed and fled. (B2r)

The third arch was that of the Dutchmen or Belgians at the Royal Exchange. Dekker describes how at "the heart of the Trophee [arch]"

> was a spacious square roome, left open, Silke Curtaines drawne before it, which (upon the approch of his Majestie) being put by, 17. yong Damsels, (all of them sumptuously adorned, after their countrey fashion,) sate as it

---

[59] Ibid., 54.   [60] Ibid., 55.

[61] For descriptions of masques using such discoveries in 1511, 1513, 1518 and 1527, see Sidney Anglo, "The Evolution of the Early Tudor Disguising, Pageant, and Mask," 21–2, 23, 27, 29, 39–40.

Figure 3.8 Arch of the Dutchmen or Belgians at the Royal Exchange, *The arch's of triumph erected in honor of the high and mighty prince James, the first of that name,* John Harrison, c. 1613

were in so many Chaires of State, and figuring in their persons, the 17. Provinces of Belgia, of which every one caried in a Scutchion (excellently pencilde) the Armes and Coate of one. (D2r)

Harrison's engraving of this arch shows the curtains after they have been opened (Figure 3.8). In both instances, James is ostensibly the cause of the revelation, and the imagery of the first, in particular, emphasizes the symbolic dimension and implications.

Lord Mayor's shows also sometimes used discoveries to encapsulate key ideas, and in none is this more apparent than *The Triumphs of Truth* (1613), "the most expensive mayoral pageant of the Renaissance."[62] Middleton's detailed description makes clear that the large investment was devoted to a show portraying a highly visual battle between Truth and Error. David Bergeron comments that:

> No other pageant-dramatist so consistently follows through on a pattern of imagery as Middleton; time and again, without being obtrusive, he presents both visually and verbally the conflict between light and darkness, a tension of symbolic import. This becomes his particular way of symbolizing the struggle for the victory of Truth and Virtue over men and nations.[63]

Not only does *The Triumphs of Truth* capitalize on the inherent theatricality of the action of discovery, it also enacts the idea of stripping away false appearances to reveal hidden truth. Several excerpts from the description and speeches indicate how Middleton combined the visual and verbal to convey a long battle and eventual victory. The show included a "Mount Triumphant" (C2r) representing London, "*but the Beauty and Glory thereof over-spred with a thicke Sulphurous Darknesse, it being a Fog or Mist raisde from Error*" (C2r). After describing the scene, Truth comments, "I see if Truth a while but turne her Eies, / Thicke are the Mists that o'er faire Citties rise"; then she commands, "Vanish Infectious Fog that I may see / This Citties Grace, that takes her Light from Mee. Vanish, give way" (C2v).

> *At this her powerful command, the Cloude suddenly rises, and changes into a bright spredding Canopy, stucke thicke with Starres, and beames of Gold, shooting forth round about it, the Mount appearing then most rich in Beauty and Glory.* (C2v)

The description of an elaborate scene of symbols and figures representing Truth continues until "*The Mount thus made glorious by the Power of Truth, and the Mist expeld, London thus speakes*":

> Thicke Scales of Darknesse in a Moments space
> Are fell from both mine Eyes, I see the Face
> Of all my Friends about me (now) most cleerely,

---

[62] David Bergeron, *English Civic Pageantry*, 179.   [63] Ibid., 197.

Religions Sisters, whom I Honour deerely;
Oh I behold the worke, it comes from Thee
Illustrious Patronesse, thou that mad'st me see
In Dayes of blindest Ignorance, when this Light
Was ee'n extinguisht, Thou Redeem'st my sight.   (C3v)

But Error is not so easily defeated and calls on her "Monsters ... Barbarisme, Impudence, Lies, Ignorance" to "once againe with Rotten Darknesse shroud / This Mount Triumphant, drop downe sulphurous Cloud" (C4r). In response, *"the Mist falles againe, and hangs over all the Beauty of the Mount, not a Person of Glory seene"* (C4v). This sequence of covering, discovering and re-covering the Mount occurs several times, for reasons that are made clear. London recognizes "Perfect Love" – "Æternity's bright Sister, by whose Light / Errors infectious workes still flye my Sight. / Receive thy Servants Thankes" (C4v) – but the subsequent action includes, *"Error by the way still busie and in Action to drawe Darknesse often upon that Mount of Triumph, which by Truth is as often disperst"* (D1r). Only at the very end (after the installation of the new Lord Mayor being celebrated – and instructed – by this show) is Error finally defeated when *"a Flame shootes from the Head of Zeale, which fastening upon that Chariot of Error sets it on Fire, and all the Beasts that are joinde to it"* (D2v).

The symbolic link between truth and light so evident here is also central to the representation of the discovery of truth in the work of early modern visual artists and dramatists (see Chapter 4). In this show, the "mist" or "cloud" of Error was probably a painted curtain or other property that could be moved without too much difficulty to cover and uncover the Mount repeatedly.[64] But when the revelations occur, the descriptions also emphasize light and brightness, suggesting another painted curtain as a backdrop or an actual lighting effect. Either way, it would need to have been impressive (like the final fire) to counter the spectacle and effect of the enshrouding mists.

From the moment James I came to the throne, the fullest potential for the discovery of spectacular *tableaux vivants* was realized in the masques created for his court, especially those by Inigo Jones in collaboration with Ben Jonson.[65] Fortunately, the descriptions of court masques are typically quite detailed so that often the visual experience of a discovery and the method of its

---

[64] The imagery of clouds, literalized in masques, is sometimes used analogously to refer to disguises in plays; see Chapter 4.

[65] This is not the place to rehearse the conflict between Jonson and Jones over the increasing dominance of spectacle in masques, although I am aware of it. But the very reason for Jonson's

staging are clearly conveyed. One aspect made evident is that over time the technique Jones used to discover a hidden scene evolved from first raising, lowering or opening a curtain, then to the use of a revolving stage, then to the use of sliding panels. Martin Butler provides an informative summary:

> Jonson's structural innovations in *The Masque of Queens* (1609) were no less dependent on Jones's technological developments. Earlier masques made use of the *machina versatilis* or "turning machine," a scenic unit which revolved to discover hidden masquers. *Queens*, however, opened with "an ugly hell" before which twelve witches danced in an attempt to curse the glory of the court; but suddenly "the whole face of the scene altered, scarce suffering the memory of any such thing," in place of which were revealed the masquers seated in the House of Fame. Jonson appears to be describing the *scena ductilis*, or system of sliding flats which enabled the entire setting, and not only one unit, to be changed at a stroke. This arrangement turned the masque from a static presentation or discovery into a dynamic action. Queen Anne and her eleven accompanying "queens" entered the action in a blaze of light before which the witches vanished as if insubstantial; their triumphant discovery mimed the victory of truth over falsehood and fame over envy under the approving and controlling gaze of the royal spectator.[66]

Given such advances in staging technology, together with the desire for a spectacle that celebrated and complimented the royal personage, it is not surprising that the mythical and allegorical elements associated with discoveries in masques were gradually supplemented by the increasingly realistic detail of what was revealed.[67] By the 1630s when William Davenant was creating court masques, for example, the discovery of a spectacularly realistic scene at the start had become conventional. His *Britannia Triumphans* (1637), created with Jones, begins:

> *A curtaine flying up discovered the first Scene, wherein were English houses of the old and newer formes, intermixt with trees, and a farre off a prospect of the Citie of London, and the River of Thames, which being a principall part, might be taken for all great Britaine.* (A3r–v)

As previously noted, the removal of clothing to uncover a hidden reality is rare in the descriptions of shows and masques. Certainly, having a figure

---

unhappiness calls attention to the emphasis on the visual in the many masques they created together for both King James and King Charles.

[66] Martin Butler, "Private and Occasional Drama," 140.

[67] For other examples of discoveries in which technology and realism dominate the spectacle, see William Davenant, *The Triumphs of the Prince D'Amour* (1635); Thomas Carew, *Coelum Brittanicum* (1633); Aston Cockain, *A Masque* (1639).

in a masque remove a disguise offered much less potential for spectacle than did the discovery of a scene or tableau. But Jonson and Middleton (who were also playwrights, after all) both used the simpler kind effectively in their occasional works. In *Hymenaei* (1616), written for the marriage of the Earl of Essex and Lady Frances Howard, Jonson presented a battle between the identically dressed figures of Truth and Opinion. When the deception is revealed, Truth describes what the spectators would have seen and understood:

> And Princes, see, tis meere Opinion,
> That in Truth's forced Robe, for Truth hath gone!
> Her gaudy Colours, peec'd, with many Folds,
> Shew what uncertainties she ever holds.　　　　　　　(F2v)

In Middleton's *The Sun in Aries*, the Lord Mayor's show for 1621, when the incumbent mayor approached the recently refurbished New Standard conduit in Cheapside, "*one in a cloudy Ruinous Habit Leaning upon the Turret, at a Trumpets sounding, suddenly starts and wakes, and in Amazement throwes off his unseemly Garments*," saying, "What Noyse is this? wakes me from Ruines Wombe / Hah? blesse me, (Time) how brave am I become?" (B2v). As a comparison of these two examples illustrates, when a figure discovers himself, the meaning is straightforward, but when the discovery is done by another, the implications are more complex. The same is generally true of disguise-discoveries in plays.

　　Two Jonson-Jones collaborations in particular balance spectacle and theme so as to make the discoveries especially meaningful. The first is *The Entertainment at Britain's Bourse*, performed for King James when he opened the New Exchange on 11 April 1609. Thomas Wilson, Robert Cecil's secretary, wrote a description of what was planned, including that an actor playing a mountebank, wearing "a vizard as they use to have," would stand before a shop containing "things of price to be covered with curtains" and "When their turn comes to be spoken of, he shall unmask as a merchant that sells not *merces adulterinas* [false wares], and then make a presentment of them as the things and persons deserve."[68] In addition to this self-discovery, "make a presentment" presumably meant drawing open the curtains to reveal the merchandise. James Knowles notes that the extant text of this show does not actually say when or where this unmasking and discovery were to happen, and he speculates that it might have been revised

---

[68] James Knowles, "Jonson's *Entertainment*," 116.

before performance.[69] Nevertheless, the intention seems clear; and as Knowles observes, "The very design of the shop, fitted out with shelves and curtains which are drawn to reveal the wonders within bears a distinct resemblance to the Renaissance *kunstkammer* or cabinet of wonders."[70]

The show called *Prince Henry's Barriers* was created by Jonson and Jones to celebrate Henry in 1610, the year of his investiture as Prince of Wales. Jonson's text gives only the most basic directions for performance, but each one signals a discovery and each discovery is different. To start there is, "*The Lady of the Lake, first discovered*" (4M3r); soon after, Arthur is "*Discovered as a starre above*" (4M3v); then there is Merlin "*arising out of the tombe*" (4M4r); and "*Meliadus* [Henry], *and his sixe assistants here discovered*" (4M4v). Near the end, Merlin might be cueing another discovery when he says, "Stay, methinkes I see / A person in yond' cave. Who should that bee? / I know her ensignes now: 'Tis Chivalrie" (4N1r); Chivalry then awakens and emerges to initiate the actual barriers combat. In performance the revelation of each important court figure was almost certainly visually impressive; but, ironically, the minimal stage directions call attention to how the discoveries both emphasize and are justified by the symbolic significance of the mythical figures from Arthurian legend.

In general, while discovery scenes (and discoveries of disguises) in occasional works shared a number of elements with those in plays – the most fundamental being the physical act of removing a cover to reveal something beneath – they were mostly quite different in purpose and effect. First, and most basically, in plays written for the commercial playhouses physical limitations meant that discovery scenes were usually fairly simple to stage, whereas in works created for one-off, no-expense-spared performance at court or in the street, discoveries were more – sometimes a lot more – complex and elaborate. Then there is the matter of who was watching. Discoveries in plays are watched by other characters and by playgoers whose responses are usually conditioned by the reactions of the characters. Discoveries in masques and shows were watched by a queen or king, prince, Lord Mayor or other authority figure, and by others in attendance who also watched his or her responses. Each situation invites possibilities for multiple levels of perception and thus for irony. But whereas the ironies available to playgoers watching surprised characters are almost certainly intended to make a discovery more meaningful, ironies perceived by those

---

[69] Ibid.   [70] James Knowles, "Cecil's shopping centre," 15.

watching a masque or show that was written to honour and flatter a figure of importance were probably unintended and therefore potentially dangerous.

Theatrical Spectacle

Perhaps because of his experience creating City pageants and court masques, Middleton also made effective use of spectacular discoveries in several plays. Besides the opening of the tomb in *The Second Maiden's Tragedy/ Lady's Tragedy*, discussed above, two of his other plays include what must have been significant revelations involving an altar. In *Hengist, King of Kent* (1618) a dumb show begins with "*Musique*" then "*ffortune is discovered uppon an Alter, in her hand a golden round full of Lotts*" (261–2). This minimalist description probably belies an elaborate staging. Fortune's costume was doubtless symbolic, while her "golden round" represents the possibility of her favour on the one hand and her instability on the other, the latter also being indicated by the "lots." Indeed, Fortune's arbitrariness is ironically the truth discovered here. *A Game at Chess* (1624) has a similar direction, the fullest version of which is "*An altar discovered, richly adorned, with tapers on it, and divers statues standing on each side.*"[71]

In *The Brazen Age* (1611), Heywood included a visual set-piece that dramatizes a mythical event, although the paucity of detail makes it difficult to see with the mind's eye: "*Two fiery Buls are discovered, the Fleece hanging over them, and the Dragon sleeping beneath them*" (G2v). This discovery is precipitated by Jason arriving and "demanding combat" (G2r) with the bulls, so the scene would have been effective in creating a sense of the formidable foe that, with Medea's help, he immediately defeats, capturing the fleece.

Less explicitly emblematic or pageant-like but equally striking as a visual discovery is this revelation in Webster's *The Duchess of Malfi* (1614): "*Here is discover'd, (behind a Travers;) the artificiall figures of Antonio, and his children; appearing as if they were dead*" (I1v). The playgoer views this scene with the Duchess and Bosola, who tells her that Ferdinand "doth present you this sad spectacle, / That now you know directly they are dead" (I2r). Again the idea of the discovery of truth is being evoked, but here the explication supports the deception rather than countering it. And playgoers, accustomed to

---

[71] See *A Game at Chess: A Later Form*, ed. Gary Taylor, 5.1.33sd.

discoveries of truth, are given no reason to doubt what they see, until later when Ferdinand says to Bosola, "she's plagu'd in Art. / These presentations are but fram'd in wax. / ... / she takes them / For true substantiall Bodies" (I2v). But only when the Duchess is dying does Bosola finally tell her that what seemed true was false: "The dead bodies you saw, were but faign'd statues" (K4v).

At the very end of the period, Brome's *A Jovial Crew* (1641) includes two set-piece discovery scenes, both of which focus on the crew of beggars. The first comes in Act 1 when Springlove is about to join the jovial crew: "*He opens the Scene; the Beggars are discovered in their postures; then they issue forth*" (C3v). Then in Act 2 "*Randal opens the Scene. The Beggars discovered at their Feast. After they have scrambled a while at their Victuals*" a song is sung (F3r). Here again the use of a discovered tableau creates the impression that the secret world of the jovial crew is being revealed to playgoers. Indeed, both scenes constitute a kind of performance within the play, on which other figures comment.

Some plays include actual masques with discoveries not unlike those in court masques when the disguised noble figures reveal themselves; but usually the theatrical versions add an ironic twist to the spectacle. Again Middleton (with Rowley) provides examples, especially but not surprisingly in *The World Tossed at Tennis*, a masque that was intended for performance at court but seems instead to have been staged at the Swan in 1620.[72] Certainly its use of discoveries on an upper level is rare in plays but common in court masques.[73] This masque begins with Pallas calling on Jove to "Unfold thy fierie Vaile, the flaming Robe / And superficies of thy better brightnesse, / Descend from thine Orbicular Chariot" and then "*Jupiter descends*" (C3v).[74] This is soon followed by:

> *Musique and this Song as an Invocation to the nine Muses; (who in the time) are discover'd on the upper Stage, plac'd by the nine Worthies, and toward the*

---

[72] *The World Tossed at Tennis*, ed. C. E. McGee in *Thomas Middleton, The Collected Works*, 1406. Lauren Shohet says that this work "uses the phrase 'courtly masque' ... in the title as a marker of genre, rather than location," noting that "Although one performance of the masque was presented to King James, at Denmark House ... others were offered to different audiences, so that 'courtly' becomes at least in part an adjective of manner" (*Reading Masques*, 196).

[73] Shohet refers to this masque having "a full range of expected generic characteristics" including "alternations of antimasque scenes with mask-like 'discovery' of gods and worthies" (*Reading Masques*, 197).

[74] Referring to the "veil" or covering, McGee says, "this suggests that the staging included a discovery of Jupiter behind a brilliant fabric embellished with flames of cloth, perhaps a curtain or perhaps the character's robe" (*The World Tossed at Tennis*, ed. C. E. McGee, note to line 223).

conclusion descend, each one led by a Muse, the most proper and pertinent to the
person of the Worthy, as Therpsichore with David; Urania, with Joshua,
&c. (C4r)

Middleton also included a masque with discoveries in two plays. The stage
direction in *Your Five Gallants* (1607) describes a masque in which everyone is in disguise:

> *Enter the maske, thus ordered, A torchbearer, a sheeld-boy, then a masker, so*
> *throughout, then the sheeld-boyes fall at one end, the torchbearers at the other;*
> *the maskers ith middle, the torchbearers are the five gentlemen: the sheeld-boies*
> *the whores in boies apparel: the maskers the five Gallants.* (I2v)

Before the end, everyone has unmasked and, as one of the gallants says, "all
our shifts are discovered" (I3v). *No Wit, No Help Like a Woman's* (1611)
includes a similar use of a masque with disguised figures who are
discovered:

> *Enter four at several corners, addrest like the four Winds, with Wings, &c. and*
> *dance all to the Drum and Fiff; the four Elements seem to give back, and stand*
> *in amaze; the South wind has a great red face, the North wind a pale bleak one,*
> *the Western wind one cheek red, and another white, and so the Eastern wind; at*
> *the end of the dance, the Winds shove off the disguises of the other four, which*
> *seem to yeeld and almost fall off of themselves at the coming of the Winds; so all*
> *the four old Suiters are discovered.* (G1r)

Dekker's experience creating City pageants with a message is reflected in
a moralizing masque in *The Whore of Babylon* (1606):

> *The Hault-boyes sounding, Titania in dumbe shew sends her Lords to fetch them*
> *in, who enter bare headed the three Kings queintly attired like Masquers*
> *following them, who doing honour to her, intreat to dance with her maides,*
> *and doe so: This done they discover.* (C1r)

Titania says, "Your painted cheeks beeing off, your owne discovers, / You
are no Fairies" and the Kings respond, "No: but wounded lovers" (C1r).
Since the three Catholic kings are suitors for Titania's (Elizabeth's) hand in
marriage, the use of a court masque is especially fitting. A final example also
occurs in a play that is heavily influenced by masque conventions. *Four*
Plays in One (1613) by Fletcher and Field even has a cloud that opens for the
discovery of a divine being:

> *Musick. Enter Delight, Pleasure, Craft, Lucre, Vanitie, &c. dancing (and*
> *mask'd) towards the Rock, offering service to Anthropos. Mercury from above.*
> *Musick heard. One half of a cloud drawn. Singers are discovered: then the other*
> *half drawn. Jupiter seen in glory.* (8F4r)

It might be said that the use of discovery actions for revelations such as this, or for those performed in the early Church, is almost inevitable and therefore unsurprising. But as virtually all these examples show, discoveries are contrived actions that require special staging, which could have been an argument against including them. In addition, one might think that the repeated and continuous use of the device in one form or another over a long period would have resulted in playgoers tiring of it. But these examples indicate a lasting playgoer interest in and appreciation of surprise (or not-so-surprise) revelations. This popularity suggests that rather than being a problem, the staging was one of the attractions. In particular, if (as I think likely) the imagery of Christian revelation inflects the action and language of dramatic discoveries and these allusions would have been registered by early modern playgoers, there are dimensions still to be perceived and analyzed if we are to really appreciate how these revelations worked, in both performance and those playgoers' imaginations.

CHAPTER 4

Revelation and Belief

The idea that "truth was originally thought of as also a kind of unveiling, a removal of the curtains of forgetfulness in the mind"[1] is evident in two examples that use curtain imagery to convey the transition from the world of time and death to eternal life. In the last speech of Peele's *David and Bethsabe* (1599), David speaks over the body of his dead son Absalom:

> Thy day of rest, thy holy Sabboth day
> Shall be eternall, and the curtaine drawne,
> Thou shalt behold thy soveraigne face to face,
> With wonder knit in triple unitie,
> Unitie infinite and innumerable. (I1v)

In Francis Quarles's emblem illustrating Psalm 42.2 – "When shall I come and appear before the Lord" – a figure stands on one side of an "envious curtaine," with a brightly haloed angel on the other side (T6r–7v; Figure 4.1). As the accompanying Epigram 12 indicates, this separation is because the figure on the right is still alive, in a fallen body:

> How art thou shaded, in this vale of night,
> Behind thy Curtaine flesh? Thou seest no light,
> But what thy Pride does challenge as her owne;
> Thy Flesh is high: Soule, take this Curtaine downe. (T8r)[2]

As to whether or how the religious revelations that give meaning to these images can be related to the use of the discovery device in plays written by Shakespeare and his contemporaries, certainly both the liturgical and the pictorial curtains are parted to reveal a truth that has been hidden, private, secret; and in plays curtains are opened to reveal figures that have been secluded, or locations or actions involving secrecy. On the one hand, the drawing open of curtains is a common method of effecting a discovery, so

---

[1] Frye, *The Great Code*, 135. See Chapter 2 for the full quotation.
[2] Francis Quarles, *Emblemes*, Book 5, number XII.

Figure 4.1 "When shall I come and appear before the Lord," *Emblemes*,
Book 5, XII, Francis Quarles, 1635

its use in church ritual and religious art as well as in secular drama might be unremarkable; but discoveries in the plays also include other elements characteristic of the overtly Christian versions. In particular, dramatic discoveries – whether of scenes or disguises – are often explicitly signalled with evocative language that emphasizes the experience of seeing and believing and calls attention to the illumination both required and achieved.

The Language of Discovery and Recognition

Theatrical discoveries are frequently signalled by "behold," "look," and "see," injunctions that emphasize (and often cue) the action, and to which both the play's characters and playgoers respond. In addition, the observing characters often react to a discovery with "wonder" and "joy," words that stress the miraculous quality of the revelation or attribute that quality to it.

One of the most moving moments in *King Leir* (1590) comes when the disguised Cordella reveals herself to her father, saying, "But looke, deare father, looke, behold and see / Thy loving daughter speaketh unto thee" (H4r). In *The Bloody Banquet* a revelation that initiates an upbeat ending to the tragedy is signalled when the Old Queen "*discovers*" first herself and then the prince who has been thought dead, saying, "behold a hopefull heire: / Stand not amaz'd" (H1v). In *The Rape of Lucrece* when Lucrece is "*discoverd in her bed*" by Sextus, he says, "Heere, heere, beholde! beneath these Curtaines lyes, / That bright enchantresse that hath daz'd my eies" (G1v). And in *The Revenger's Tragedy* Antonio, "*Discovering the body of* [his wife] *dead to certaine Lords*," says, "behold, my Lords / A sight that strikes man out of me" (C1v). Near the end of *The Custom of the Country* (1620) when the disguised Duarte reveals himself to his mother, he signals the action with "Yet turne and see good Madam." Her response is indicated by the watching governor's words: "Do not wonder" and "Pray do not stand amaz'd, it is Duarte." And his mother is content to believe what she sees: "O my sweete Sonne. / I will not presse my wonder now with questions" (C4v). The corrupt world of *The Queen and Concubine* (1635) is countered when the disguised Sforza "*Discovers himself*" and the king responds, "I am all wonder" and "Shew me, shew me yet the face of glorious Truth; where I may read / If I have err'd, which way I was misled" (H4r; see Chapter 6).

The extended denouement of *The Costly Whore* (1619–32) has a Duke and father confronted with the ostensible deaths of his son and his daughter and her husband, all of whom he has sentenced to execution. The play concludes with a series of cued discoveries that surprise the Duke into repentance. The sequence of revelations begins with the entrance of the son, Frederick, on a "*hearse . . . covered with a blacke robe*" (G3v). Then come Julia and Otho, both veiled, pretending to be Euphrata the Duke's daughter and Constantine her husband. When Otho removes their veils, the Duke says, "Am I deluded, where is Euphrata. / And that audacious traitor Constantine?" (G4v), whereupon a bier is brought on "*with the bodies of Euphrata, and Constantine covered with blacke*" (H1r). Presumably Alberto uncovers the two when he tells the Duke these are "The bodies of the drowned Constantine. / And the faire Euphrata, behold them both" (H1r). Seeing them (as he thinks) dead, the Duke finally realizes the truth of their innocence and collapses. This causes Valentia to uncover Frederick:

> Behold my Lord, behold thy headlesse Sonne:
> Blest with a head, the late deceased living,
> As yet not fully waken'd from the sleepe:
> My drowsie potion kindled in his braine,
> But much about this houre the power should cease,
> And see he wakes.   (H2r)

The Duke's "O happinesse 'tis hee" (H2r) begins the process of truth-telling that punishes the bad, rewards the good and leads to a happy ending.

Just as Shakespeare makes a virtue of necessity with other requirements of early modern performance, when he includes a discovery he effectively capitalizes on a practical aspect of staging to emphasize thematic significance. In particular, the words of the figure in control of a revelation not only cue the action but also describe what is being revealed. Moreover, the language cues the responses of other figures while, at another level, telling playgoers what has been revealed and how to "see" it. Sometimes, indeed, the primary or only indication of a discovery is verbal, as at the end of *The Comedy of Errors* (1592) when the Abbess brings Antipholus out of the priory where she has hidden him, saying, "Most mightie Duke, behold a man much wrong'd" and "*All gather to see them*" (TLN 1813–15).[3] Similarly, at the end of *All's Well That Ends Well* (1605?) Diana cues the

---

[3] Bevington says that here the tiring house façade "becomes the means of revelation and discovery. It is through the stage door representing the Abbey that the Abbess emerges with Antipholis and Dromio of Syracusa to undeceive all those who have begun to question their own sanity" (*Action Is Eloquence*, 109). Bruce R. Smith describes the Abbess as a "*dea-ex-machina*" and says that opening a curtain "would have turned the Abbess's appearance into an epiphany appropriate for Christmas, a physical discovery that inaugurates all the ensuing discoveries of true identities" (*The Key of Green*, 214).

entrance/discovery of Helen – "So there's my riddle, one that's dead is quicke, / And now behold the meaning"[4] – at which the surprised King responds, "Is there no exorcist / Beguiles the truer Office of mine eyes? / Is't reall that I see?" (TLN 3037–42). In *Richard III* (1593) Anne probably uncovers Edward's bleeding wounds when she says to Richard, "If thou delight to view thy hainous deedes, / Behold this patterne of thy butcheries" (A4v). And later Richard probably uncovers his arm as he tells onlookers, "Then be your eies the witnesse of this ill, / See how I am bewitcht, behold mine arme / Is like a blasted sapling, withered up" (G2r). Wounds are certainly exposed in *Julius Caesar* (1599) when Antony says, "Kinde Soules, what weepe you, when you but behold / Our Caesars Vesture wounded? Looke you heere, / Heere is Himselfe, marr'd as you see with Traitors" and the Plebians exclaim, "O pitteous spectacle!" and "O most bloody sight!" (TLN 1732–5, 1739). When Julia, disguised as a page, discovers herself in *The Two Gentlemen of Verona*, only her vague "Behold her, that gave ayme to all thy oathes" (TLN 2225) and Proteus's surprised "How? Julia?" (TLN 2224) signal the action. But given the quite specific earlier information about Julia not cutting her hair for the disguise (TLN 1019–20), it seems probable that here she removes her page's cap to release long hair.[5] As curtains are opened to show the caskets in *The Merchant of Venice*, Portia says to Arragon, "Behold, there stand the caskets noble Prince" (D3v).

The miraculous quality of some discoveries is emphasized in three of Shakespeare's romances. In *The Tempest*, when "*Prospero discovers Ferdinand and Miranda, playing at Chesse*" (TLN 2141–2), his words both direct the onlookers' sight and anticipate their response:

> pray you looke in:
> My Dukedome since you have given me againe,
> I will requite you with as good a thing,
> At least bring forth a wonder, to content ye
> As much, as me my dukedom.   (TLN 2136–40)

And in *The Winter's Tale*, as Paulina opens a "curtain" to reveal the "statue" of Hermione, she says "prepare / To see the Life as lively mock'd, as ever /

---

[4] "Quick" probably puns on the fact that she is visibly pregnant (as well as alive); if so, she would resemble della Francesca's Madonna del Parto (Figure 3.5).

[5] Michael Shapiro refers to "the possibility of staging the undisguising through the falling or sudden release of Julia's hair, as in narratives by Ariosto, Tasso, and Spenser" (*Gender in Play*, 72). Hyland says, "for disguised girls the discovery of long hair seems, in cases where any direction is given at all, to have been the conventional way" to "engineer" these discoveries (*Disguise on the Early Modern Stage*, 55).

Still Sleepe mock'd Death: behold, and say 'tis well" (TLN 3206–8).[6]
In *Pericles*, after the "chest" holding Thaisa is brought on, Cerimon
twice says, "Wrench it open," then signals the discovery: "what's here,
a Corse?" Presumably the body, "Shrowded in Cloth of state" (E3v), is
lifted out of the coffin, because her revival seems to be visible to all when
Cerimon says, "behold her eyelids, / Cases to those heavenly jewels which
Pericles hath lost, / Begin to part their fringes of bright gold" (E4r) – which
also uses the metaphor of a curtain to describe Thaisa's eyes opening to
discover that she is alive.[7]

One plot in *The Trial of Chivalry* (1601) deals with Bellamira, who is
loved by both Philip and Bourbon and whose beauty is repeatedly
described with superlatives. When she accepts Philip, Bourbon scars
her face with poison in the hope that Philip will then reject her; but
Philip says he loves her for her inner beauty and will marry her anyway.
Bellamira then flees to the woods, where she meets a woman who heals
the scars. This prepares for the end of the play when Bellamira enters
"*with a Scarfe on her face*" (K1v) accompanied by the Clown, who tells
Philip, "Heere is a poore kinswoman of mine would desire some private
conference with you"; presumably she removes the scarf, discovering her
renewed beauty, because a surprised Philip asks, "whom see I?
Bellamira?" And Pembroke says, "Looke not so strange, it is thy lovely
Love, / Thus manag'd, to approve thy constancy" (K1v–2r). Pembroke's
words to Navar and France encourage belief and emphasize the comic
resolution: "Here end your strife, and let all hatred fall, / And turne this
warre to Hymens festivall" (K2r).

In some cases the discovery of a female is described using language
suggestive of a religious revelation. In the last act of Heywood's *The Fair
Maid of the West, part 1* (1604) Bess enters "*vail'd*" (H3v) to meet
Mullisheg, the explicitly pagan King of Fez. When she unveils, he uses
the language of Christianity to thank his Muslim god:

---

[6] Snyder and Curren-Aquino (*The Winter's Tale*, 5.3.20sd note) say that "The atmosphere surrounding
the unveiling of Hermione's 'statue' may be related to similar veneration in remembered scenes of the
old religion (as in Roger Martyn's nostalgic recollection of the ceremonial uncovering of sculpture at
Long Melford church, quoted in David Cressy and Lori Anne Ferrell, eds., *Religion and Society in
Early Modern England: A Sourcebook*, 1996, 11)." Smith says that this opening of the curtain is like
"the religious custom of shrouding the crucifix during Lent with a curtain ... and opening it on
Easter" (*The Key of Green*, 235).

[7] Compare this with Prospero's words as he awakens Miranda – "The fringed Curtaines of thine eye
advance, / And say what thou see'st yond" (TLN 551–2) – and her response when she first sees
Ferdinand: "It carries a brave forme. But 'tis a spirit" and "I might call him / A thing divine, for
nothing naturall / I ever saw so Noble" (TLN 555, 562–4).

I am amaz'd,
This is no mortall creature I behold,
But some bright Angell that is dropt from heaven,
Sent by our prophet. (H4r)

In *The Two Noble Ladies* (1622) Cyprian, a conjurer, has charmed Justinia and when she is "*discovered in a chaire asleep, in her hands a prayer book, divells about her,*" he says:

Let me see
this Christian Saint which I (in spite of hell)
am forc'd to worship.
O how heav'nly sweet
she looks in midst of hells enchantments. (1750–4)

And Fletcher's *The Lovers' Progress* (1623) has "*Caliste sitting behind a Curtaine*" before Lisander draws it open and says:

Shee is asleepe,
Fierce love hath clos'd his lights, I may looke on her,
Within her eyes 'has lock'd his graces up,
I may behold and live; how sweet she breathes?
The orient morning breaking out in odors,
Is not so full of perfumes, as her breath is;
She is the abstract of all excellence, and scornes a paralell. (3K4v)

In each case the immediate context is unequivocally secular, even sexual, but for the original audiences the evocative language must have added a spiritual dimension (ironic or not) to these moments of recognition and admiration.

From Darkness to Enlightenment

The motto and haloed angel of the Quarles emblem (Figure 4.1) are reminders that the metaphor of light as spiritual enlightenment is an essential aspect of Christian apocalyptic imagery:[8]

Sende foorth thy light and thy trueth: that they may leade me and direct me unto thy holy hyll, & to thy tabernacles. (Psalm 43.3; B6r)

For every one that evyll doeth, hateth the lyght: neither commeth to the light, lest his deedes should be reproved. But he that doeth trueth, commeth

---

[8] Quoted from the 1568 "Bishops' Bible," the version read aloud in church and with which playwrights and playgoers would have been most familiar, until at least 1604 when the version authorized by King James gradually replaced it.

to the lyght, that his deeds may be knowen, howe that they are wrought in God. (John 3.20–21; G7r)

Then spake Jesus agayne unto them, saying, I am the light of the world: he that foloweth me, doth not walke in darknesse, but shall have the light of life. (John 8.4; H3v)

Therefore judge nothyng before the tyme, untyll the Lorde come, who wyl lyghten thynges that are hyd in darkenesse, & open the counsels of the heartes, and then shall every man have prayse of God. (1 Corinthians 4.5; N3r)

The association of Christ with light is literal in a number of Adoration paintings that depict Mary in the act of discovering her child to the shepherds. In these works, light illuminates Christ, and sometimes one of the onlookers also carries a torch or candle.[9]

The concept of truth as light is depicted in Cesare Ripa's emblem of *Veritas*, in which she stands with arm extended, holding a sun in her hand. Gian Lorenzo Bernini's sculpture of *Veritas*, also with a sun in her out-stretched hand, captures the moment of discovery.[10] And a similar figure of Truth on the title page of *Truth brought to light and discovered by Time* (Figure 2.4) explicitly combines Ripa's image with the action of discovery. In several pictorial images an actual discovery of truth is lit by a torch or candle, both to highlight what is being discovered and to symbolize the idea of spiritual illumination. In a painting by Theodore van Thulden, *Time Revealing Truth*, Time lifts a cloth from naked Truth, who holds a sun in her hands. The partly visible title page of the book behind Truth probably says *Sol et Tempus, Veritas Detegent* (Sun and Time, Reveal Truth).[11] The use of literal illumination to represent spiritual enlighten-ment is central to Piero della Francesca's fresco of *The Vision of Constantine*:

Inside his large tent, the Emperor lies asleep. Seated on a bench bathed in light, a servant watches over him and gazes dreamily out towards the onlooker, as though in silent conversation ... [T]he two sentries in the foreground stand out from the darkness, lit only from the sides by the light projected from the angel above. The divine messenger descends from on high, showing the Cross made of light to the emperor deep in sleep, to

---

[9] See, for example, Cigoli, *Adoration of the Shepherds*, www.metmuseum.org/art/collection/search/435900.

[10] For the Bernini, see http://galleriaborghese.beniculturali.it/it/node/200.

[11] This information is paraphrased from the website of Lawrence Steigrad Fine Arts, New York, 2015; the suggestion about the book's title is from Dr. Paul Huys Janssen, www.steigrad.com/thulden-time-revealing-truth.

Figure 4.2 *Tarquin Attacking Lucretia*, Giorgio Ghisi, c. 1450

whom he communicates the certainty of victory if the army moves under the sign of the Cross: 'In hoc signo vinces'.[12]

By contrast, an engraving by Georgio Ghisi (Figure 4.2) and a fresco by Giulio Romano[13] show a man entering with a torch that illuminates the discovery of Tarquin subduing a resisting Lucrece. In both these images the torch not only provides light but probably also symbolizes the fires of lust.

On the early modern stage the most general function of property candles and torches was to signal fictional darkness, and theatre historians have suggested that these props were not actually lit. And since the idea of metaphoric darkness and enlightenment is at the heart of many discovery scenes, we should not find it surprising that torches or candles need not have been lit to serve this symbolic function. But discovery scenes typically involve the opening of a curtain or door to reveal an enclosed space, which in the early modern playhouse would almost certainly have been darker than the open stage. This staging would have made it difficult for playgoers

---

[12] The Latin translates, "By this sign shalt thou conquer." The description is quoted from the Web Gallery of Art.
[13] *Tarquin and Lucretia*, in the ducal palace, Mantua. For the image and information see the Web Gallery of Art.

to see what had been discovered, but these discoveries are usually essential to the plot – highly anticipated and with important consequences. Perhaps, therefore, the lights called for in discovery scenes were lit and used not only to signal darkness and symbolize the idea of enlightenment, but also literally to illuminate what had been discovered.[14] If so, their function was simultaneously practical and symbolic.[15]

Several of the plays most overtly concerned with the business and idea of revelation feature discovery scenes that expressly include the use of a torch or candle. Primary among these is *The Spanish Tragedy*, specifically two of the five additions that appear in the fourth quarto (1602). Coming just after Hieronimo has found Horatio's body, the first addition draws out the process of recognition. He says to Isabella, "If it should proove my sonne now after all, / Say you, say you, light: lend me a Taper, / Let me looke againe" (D3v), and both see that it is their son.[16] The fourth and longest addition is a scene in which Hieronimo tells a painter how he should depict his finding of Horatio's body:

> And then at last, sir, starting, behold a man hanging: And tottering, and tottering as you know the winde will weave a man, and I with a trice to cut him downe. And looking upon him by the advantage of my torch, finde it to be my sonne Horatio. (H4r)

Perhaps this description reflected how the scene had always been performed, or perhaps it was a revised version; whichever, it is pictured in the 1615 title page woodcut that shows Hieronimo holding up a torch as he finds Horatio's body. If, as I have earlier suggested (see Chapter 2), the body has been hidden by the departing murderers and Hieronimo literally discovers it here, the property light he carries would have both symbolized his enlightenment and illuminated the discovered space for him and for playgoers. Certainly these repeated emphases on the use of light for this event require its presence and signal its importance.

In *Hoffman* the combination of lights and a discovery scene is spelled out in a stage direction: "*Enter Ferdinand and Sarlois, open a curtaine: kneele*

---

[14] Keith Brown considers the possibility that lights were used for illumination: "place a lighted candle in the shadowed angle of two house-walls, even on a brightly sunny day, and then stand back into the sunshine yourself, and the little point of light remains remarkably visible even at a considerable distance" ("More light, more light," 4).

[15] One of the early modern meanings of *discover* is "To expose to view (something hidden or previously unseen); to allow to be seen; to reveal; to bring to light. Now *rare* (chiefly *arch.* and *literary* in later use)" ("discover, v." *OED Online*, Oxford University Press, September 2016).

[16] Nothing indicates that Hieronimo is given the light he asks for, but nothing indicates that his request has not been answered, and two servants are on stage with him and Isabella.

Saxony, the Hermet and Mathias: tapers burning" (G1r). The location is referred to variously as "this tomb" and "this monument," and as Sarlois makes the discovery he says, "See Princely uncle the blacke dormitory, / Where Austria and Prince Lodowick are layd" (G1r). One function of the tapers in such a context would have been to help create an atmosphere of solemnity and mourning; but they could also have provided additional light. At the start of *Alphonsus, Emperor of Germany* (1594?) Alphonsus enters with *"a torch in his hand"* (B1r), saying, "Within this Chamber lyes my Secretary" (B1v). Presumably he is referring to a doorway in the tiring house wall, because next he *"opens the door"* (B1v) and finds his secretary asleep on what is referred to as a "bed" (B2r). Eventually the secretary awakens and Alphonsus sits beside him. Nothing in the text indicates that they move out of the space where this long scene seems to have begun, so Alphonsus's torch would have been very useful in helping playgoers to see, especially since before the scene is over Alphonsus poisons his secretary. But even if the bed was moved forward after the secretary awakens, Alphonsus's initial discovery of the chamber and its contents would have been illuminated by his torch.

In 3.5 of *The Revenger's Tragedy* when Vindice is stage-managing the scene in which he uses the *"skull of his love drest up in Tires"* (F1r) to deceive and poison the Duke, he first tells Hippolyto to go "Back with the Torch; brother; raise the perfumes" (F2v) to hide the truth. Then when he is about to reveal the skull, he says:

> Brother – place the Torch here, that his affrighted eyeballs
> May stare into those hollowes, Duke; dost knowe
> Yon dreadfull vizard, view it well, tis the skull
> Of Gloriana, whom thou poysonedst last.   (F2v)

The torch ensures that the Duke understands the just deserts of his death and, in keeping with Vindice's theatrical ambitions, lights his moment of revenge. In the much later *Love's Sacrifice* (1632) the directions for two discovery scenes include property lights. The first is in Act 2:

> *Enter Biancha, her haire about her eares, in her night mantle; she drawes a Curtaine, where Fernando is discovered in bed, sleeping, she sets downe the Candle before the Bed and goes to the Bed side.* (F1v)

In this case the candle is to help Fernando see Bianca; she says, "'Tis I: / Have you forgot my voyce? or is your eare / But usefull to your eye?" (F1v). He remains on the bed for the long scene that follows, during which each confesses love for the other, a revelation of truth for which that candle could have provided some actual illumination. Later in the play when a tomb is *"discovered,"* four figures enter *"with Torches,"* then *"One goes to open the Tombe, out of which riseth Fernando"* (Lɪv). The torches probably added a ceremonial dimension to the funeral procession, but they also would have helped to light a scene located in or at the opening of a darker space.

Other plays use property lights for the staging of discovery scenes in ways both practical and thematic. In the last act of Marlowe's *Edward II* (1591–2) the deposed king is imprisoned in a "dungeon" (L3v) when Lightborn comes to murder him. Critics have long noted the irony that "Lightborn" is an English version of "Lucifer," so it is worth emphasizing that the name has no historical source but was given to Edward's murderer by Marlowe. And Mortimer uses the name twice when Lightborn first enters, an indication that Marlowe wanted playgoers to hear and register the irony. But the name is also a description: Lightborn carries a "light" given to him by Gurney "to go into the dungeon" (L3v). Lightborn's "Foh, heeres a place in deed" probably indicates that he has opened a curtain or door to reveal Edward. At the same time, Edward asks, "what light is that?" So the light allows the one to see the other, and it would have helped playgoers to see what Lightborn sees. In addition, the exchange between the two that follows makes it clear that Edward has also seen the truth: "Villaine, I know thou comst to murther me" (L3v).

In the 1622 quarto of *Othello* (1602?) the last scene begins, *"Enter Othello with a light"* (Mɪr), and in the Folio, *"Enter Othello, and Desdemona in her bed"* (TLN 3239). Since Othello later closes curtains to hide Desdemona on the bed, here he must open them or they are open already. Whether the curtains were hanging on a thrust-out bed or the bed was behind curtains hanging in front of the tiring house wall, they would have made the semi-enclosed bed darker than the rest of the stage. Thus although the light is clearly the stimulus for Othello's meditation on the light–life metaphor, it would have shone into the space where Desdemona lay, allowing playgoers to see what Othello describes.

Few plays more obviously and repeatedly use light and dark imagery than *Romeo and Juliet* (1596–7), in which the metaphors seem intended to heighten playgoer awareness of the multiple implications of the trope. But in Act 5 when Romeo comes to the Capulet tomb, Shakespeare followed Arthur Brooke's *Romeus and Juliet* in emphasizing the use of lights to see. As Romeo approaches the tomb, Paris sees his "torch." Romeo tells Peter to "Give me the light" (L2r), then opens the tomb, which was probably a doorway or other curtained space. Romeo's description of what he sees – the bodies of Tybalt and Juliet – helps playgoers to imagine the scene; but the torch he carries might also have let them see for themselves. The irony is that what Romeo thinks he sees is partly true: Tybalt is dead; and partly false: Juliet only seems dead. After Romeo has acted on this apparent truth and killed himself, Juliet awakens, seemingly still in the tomb, so any additional light would have helped make her visible when she too commits suicide. When the Friar enters with a "Lanthorne," he asks Balthazar about the "torch" (L3v) burning in the tomb, so it is still lit; and when the Watch enters, the Boy also mentions the burning torch, which allows them to see the "Pittifull sight" (L4r).

In *The Rape of Lucrece* (1607) Heywood follows Shakespeare in having Sextus/Tarquin carry a light when he comes to Lucrece's bed – in the poem it is a "flaming torch" (D3v), in the play, a "*Taper light*" (G1r). But whereas Shakespeare makes much of the "fires of lust" metaphor, Heywood does not. Instead he provides both a stage direction and dialogue making it clear that Sextus discovers Lucrece in a curtained bed:

> *Lucr. discoverd in her bed.*
> Heere, heere, beholde! beneath these Curtaines lyes,
> That bright enchantresse that hath daz'd my eies.   (G1r)

Even when partly opened, those curtains would have darkened the interior where Lucrece lay, and although a taper would have provided very little light, that Heywood has Sextus carry one leads me to think that it served a practical purpose. Certainly Sextus's "behold" makes one want to see the "enchantress" in the bed. Another play with a figure discovered on a bed is Fletcher's *Monsieur Thomas* (1615), with a bed-trick in which the playboy Thomas arrives for an assignation expecting to find the woman he loves in bed waiting for him, but instead finds he has been tricked, although it takes time – and light – for him to realize the truth. The episode begins, "*a bed discovered with a black More in it*" (L1r), but Thomas comments that the figure on the bed has "pull'd it selfe together" (L1r), so he is unable see her very well. His "by your leave, candle" and "by this light it moves me" (L1v) both signal his use of the candle to get a better look. But when he sees black skin, he exclaims, "Holy saints, defend me, / The devill, devill, devill, devill O the devill" (L1v). Again, it seems unlikely that an experienced playwright would set such a scene in near-darkness, and the candle that helps Thomas to see the truth would probably also have helped playgoers to see and enjoy the reason for his fearful exclamations.

As we have seen, it is not unusual to find property lights being used in tomb scenes; indeed, the tomb scene in Fletcher, Field and Massinger's *The Knight of Malta* (1618) is reminiscent of that in *Romeo and Juliet*, especially in the way one figure after another enters with a light and looks into the tomb. In the 1647 Beaumont and Fletcher folio the stage direction *"Discover Tombe"* (5L4v) at the end of 4.1 anticipates the beginning of 4.2, when Miranda and two others arrive at the church and one observes, "the door is open." Miranda says, "Give me the light" (5L4v), then they hear groaning from the tomb and find Oriana in a coffin, awakening from a death-like sleep. The men lift the lid off the coffin, free Oriana from it and take her away. Next Rocca and Abdella enter with Mountferrat, expecting to find Oriana awakening from the potion they have administered. Rocca says, "Let me go in first, / For by the leaving open of the door here / There may be some body in the Church: give me the Lanthorne" (5M1r); but then a long discussion among the three follows, until this discovery:

MOUNTFERRAT   Where is the monument?
                        Thou art sure she will awake about this time?
ABDELLA   Most sure, If she be not knockt oth' head: give me the
                        Lanthorn,
                        Here 'tis, how is this, the stone off?
ROCCA   I, and nothing
                        Within the monument, that's worse, no body
                        I am sure of that, nor signe of any here,
                        But an empty Coffin.   (5M1r)

They argue among themselves until Rocca says, "I see a light, stand close"; then Gomera and a *"Page with Torch"* enter, Gomera asks for the torch, and at the direction *"The tomb wide open"* makes a second discovery: "The Stone off too? the body gone" (5M1v). He also sees Mountferrat and the others, who have probably hidden in the tomb, because Gomera says, "Prethee come out, this is no place to quarrell in" (5M1v). If as seems likely the tomb was a doorway or curtained space and the coffin was within it throughout this scene, the sequence of light, lantern and torch would have repeatedly introduced some illumination into that space.

In Massinger's *The Guardian* (1633) the property lights are not brought on by the discoverer but are part of the scene that is discovered. At the beginning of 3.6 a tableau is pre-set: *"Enter Jolante (with a rich banquet, and tapers) (in a chair, behind a curtain.)"* (K6v). The action begins with Jolante speaking from behind the curtain before she is discovered by Severino, who thinks she is in mourning but finds the truth – "What do I behold?" (K7r) – that she is actually waiting for an assignation. A scene in Davenant's *The Platonic Lovers* (1635) begins, "*Enter Amadine with a Taper, and Theander*" (D2v). Then Theander "*Drawes a Canopie; Eurithea is found sleeping on a Couch, a vaile on, with her Lute*" and he tells Amadine, "Give mee the light" before describing what he sees: "Shee lies as in a shady Monument" (D2v).

Very near the end of the period, Heywood wrote *Love's Mistress* (1634) which, like *The Rape of Lucrece*, includes an episode taken from non-dramatic narrative. In this case it is a famous scene from Roman myth: Psyche's discovery of the sleeping Cupid. Married to Cupid but forbidden to see him, Psyche is persuaded by her sisters that he is a monster, so she decides to look at then kill him. As he sleeps, she comes to his bed with a lamp and razor, but when she opens the curtains and sees him, she is so startled by his beauty – the truth – that she spills some of the lamp oil on him and he awakens. Heywood calls for a "*Lampe*" rather than another kind of property light because of its oil, but the "Bright lampe" could also have helped playgoers see into the curtained bed where Cupid lay. And the reaction of Psyche to what she sees – "Wonderous amazement! what doe I behold?" (F2r) – is very much like that of Sextus when seeing Lucrece. Heywood seems to have twice used the same methods to stimulate playgoers to want to see into a bed.

If, as I have argued, candles and other lights were used to illuminate discovery scenes, it is not surprising that disguise-discoveries call for these props much less often. But the verbal imagery of darkness and light sometimes also accompanies the removal of a disguise. In particular, references to a disguise as a "cloud" are used to set up the revelation of true identity.[17] When Jupiter "*puts off*" his peddler disguise in Heywood's *The Golden Age* (1610), he says, "Hence cloud of basenesse, thou hast done inough" (I1v), and in Dekker's *If It Be Not Good, the Devil Is in It* (1611) when the king disguised as a friar is threatened, he signals his self-discovery with a question: "thinkst thou (base Lord) / Because the glorious Sun behind blacke cloudes / Has a while hid his beames, hees darkned forever?" (L1r). The idea of bright nobility hidden by a cloud is also present in Massinger's *The Bondman* (1623) when Pisander, a nobleman disguised as the bondman, reveals himself: "Let fury then disperse these clouds, in which / I long have mask'd disguis'd" (L2v–3r).

---

[17] For the use of cloud imagery in masques, see Chapter 3.

In *The Antipodes* (1638) Brome seems to acknowledge the convention when the Doctor says to Peregrine,

> Now sir be pleas'd to cloud your Princely raiment
> With this disguise. Great Kings have done the like,
> To make discovery of passages
> Among the people: thus you shall perceive
> What to approve, and what correct among 'hem.   (H1v)

And in *Bartholomew Fair* Justice Overdo refers to his mad Arthur disguise as "this cloud that hides me" (D1v). But when the imagery recurs during Overdo's disguise as a porter, the implications are ironic: "Neither is the hour of my severity yet come, to reveal myself, wherein, cloud-like, I will break out in rain and hail, lightning, and thunder, upon the head of enormity" (K3v).

Two further examples use cloud imagery to emphasize the miraculousness of the discovery. In Ford's *Love's Sacrifice* (1632) when the disguised Roseilli discovers himself, he says, "here behold the man" and "Thus long I have bin clouded in this shape," to which Fiormonda responds, "Strange miracle!" (L1r). Much more inventive and complex is the sequence in Berkeley's *The Lost Lady* (1637), after the Moor has been poisoned and seems to have died:

IRENE   Bring some water here, she does but swoone:
   So chafe her Temples, – Oh Heavens! what prodigie
   Is here! her blacknesse falls away: My Lord, looke on
   This Miracle, doth not Heaven instruct [us] in pittie
   Of her wrongs, that the opinions which prejudice
   Her vertue, should thus be wash't away with the
   Blacke clouds that hide her purer forme.
HERMIONE   Heaven hath some further ends in this
   Than we can pierce: More water, she returnes to life,
   And all the blacknesse of her face is gone.
IRENE   Pallas, Apollo, what may this portend! My Lord,
   Have you not seene a face like this?
LYSICLES   Yes, and horrour ceazeth me: 'Tis the Idea
   Of my Milesia. Impenetrable powers,
   Deliver us in Thunder your intents,
   And exposition of this Metamorphosis.   (M1r)

Significantly, this moment of revelation, illumination and belief is shared by playgoers, who, like the characters, have not known of the Moor disguise.

Revelations and Recognitions

The visual dimension is basic to all the discoveries dealt with in this study, but some seem to have been engineered to emphasize how and why the action of revelation permits an important recognition of the truth. In this context it is useful to consider some roughly contemporary works of both sacred and secular art that seem constructed to emphasize their revelatory purpose by explicitly including the viewer who is outside the painting, in the real world. The secular discoveries are often of morally compromised mythical figures and seem intended both to titillate and to warn the viewer. In Correggio's *Venus and Cupid Discovered by a Satyr*, the lustful satyr seems to be exposing a sensuous Venus for our pleasure as well as his own. Significantly, though, we are also in a position to watch the satyr.[18] Similarly, in *Tarquinius and Lucretia* by Hans von Aachen, a man opens a curtain, allowing him and us to see the infamous rapist and frightened victim.[19] The much busier *Mars and Venus Discovered by the Gods*, by Joachim Wtewael,[20] depicts figures exposing the adulterous lovers or enjoying the show. Especially worth noting are the figure at the far right and the putto top left, who both look out of the picture at the viewer. One of the most spectacular versions of such a discovery is Bronzino's complex *Allegory with Venus and Cupid* (Figure 4.3), in which (according to one interpretation) Time seems to be uncovering a salacious scene at the centre of which is Venus embraced by Cupid.[21] One finds it hard to look away. This could also be said of a completely contrasting sacred painting, *Man of Sorrows* (Figure 4.4) by Petrus Christus, in which two angels hold back curtains through which Christ seems just to have come. The angels look at him and he looks at the viewer as he opens his wound. The similarities between this work and della Francesca's *Madonna del Parto* (Figure 3.5) are striking, although in the latter the angels look out at us, as if insisting that we look at the Madonna. In Raphael's *Madonna del Baldacchino* (Figure 4.5), unlike all the other figures, Saint Augustine looks out at the viewer, while with his right hand he directs our gaze. This attention-getting device can also be found in two

---

[18] See www.louvre.fr/en/oeuvre-notices/venus-satyr-and-cupid.
[19] See www.khm.at/de/object/ea119a40c1.
[20] See www.getty.edu/art/collection/objects/715/joachim-anthonisz-wtewael-mars-and-venus-surprised-by-vulcan-dutch-1604-1608.
[21] See the descriptions (and the painting in colour) on the National Gallery website, www.nationalgallery.org.uk/paintings/bronzino-an-allegory-with-venus-and-cupid; see also Panofsky, *Studies in Iconology*, 86–91.

Figure 4.3 *An Allegory with Venus and Cupid*, Bronzino, 1545–6

Adoration paintings, in which Mary uncovers Christ, showing him to the shepherds, one of whom looks out at the viewer.[22] The device of including a figure who seems to be partly in the painting and partly

---

[22] See Francisco de Zurbaran, *Adoration of the Shepherds* on the Web Gallery of Art and Jacob Jordaens, *Adoration of the Shepherds* www.liechtensteincollections.at/en/pages/zoom.asp?img=/asse ts/images/1CB74.jpg.

Figure 4.4 *Man of Sorrows*, Petrus Christus, 1450

outside it with us is an essential feature of the van der Goes *Nativity* (Figure 3.3), discussed in Chapter 3. And Rembrandt's *Holy Family with a Curtain*,[23] uses a *trompe l'oeil* effect to give the impression of a curtained painting. Each of these works forces viewers to register the artifice of the art and to acknowledge their role as interpreters.

Discoveries in some plays function in a similar way to make playgoers aware of how the revelation creates a role for them as viewers and inter-preters. Sometimes the playgoer is as unprepared for the discovery as the

[23] See http://altemeister.museum-kassel.de/33765/%20.

Figure 4.5 *Madonna del Baldacchino*, Raphael, 1507–8

figures in the play; but in other cases what the playgoers see has the effect of separating them and their experience of the discovery from that of the characters. Typically, a reaction of surprise signals the mental adjustment that must be made as a consequence of the action, but that might be said of many – perhaps most – discoveries. Those discussed below are distinguished by the verbal emphasis put on surprise or new awareness, the reasons for it and the effect it has on the experience that is the play. Examples in this category include not only disguise-discoveries but also discovery scenes; that is, they are not simply or primarily based on the appearance–reality dichotomy.

An early Shakespeare play that capitalizes on how the discovery device can lead to an awareness of the truth for characters at one level and playgoers at another is *The Merchant of Venice* with its unique sequence of three identically staged discovery scenes. Two of these dramatize the experience of being faced with an unpalatable truth, while also creating suspense for the third, which reverses the earlier experience and relieves the anticipation. Furthermore, these are actually double discoveries because first curtains are opened to reveal the three caskets, then the gold, silver or lead casket is opened to reveal the contents. This series of discoveries and responses begins with Portia's command: "Goe, draw aside the curtaines and discover / the severall caskets to this noble Prince" (D2v). After mulling over each of the inscriptions and their implications at length and opening the gold casket, Morocco realizes the truth immediately: "O hell! what have wee heare, a carrion death, within whose emptie eye there is a written scroule" (D3v). This scroll only confirms what is already clear – "All that glisters is not gold" – and Morocco departs a "looser" (D3v). That Shakespeare intended this unique two-level discovery format is evident from Portia's "draw the curtaines" (D3v) at the end of this scene. Thus the curtains are closed when Nerissa enters for the next casket scene, telling a servant "draw the curtain strait" (D4v). Arragon also accepts the conditions before choosing; but when he opens the silver casket, Portia's comment – "Too long a pause for that which you finde there" – suggests that he is having difficulty accepting what he sees: "the pourtrait of a blinking idiot" (E1r). Having read the explanatory verse, Arragon acknowledges, "With one fooles head I came to woo, / But I goe away with two." Again at the end of this scene Portia has the curtains closed – "Come draw the curtaine Nerrissa" (E1v) – so although no subsequent signal is given, they would have to be opened again when Bassanio arrives to make his choice. Having watched two previous scenes of choosing and discovery of course means that Portia and the playgoers know what the gold and silver caskets contain, thus at the very least the repetitions are a means of building suspense and dramatic irony. But by the time the three caskets are shown to Bassanio, playgoers are also attuned to statements such as Portia's "If you doe love me, you will finde me out" (E4r), which suggest that each suitor's discovery is deserved. Certainly, when Bassanio opens the lead casket and exclaims, "What finde I heere? / Faire Portias counterfeit" (F1r), only he is surprised. Moreover, the emphasis of Bassanio's musings about deceptive "outward showes" – "The seeming truth which cunning times put on / To intrap the wisest" (E4v) – explains not only why he chooses the lead casket but also more generally articulates Shakespeare's perennial interest in the difficulty of discovering and recognizing an ugly truth hidden below an appealing surface – or, in this instance, vice versa.

Shakespeare was adept at using discoveries in ways that capitalized on their inherent theatricality, although each is different because pertinent to the particular thematic context in which it occurs. In *Macbeth* (1608) the use of a discovery to foster belief begins with the words of the third apparition: "Macbeth shall never vanquish'd be, untill / Great Byrnam Wood to high Dunsmane Hill / Shall come against him" (TLN 1635–7). Macbeth confidently insists that this is impossible, but of course it comes to pass. And when the inevitable happens, although the event could simply have been reported, it is first prepared for and then staged. Malcolm spells out what is effectively a disguise – "Let every Souldier hew him down a Bough, / And bear't before him, thereby shall we shadow / The numbers of our Hoast" (TLN 2296–8) – and signals its discovery: "Now neere enough: / Your leavy Skreenes throw downe, / And shew like those you are" (TLN 2381–3). In this play so obsessed with time, it should not be surprising to see truth discovered so literally to effect a turning-point in the action.

Additional Shakespearean examples include the moment in *Hamlet* (1600–1) when Hamlet realizes he has killed Polonius, hidden behind the arras. When Gertrude asks Hamlet, "what hast thou done?" he replies, "Nay I knowe not, is it the King?" (I2r) and only after he has lifted the arras does he see the truth. In *Twelfth Night* a discovery highlights the verbal and visual artifice that characterizes the first meeting between Olivia and Viola in disguise as Cesario. Before Viola enters, Olivia puts on a veil, prompting Viola's (probably) disingenuous first question: "The honourable Ladie of the house, which is she?" (TLN 462). When an increasingly impatient Viola/Cesario says, "Good Madam, let me see your face," Olivia cues her unveiling: "we will draw the Curtain, and shew you the picture," and asks, "Ist not well done?" (TLN 521, 524, 525–6). But Viola retorts, "Excellently done, if God did all" (TLN 527). And when Olivia persists in speaking of her face as if it were a painting, Viola says, "I see you what you are, you are too proud: / But if you were the divell, you are faire" (TLN 541–2). By using the analogy to the unveiling of a painting, Shakespeare emphasizes Olivia's superficiality at this point in the play; and Viola's comment exemplifies her ability to see and speak the truth. When the veil device occurs in *Troilus and Cressida*, it is even more obviously a ploy. Having finally brought Cressida and Troilus together, Pandarus manages their initial physical interaction and is clearly exemplifying his name when he tells her, "Come draw this curtaine, and lets see your picture" (F2r). The absence of stage directions or informative dialogue leaves open whose idea the veil was, Pandarus's or Cressida's, and which of the two removes it; but however it is played, the discovery is obviously contrived. And Troilus's response – "You have bereft me of all wordes Lady" (F2r) – indicates how well it has worked.

In *A Looking-Glass for London and England* (1589) Lodge and Greene set up a moralizing discovery scene when the tyrannical King Rasni is about to enter an incestuous marriage with his sister Remilia. In the buildup to the event, both brother and sister have defiant speeches of self-celebration that make clear their refusal to obey any laws but their own. As Remilia ends her speech she tells her women to "Shut close these Curtaines straight and shadow me, / For feare Apollo spie me in his walkes, / And scorne all eyes, to see Remilias eyes," and "*They draw the Curtaines, and Musicke plaies*" (C2r). But as the ceremony is about to begin there is "*Lightning and thunder wherewith Remelia is strooken*" (C2v). Rasni and the other figures on stage, and the playgoers, hear but do not see this because the curtains are still closed, allowing for a buildup to the moment of revelation. Rasni says,

> What wondrous threatning noyse is this I heare?
> What flashing lightnings trouble our delights?
> When I draw neare Remilias royall Tent,
> I waking, dreame of sorrow and mishap. (C2v)

But the flatterer Radagon reassures him: "These are but common exalations / ... / Tut, be not now a Romane Angurer, / Approach the Tent, looke on Remelia" (C2v). This is followed by Rasni's description of what he expects to see, that begins "Now ope ye foldes where Queene of favour sits," but ends "Cloud not mine eyes whilst I behold her face. / Remilia my delight, she answereth not" (C2v). Finally, "*He drawes the Curtaines and findes her stroken with Thunder, blacke*" (C2v) – a sight that playgoers would expect but that it takes Rasni some time to believe. Saying, "How pale? as if bereav'd in fatall meedes, / The balmy breath hath left her bosome quite" (C2v), he tries to revive her; but when nothing works and he finally accepts the truth, he also has it removed: "beare her from my sight" and "*They beare her out*" (C3r).

The plot of Middleton's *The Phoenix* (1603–04) revolves around a dying Duke's son who disguises himself so he can learn about Ferrara before he becomes its ruler. Thus it is usually grouped with so-called "disguised ruler" plays, especially those written during the early years of King James's reign: *The Malcontent, Measure for Measure* and *The Fleer*.[24] But despite some common elements – most notably the adoption of a false identity for the purposes of observation and commentary – in *The Phoenix* the disguised figure is not yet a ruler so less is at stake. Also, unlike most other disguised dukes, Phoenix adopts several different disguises through the play and he has a partner in those disguises, Fidelio. Early in the action, Phoenix enlists Fidelio to join him in pretending to leave Ferrara but actually to disguise themselves and remain to observe the people Phoenix will soon rule, so when the two next appear as "Gentlemen" (B3v), playgoers know who they are. In this disguise they learn that the Captain is trying to sell his wife (Fidelio's mother) and to prevent this they take on new disguises: Fidelio as a scrivener and Phoenix as "that common folly of Gentry, the easie-affecting venturer" (D2r). During their gulling of the Captain, Phoenix has a series of asides commenting on the man's corruption and forging a connection with the playgoers. This sequence ends when Phoenix and Fidelio discover themselves first to the Captain, then to Fidelio's mother. Although there is no stage direction, the Captain's exclamation, "ha, who? oh" and her plea, "I do beseech your pardon good my Lord" (E2v), make it clear that something has happened physically to make them recognizable. When Phoenix and Fidelio next appear, they identify themselves as travelling businessmen[25] and after a series of encounters in this disguise Phoenix meets Proditor, who tells him of his plan to accuse the Duke's son (i.e., Phoenix) of plotting to murder his father, after which Proditor will be able to justify killing Phoenix. As often in such instances, the disguise allows playgoers to enjoy multiple levels of deception and intrigue inflected by dramatic irony. In preparation for the denouement, Fidelio enters not in disguise but as himself, which avoids having his discovery undercut Phoenix's when it comes. Fidelio tells the Duke that Phoenix has returned and gives the Duke a letter from his son, ostensibly a report of his travels. In fact, though, the letter is a series of accusations, or truths told just in time. When the Duke reads that Proditor has hired a man to kill him, the still-disguised Phoenix confesses, "I am the

---

[24] See, for example, Quarmby, *The Disguised Ruler*.

[25] In their edition Lawrence Danson and Ivo Camps have Phoenix and Fidelio enter "[*disguised in robes*]" (sc. 10.71.1).

man" (I2v) and confirms Proditor's plot. As the Duke continues reading
the letter, each of the evils Phoenix has encountered while in disguise is
exposed. Finally the moment for which playgoers have been primed arrives
and Phoenix discovers himself:

PHOENIX   Behold the Prince to approove it.
PRODITOR   Oh, where?
PHOENIX   Your Eyes keep with your Actions, both looke wrong.
PRODITOR   An infernall to my spirit.
ALL   My Lord the Prince.   (I4r)

The play ends with the Duke giving up power to Phoenix who, now aware
of the truth about the various schemers, sentences them to well moralized
and fitting punishments untainted by irony.

In Beaumont and Fletcher's *Philaster* (1609) playgoers are not told
until the last scene that the player in the role of the page Bellario is
actually the female character Euphrasia.[26] Interestingly, the more
authoritative second quarto (1622) version of the play does not indicate
whether or not Euphrasia literally discovers herself here; but the first
quarto (1620) version has "*Kneeles to Leon, and discovers her haire*" (I4v),
more evidence of how this and probably other similar discoveries were
performed.[27] As we have seen, a usual consequence of staged discoveries is
the truth-telling that permits the resolution of conflicts, and certainly this
is central here when the discovery that Bellario is a female means that
Philaster's jealous suspicions about Arethusa and her page are groundless.
As this suggests, one effect of not revealing Bellario's "true" gender and
identity is to add sexual titillation to the tragicomic mix; the device also
preserves the (false) possibility of tragedy until this point because playgoers do not have the one piece of knowledge that will determine the
tragicomic denouement. The playwrights got mileage out of Bellario-as-
male until the moment of revelation and recognition, with its comic
consequences. But they also evidently understood how the physical,
visual business of discovery could be emphasized with dialogue about
the revelation of truths: in the second quarto version of the scene, "all is
discovered" occurs twice (I2v).

From the beginning of Middleton and Dekker's *The Roaring Girl* (1611)
to the last scene, Moll appears dressed in men's clothing, troubling the

---

[26] Muriel Bradbrook may be right that although "Bellario's true sex is not revealed till the end . . . by
this time any theatrical page might be assumed to be a woman in disguise" ("Shakespeare and the
Use of Disguise," 167). For a similar view see Shapiro, *Gender in Play*, 187–8.

[27] See the discussions of *The Two Gentlemen of Verona* above and of *Antonio and Mellida* in Chapter 6.

other characters in a way analogous to how the real Moll Frith doubtless confused contemporary Londoners, perhaps including members of the audience. But in 4.1 Moll joins in a plot that leads to a fifth-act disguise and discovery. Sebastian's father, Sir Alexander, has prevented his son's marriage to Mary Fitz-allard, so Sebastian pretends he wants to marry Moll. This prospect so horrifies Sir Alexander that when in the last scene he is told that Sebastian has decided to marry someone else, he readily agrees, setting up the deception planned by Moll, Mary and Sebastian. Playgoers will know it is Moll who enters dressed as a woman – ostensibly Sebastian's bride-to-be – and "*maskt*" (L4v). Sebastian says to his father, "Before I dare discover my offence, / I kneele for pardon" (L4v), but Sir Alexander is completely fooled into thinking his son is about to marry a woman who is *not* Moll. He says, "Hide not my happinesse too long, al's pardoned, / Here are our friends, salute her, Gentlemen," at which they "*unmaske*" Moll (M1r). Sir Alexander is so upset that he agrees Sebastian can marry Mary Fitz-allard, and asks her forgiveness using language that links the business of discovery with the imagery of blindness and sight:

> Forgive me worthy Gentlewoman, 'twas my blindnesse
> When I rejected thee, I saw thee not,
> Sorrow and wilfull rashnesse grew like filmes
> Over the eyes of judgement, now so cleere
> I see the brightnesse of thy worth appeare.   (M1v)

The later plays to which I now turn make description difficult because of their winding plots based on contrived situations more relevant to another time. But these very qualities can make such plays worthy of attention. Their extensive – even excessive – uses of discoveries are evidence not simply of the longevity of the device but also (presumably) of playgoers' tolerance for it. More particularly, while the kinds of situation that lead to discoveries reflect contemporary topical concerns, playwrights were still using the same language of revelation and recognition to signal and respond to those discoveries.

When the disguise-discovery formula occurs three times in Davenport's *The City Nightcap* (1624), its use for dramatizing erroneous judgements based on false appearance is explicit. Rather than being surprised along with the characters, playgoers are put in a position to anticipate the discoveries and consequent realizations. In the complicated main plot,[28] Lorenzo is irrationally jealous of his wife, Abstemia, and sends his friend

---

[28] I gratefully acknowledge the help provided by the plot synopsis on Wikipedia: http://en.wikipedia.org/wiki/The_City_Nightcap.

Philippo to try to seduce her; she refuses him, but Lorenzo is unconvinced and suborns two slaves to testify that they saw Philippo and Abstemia in bed together. Found guilty in the play's first trial scene, Philippo is banished from Verona, while Abstemia is divorced from Lorenzo and leaves. But then Lorenzo's deception is found out and in the play's second trial scene he too is banished and told he cannot return until he finds Abstemia. The action then moves to Milan, where Abstemia has been taken into a brothel against her will and goes by the name of Millicent. Hearing of this new prostitute, Philippo wants to be her first customer, but before he can see her he is ejected by Antonio, son of the Duke of Milan, who also wants to be first. But "Millicent" manages to dissuade Antonio and he departs, only to switch clothes with his slave so he can return and try again. When Philippo meets the slave disguised as Antonio, he shoots him in revenge for their encounter at the brothel. The dead slave, who has been shot in the face, is found by the Duke of Milan who, of course, mistakes him for his son. At the same time, a guilt-ridden Lorenzo has come to Milan looking for Abstemia and, when accused of killing Antonio, he confesses in order to end his life. Hoping to save her husband, Abstemia also confesses. The final scene begins with Philippo "*putting on a disguise*" (F4v) to escape arrest for Antonio's murder. No sooner does he relinquish a pistol than Antonio, still in slave's clothing, enters, picks up the weapon and takes Philippo away. Antonio then appears where Lorenzo and Abstemia are imprisoned for a bizarre final test of both the jealous husband and constant wife. When she again shows that she is what she seems and Lorenzo finally accepts this truth, Antonio "*Discovers himself.*" After expressions of recognition and relief all round, the Duke asks Antonio, "who is it was slain / In your apparel?" (H3v) and the disguised Philippo explains how he came to shoot the slave. When Antonio agrees that the killing was justified, Philippo responds, "let me / In mine own person thank you" and – as the surprised exclamations of "*Omnes*" (H4r) indicate – he too discovers himself. He produces a letter proving that the dead slave was planning to kill Antonio, and tells him "we all have happily / Been well deceiv'd; you are noble, just and true; / My hate was at your cloathes, my heart at you" (H4r).

   In the contrasting subplot Lodovico refuses to see that his wife Dorothea is unfaithful, although her adultery with their servant Francisco and subsequent pregnancy are apparent to all. His friends finally persuade him to disguise himself as a friar, in which role he hears his wife's confession. As with Lorenzo in the main plot, what he expects to hear is the opposite of the truth he is told. Lodovico tells Dorothea that as penance she must publicly confess, then when she dissembles, he returns as the Friar to confront her. Those present refuse to believe the truth and turn on him, "tear[ing] those holy weeds off" (F3v). The surprised Duke asks, "Who's this?" and the rest recognize him: "'Tis Count Lodowick" (F3v). Once the truth is out, the Duke sentences the adulterers, saying to Francisco, "You sir that do appear a gentleman, / Yet are within slave to dishonest passions" (F4r). The end of this plot is signalled with familiar language and imagery: "Vice for a time may shine, and vertue sigh; / But truth like heavens Sun plainly doth reveal, / And scourge or crown, what darkness did conceal" (F4v).

The main plot of Arthur Wilson's *The Inconstant Lady* (1630) is also a complex and convoluted web woven of at least two, and probably three, different versions of disguise that lead to a series of revelations and recognitions, which result in thematically significant reunions and reconciliations. The lady of the title is Emilia, who was betrothed to Aramant until his father disowned him in favour of Millecert, his younger brother; as a consequence, Emilia seduces and marries Millecert. At the same time, Emilia is afraid that the beauty of Cloris, introduced as Emilia's sister, will outshine her own, so she keeps Cloris hidden. Cloris loves Aramant and escapes to be with him; but when the Duke sees her, he wants her for himself and takes her captive. Unhappy in his marriage to Emilia, Millecert wounds a man in jealousy and adopts a disguise to escape arrest. As "Gratus" he advertises his skill at tempting women and the Duke hires him to seduce Cloris on his behalf. In a soliloquy, Millecert vows he will use his disguise to repair the wrongs he did to his brother. This sets up encounters in which neither Aramant nor Emilia recognizes Millecert – but even this late in the period nothing works against a playgoer's willingness to believe in the disguise device and everything encourages it. As Gratus, Millecert plots with his brother to free Cloris from the Duke. Emilia also enlists Gratus's help in persuading the Duke to want her instead of Cloris. Emilia also confesses to Gratus that Cloris is not in fact her sister but a foundling taken in by her father. As the fifth act begins, Millecert, still disguised as Gratus, tells Emilia that her plot to poison Cloris has succeed and she is dead; they arrange for Emilia to pretend to be Cloris in the Duke's bed. On the other side of this deception, when Gratus tells Aramant that Cloris will be his, Aramant asks how he can thank him and "*Mill[ecert] discovers*" (5.2.36.s.d.). But he becomes Gratus again for the bedtrick of the Duke and Emilia, which begins, "*Emilia with a vaile on her face, lying on a bed*" (5.3.0.s.d.).[29] When Gratus enters to tell the Duke that Cloris

---

[29] In the Lambarde manuscript of the play (in Wilson's hand) at the Folger Shakespeare Library, the stage direction is "*Emilia in a bed the Duke comes to her*" (Fo 29a), 5.3.0.s.d. note.

has been murdered, the Duke says, "Unshroud thy selfe," and when he sees Emilia's face, asks, "Where is my Cloris?" (5.3.36–7).[30] The Duke wants to punish Emilia for Cloris's murder, but Millecert's plan has been to reform her; in an aside he says, "There is a way, / That may recover all yett" (5.3.59–60). Still as Gratus, he reveals that the Duke's long lost daughter Bellaura was given to a slave. Then just as Gratus says that Cloris is still alive, she enters with Aramant, prompting another aside from Millecert: "then I must / Discover all" (5.3.171–2). When the Duke says he still wants Cloris for his wife, Gratus announces that Cloris is actually Bellaura; the Duke says his daughter had "a strange blue mark upon her arm," then exclaims, "'Tis she!" which probably signals the play's second discovery. Finally, once all the other secrets have been revealed and truths told, "*Mille[cert] discovers*" (5.3.242.s.d.). Emilia's reaction – "My much abused husband! With what shame / Can I behold him?" (5.3.244–5) – implies a potential for reformation, which is confirmed by their reconciliation. Although we have no record of this play's success or failure on stage, it was performed both at Court and at Blackfriars, and its seemingly unironic use of so many romance conventions is evidence that even after decades they were still accepted and enjoyed by even the most sophisticated playgoers.

Carlell's *The Fool Would Be a Favourite* includes two discoveries that emphasize the experience of seeing the truth. Both focus on Philanthus, although in one case he experiences a discovery and in the other he effects one. In Act 3 he has been blindfolded and told he is in a prison, but when his captors "*unvail him*" (D4r), he says, "Amazment seizes me, is this a loathed Prison?" because he is actually in a woman's grand house. In the last act Philanthus is disguised as a ghost until he "*discovers himself*." When Agenor asks, "Ha! is't possible," Philanthus says, "Be not amazed, but trust your eyes." Agenor's "How can this be?" (G3v) of course brings forth explanations that permit a happy conclusion. Another Carlell play, *Osmond the Great Turk* (1637), has two early scenes in which a woman is revealed by lifting a veil, so that although the women and the situations seem quite different, the parallel actions imply a connection. First Osmond brings on Despina as a "present" for Melchshus, the Tartar emperor, who asks, "Ist a boy or a woman, unvaile and shew me?" (A3v). But Osmond warns him, "let her be covered still, for if I draw this vaile, you then must yeeld" (A3v). Heedless of the warning, Melchshus "*unvailes her*," saying, "More, more, by all my glories, than was delivered! Osmond so well I like,

---

[30] The Lambarde MS includes a direction for the discovery: "*Pulls of her scarfe*" (Fo 29b), 5.3.35.s.d. note.

cover her face lest I doe surfet with beholding" (A4r). The next scene introduces Ozaca, whose husband fears being cuckolded by Orcanes and has made her put on a veil. When "*Shee unvailes,*" Orcanes's words emphasize the metaphor implicit in the action: "The Painter was a niggard of his skill, or grossely ignorant that drew your picture, but Art must ever yeeld to Nature in a peice so excellent, and come far short, since 'tis but imitation" (A5v). In the first instance a powerless woman is unveiled by a man who owns her; in the second, a woman unveils herself. But in both cases, when the woman's beauty is revealed, it overpowers the man.

By the time of *Brennoralt* (1639–41) the discovery device had been used so often that playwrights doubtless wanted to find new ways to make it interesting. In this tragedy, Suckling included several discoveries, each different from the others, but all emphasizing the reactions to what is shown. In Act 4, "*Francelia (as in a bed)*" is immediately followed by the entrance of Brennoralt, who "*drawes the curtaines*" (C2v) to reveal her, saying:

> So Misers looke upon their gold,
> Which while they joy to see, they feare to loose:
> The pleasure of the sight scarse equalling,
> The jealousie of being dispossest by others;
> Her face is like the milky way i'th' skie,
> A meeting of gentle lights without name.   (C2v)

Then at the end of the play comes a sequence of discoveries linked to Iphigene, who has been presented as a male from the start (although the name might have been intended to hint otherwise). First the jealous Almerin "*throwes open the dore*" (D1r) to show Francelia with Iphigene in what looks like a compromising situation. He says, "Ha! mine eyes grow sick" and attacks them both. When Iphigene is wounded, she tries to protect Francelia by confessing the truth, warning "I will discover all." Almerin says, "Ha! – what will he discover?" and Iphigene responds, "That which shall make thee curse / The blindnesse of thy rage. – *I am a woman*," then faints (D1r; original italics). With mixed motives, Almerin opens her clothing:

> For curiosity
> Ile save thee, if I can, and know the end
> If't be but losse of Blood, – Breasts!
> By all that's good a woman! – Iphigene.   (D1v)

The sequence ends when Brennoralt enters and "*drawes the curtain,*" thinking he will see Francelia sleeping, but quickly realizing the tragic truth: "Awake fair Saint and blesse thy poore Idolator / Ha! – pale? – and cold? – dead" (D2v).

Shirley's *The Sisters* was written and performed in 1642, making its several disguise-discoveries the last before the closing of the theatres. And while it might seem that the uses of the convention in this play are merely formulaic, a closer look suggests that Shirley is both playing with and relying on expectations created by a half-century's use of recognitions made possible by literal discoveries.[31] This play's longest-lasting disguise is that of Pulcheria, the Viceroy of Sicily's daughter, who appears from the start as Vergerio. The list of Dramatis Personae gives readers this information, but it is kept from playgoers until she discovers herself in Act 5. Before that time comes, Vergerio is a young man in the service of Contarini. But the action begins with three bandits who invite a gullible Piperollo to join them; Frapolo, the bandits' leader, says, "fit him instantly / With a disguise, and let him have that face / The Devill wore in the last anti-masque" (B3r). When the thieves rob his parents, Piperollo is so ruthless that the other three tie him up and leave him with his victims. The mother says, "I'l see his complexion; / Who's this?" and the father says, "Our own Son Piperollo?" When Piperollo pleads, "Pray Father give me your blessing, ah – / Mother do not stone me to death with that / Money bag, I am your Son," his mother rejects him: "My Son? I know thee not" (B6v). Many playgoers would doubtless have recognized this as an ironic and amusing reworking of so many scenes in which a disguised son reveals himself to relieved parents. After this oblique introduction, the plot of the play's titular sisters, Paulina and Angelina, begins. Paulina is vain and intends to marry Prince Farnese, while Angelina is modest and wants to become a nun. When Frapolo and the other thieves reappear disguised as astrologers, he predicts that Paulina will indeed marry the prince; then they return with Frapolo disguised as Farnese and the other thieves as his courtiers. Just as Paulina is about to leave with him, the real prince arrives. He had intended to arrange a marriage between Angelina and Contarini, but falls in love with Angelina himself. She refuses him because she has fallen in love with Vergerio. When Contarino asks Angelina, "how canst thou / Expect a truth from him, betrays his Master?" she responds that what has happened "Was meant by Providence to wake your faith, / That's owing to another." Farnese says, "Possible? / The Vice-roy of Sicilies

---

[31] Hyland says, "I think we are seeing in this ... example of transvestite disguise the death throes of a device that had outrun its time" (*Disguise on the Early Modern English Stage*, 67).

Daughter? Pulcheria" and Contarini asks, "Pulcheria here?" (E2v). Then the truth comes out:

VERGERIO   Here Contarini.
CONTARINI   Ha, prov'd a Woman, oh my shame and folly![32]
VERGERIO   Pardon my too much love, that made me fear
            You had forgot Pulcheria, though you left
            Your vowes and me at Sicily, when you were
            Embassadour from the Prince.
CONTARINI   Whence embarqu'd
            Thou brought'st me news Pulcheria was dround,
            And thou for her sake entertain'd my servant,
            Welcome, at once receive me and forgive me.   (E2v)

Pulcheria's explanation and Contarini's realizations serve as necessarily belated exposition; but they also articulate the kind of deeper recognition that a physical discovery so often fosters.

As should be apparent by now, on the early modern stage discoveries were a non-realistic theatrical convention, used in an equally non-realistic form of drama. Moreover, the visual and verbal elements discussed in this chapter functioned as a kind of italics, repeatedly emphasizing the moments of discovery, both for figures within the play and for playgoers. In performance, this combination of action and language would typically have created a dual experience for playgoers, who shared the moment of discovery with figures in the play, but also watched and assessed their reactions to it. Furthermore, in making playgoers aware of themselves as watchers, performed discoveries heighten the artifice in both the play's manner and matter. It is important to be aware of how simultaneously detaching and engaging these events would have been for early modern audiences, who did not expect realism and seem to have enjoyed contrived metatheatre.

---

[32] Does Pulcheria remove a boy's cap to let down hair? Whatever happens it makes possible Contarini's instant recognition of her. For examples of the release of hair to end a girl-as-boy disguise see the discussions of *The Two Gentlemen of Verona* and Q1 *Philaster* in Chapter 4 and of *Antonio and Mellida* and *The Wise Woman of Hogsdon* in Chapter 6.

CHAPTER 5

Private Places and Hidden Spaces

Some discoveries are of one or more figures and properties that together create a particular fictional location, especially a private place with restricted entry. Such discovered spaces include a study, closet or counting house; a tomb, cave, tent or private chamber (sometimes with a bed or chair). In calling for such places to be discovered by opening a curtain or door, playwrights could create scenes that were partly visible and partly hidden, with consequent realistic and emblematic qualities. In particular, for early modern playwrights and playgoers the staging of these scenes as discoveries could capitalize on contemporary events, interests, beliefs, concerns and fears about rumours and reports of illicit, sinful behaviour, especially religious or sexual; occult practices, including necromancy, magic, conjuring and consorting with the devil; intrigue and deception; hidden wealth; and death. It might be thought that the reason for using discoveries in these cases was largely practical – required by the presence of sizeable props – rather than to create the impression of restricted access and to dramatize the revelation of truth. But this convention for staging locations that were private or hidden in the real world can be contrasted with the staging of almost all banquets – equally prop-heavy but public events that directions repeatedly specify are "set/put out" on the stage.[1] It might also be objected that setting these scenes in a semi-enclosed space would have introduced a staging literalness that seems at odds with the concept of the "unlocalized stage" on which dialogue could, and usually did, designate the main playing area as any place the plot called for. Furthermore, discovering such scenes would have added to the staging requirements and doubtless created sightline problems. So why were discoveries evidently the conventional way to stage private locations? I offer an answer with two interrelated parts: one lies in the ideas associated with

[1] See Chris Meads, *Banquets Set Forth*, 240–6.

151

these spaces in the real world of the playgoer; the other in the kinds of character and action typically associated with discovery scenes in plays.

Any discussion of the staging of study and similar discovered locations is, however, necessarily limited both by stage directions that are open to more than one interpretation and by how little we know about the configuration of the tiring house wall, a problem I address in the Appendix. Alan Dessen has noted that a direction for a figure to "*enter in*" a study might mean that a curtain was opened to reveal him or her with the appropriate properties in an enclosed space at an opening in the tiring house wall, or it could mean that the figure came out onto the stage where the props were placed.[2] However, there are also directions that specify a figure is to be "*discovered*" in his study, which make it possible to speculate that the less explicit directions call for the same staging, and that some kind of discoverable space was used. As I discuss in the Appendix, most modern theatre historians have argued or assumed that such scenes were located in a permanent "discovery space" in the centre of the tiring house wall, so it is important to be aware that this too is not certain. Therefore, as I explain in the Introduction, while it would certainly be convenient and much easier to assume the existence of such a location, I have not done so. When it seems reasonably evident that one of these scenes was discovered (rather than put out on the stage), I show why and categorize it as a scene that probably used curtains to effect a discovery, but I do not (because I cannot) describe exactly how it was staged or where it was located. A related question is how literally we should interpret stage directions, and whether they might reflect what a playwright imagined rather than playhouse reality. Fortunately, enough similar directions for similar kinds of discovery scene exist to warrant the inference that, when possible, such scenes were set in a way that recognizably represented a real world place of privacy by using an enclosable space either in a doorway or other opening in the tiring house wall or in a space created by curtains in front of the wall. Again, I refer readers to the Appendix.

Studies, etc.

There are thirty-plus plays in which a figure is discovered (sometimes more than once) in what is usually referred to in the text as his study, but is sometimes called a counting house, closet or cell. This total includes about

[2] See especially Alan C. Dessen, *Recovering Shakespeare's Theatrical Vocabulary*, chapter 8, "The vocabulary of 'place'."

fifteen plays in which a discovery is unambiguous and about the same number in which a discovery can pretty confidently be inferred from dialogue and other supporting evidence. Some examples of both kinds will show what I mean. As we have seen, *The Merry Devil of Edmonton* has a direction to "*Draw the curtains*," followed by the Prologue's vivid description of the scene, which includes references to the "couch," "chime," "sable slights" and "Necromantic chaire" (A3v; see Chapter 3). Together this direction and dialogue make it clear that Fabell is discovered with properties that characterize him. A similar scene prefaced by a Chorus in *Thomas, Lord Cromwell* (1601) begins, "*Cromwell in his study with bagges of money before him casting of account*" (B1v). Although a discovery is not specified here, the properties suggest one, and later in the play Hodge "*sits in the study*" disguised as Cromwell and unseen until the Governor says, "Goe draw the curtaines, let us see the Earle, / O he is writing, stand apart awhile" (D1r). Thus a later direction – "*Enter Gardiner in his studie, and his man*" (E4v) – probably signals that the same stage location – a doorway or curtained space – was used for all three study scenes. These directions can be contrasted with another in this play – "*they bring out the banquet*" (D2r) – which very clearly does not signal a discovery. The idea that a figure with properties was discovered is explicitly supported by a direction in Davenant's *News from Plymouth* (1635): "*A Curtain drawn by Dash (his Clerk) Trifle discover'd in his Study, Papers, Taper, Seale and Wax before him, Bell*" (4C3v). This in turn provides evidence that another direction in this play also signals a discovery even though it is not specified: "*Enter Signior Sharkino in his study furnished with glasses, vials, pictures of wax characters, wands, conjuring habit, Powders, paintings, and Scarabeo*" (E3v). A number of directions for study scenes, such as "*Enter Barnavelt (in his Studdy)*" (1883), in *Sir John van Olden Barnavelt*, are not as detailed, perhaps because they refer to a conventional staging: the opening of curtains to show a figure with relevant properties. In the speech following this direction, Barnavelt refers to "rewards" of service (petitions) with repeated uses of "this" and "these," which presumably refer to property papers. For two similar study scenes in Day's *Law Tricks* (1604), the first direction is "*Discover Polymetes in his study*" and the second, "*Polimetes in his study*" (G1v, H3r; see Chapter 6).

All of the study scenes under discussion here can be distinguished from at least as many occasions when properties such as a table and books are "set out" on the stage (like banquets) rather than being discovered – and it might be significant that such scenes are rarely if ever referred to in the playtext as being in a "study." In addition, while a few references to a figure being "in a study" might mean only that he is reading a book or that he is deep in thought,[3] the phrase can also designate an actual scene, as in Dekker's *Satiromastix* (1601): "*Horrace sitting in a study behinde a Curtaine, a candle by him burning, bookes lying confusedly: to himselfe*" (B4r); and in Beaumont's *The Woman Hater* (1606): "*Enter Lazarello, & two Intelligensers, Lucio being at his study,*" then "*Secretarie drawes the curtaine*" (I1r). Also important to note is that, beginning with John Cranford Adams some theatre historians have used "study" as a term for an opening in the centre of the tiring house wall.[4] But even if we set aside the question of whether or not there was such an opening, we have no hard evidence to support the idea that "study" was a generic term.[5] The only playwright who might have used it in such a way is Ben Jonson, and then only once or twice.[6] Otherwise he uses it the way other playwrights do, to designate a particular kind of room, as in *Catiline* (1611) when Sylla's ghost "*Discovers Catiline in his study*" (3L4r).

The other reason to suppose that study scenes were set in a discoverable space has to do with how the study was understood in the real world of the playgoer, together with the dramatic contexts in which study scenes occur, both of which depend on contemporary ideas of privacy. The *OED* provides definitions that help to convey how the study and similar locations were used and perceived in early modern London; particularly significant is the emphasis on seclusion:

Study	A room in a house or other building, intended to be used for private study, reading, writing, etc., esp. by one particular person.[7]
Cell	A small apartment, room, or dwelling. A dwelling consisting of a single chamber inhabited by a hermit or anchorite.[8]
Closet	A room for privacy or retirement; a private room; an inner chamber.[9]

---

[3] See Dessen, *Recovering Shakespeare's Theatrical Vocabulary*, 161.

[4] John Cranford Adams, *The Globe Playhouse*, 169. William A. Armstrong says that "Adams took over the word [study] as a generic term to describe an alleged curtained recess or inner stage at the Globe" ("Actors and Theatres," 200).

[5] Nevertheless, Scott McMillin and Sally-Beth MacLean, perhaps echoing Armstrong, refer to "the curtained space, or 'study' (as it seems to have been known generically in the Elizabethan theatre)" (*The Queen's Men and their Plays*, 139).

[6] See *Staple of News*, D4v, E1r and *Epicoene*, 3C1r.

[7] "Study, n." *OED Online*, Oxford University Press, September 2016.

[8] "Cell, n.1." *OED Online*, Oxford University Press, September 2016.

[9] "Closet, n." *OED Online*, Oxford University Press, September 2016.

Counting-house   a. A building or apartment appropriated to the keeping of accounts; a private chamber, closet, or cabinet appropriated to business and correspondence; an office.[10]

The architecture historian Peter Thornton notes that "The closet was a room to which the occupant of the bedchamber could retire and where he or she could normally expect to enjoy complete privacy to rest, read, study, write letters or entertain intimate friends." He adds that in a large house "the closets were usually placed beyond the bedchamber with which they were associated, so that they formed the innermost and therefore most secluded room of the apartment concerned."[11] Quoting Angell Day, writing in 1592 – "We doe call the most secret places in the house appropriate to our own private studies ... a Closet"[12] – Thornton comments, "he might have added that one could also call it 'a study'."[13] Referencing Cotgrave's 1632 *Dictionnarie*, Thornton says that "the French word *cabinet* could mean 'a closet, little chamber, or wardrobe wherein one keeps his best, or most esteemed, substance', so one could expect to find there precious belongings of all kinds."[14] Lena Cowen Orlin notes that the study was unusual in being a truly private (almost exclusively male) space: enclosed and lockable, "the study was a domestic space without precedent in the Elizabethan and Jacobean household, the chambers of which were otherwise communal and multipurpose."[15] Orlin argues that the study or closet originated as a place to store valuables safely and that

> privacy was a by-product of architectural ambitions to protect and preserve records and objects of value. Further, the association of the study with the strongbox imported with it the notion that the room, like its lesser antecedent, required a lock and key. This accessory to the function of the study, its capacity to be locked and its concern with the keeping of the key, in yet another way distinguished it from other household spaces and practices.[16]

To support her descriptions of and conclusions about the early modern study, Orlin refers to Ralph Treswell's "surveys of tenanted properties owned by Christ's Hospital and the Clothworkers' Company," noting that "Treswell catalogues twenty-six closets, twenty-three studies, two rooms which he says might be either a 'closet or study', and seven

---

[10] "Counting-house, n." *OED Online*, Oxford University Press, September 2016.
[11] Peter Thornton, *Seventeenth-Century Interior Decoration*, 296.
[12] Angell Day, *The English Secretorie* (1592), part 2, Q1r.
[13] Thornton, *Seventeenth-Century Interior Decoration*, 303.   [14] Ibid, 302.
[15] Lena Cowen Orlin, *Private Matters and Public Culture*, 184–5.   [16] Ibid., 185.

countinghouses."[17] Several of Treswell's drawings include rooms labeled "study," "closet" or "countinghouse." His plan of 3–4 Pancras Lane (Figure 5.1), for example, includes a "study" upper left, "Baber / study" middle right and "counting / howse" lower right.[18] Each of these rooms has only a single means of access and all but one are sequestered in a corner.

Based on her examinations of many wills, letters and other household documents, Orlin concludes that in early modern England

> the closet was primarily about control of access, whether for possessions or for persons. One effect of this control was security, one was possessiveness, one was exclusivity, one was privacy, one was secrecy, and so on. A number of effects could be in play, depending upon the nature of the space, the wealth of its owners, the objects and pursuits those owners valued, the time of year, the time of day, and the variable intentions of the key-holder – among other things.[19]

Orlin also notes that "In the discourse of the archives, solitude and secrecy were inevitably described as accidental in order to inoculate them from the stigma of sinister intent."[20] It therefore seems reasonable to speculate that staging a study, closet or counting house as a discovery scene would have emphasized the idea of privacy, capitalized on curiosity about those spaces in the real world, and created an ideal setting for the revelation of secrets hidden within. A study scene in *Captain Thomas Stukeley* (1596) provides a good example: a Page is trying to prevent Stukeley senior from seeing into his son's "study" because he knows what the father now sees: instead of law books the study contains weapons.

PAGE	Ile devise some scuse
OLD STUKELEY	Sirra heare yee me, give me the key of his studdy
PAGE	Sir he ever carries it about him,
OLD STUKELEY	how let me see methinks the doore stands open
PAGE ASIDE	A plague one it, he hath found it: I was not war Sir, be like he had thought he had lock it and turnd the key to short. now we shall see this old cutter play his part for in faith hees furnished with all kind of weapons,
OLD STUKELEY	what be these my sons bookes I promise you A studdy richly furnisht. (B1r)

---

[17] Lena Cowen Orlin, *Locating Privacy in Tudor London*, 306–7.
[18] John Schofield, ed., *The London Surveys of Ralph Treswell*, Plate 3; for another two plans with studies see Schofield's figures 5 (middle) and 6 (upper left).
[19] Orlin, "Gertrude's Closet," 65.   [20] Orlin, *Locating Privacy in Tudor London*, 324.

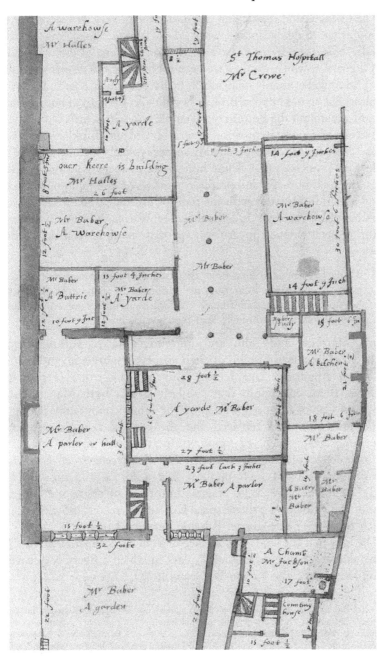

Figure 5.1 Survey of 3–4 Pancras Lane, detail, Ralph Treswell, 1611

The dialogue and the staging emphasize the privacy and secrecy of this "study" that could be locked with a key. And if "door" can be taken literally, this scene seems to have been located in one of the tiring house wall doorways, which would have been set up with the property weapons that Old Stukeley angrily itemizes: "If he have so much as a candstick I am a traitor, but an old hilt of a Broken sword to set his light in not a standish as I am a man, but the Bottom of a Temple pot, with a little old sarsnet in it. heeres a fellow like to prove a Lawier, if sword and, Butkler hold" (B1v).

As I have noted, discovered study scenes typically include a figure and table with properties that define him: books, papers, gold or, in several cases, the tools of magic and prophecy. Images of a curtain pulled back to reveal a man in his study with the tools of his trade can also be found in visual media of the time. Indeed, there seems to have been a tradition of picturing great thinkers in this way, perhaps alluding to these words of Seneca:

> To-day I have some free time, thanks not so much to myself as to the games . . . No one will interrupt me or disturb the train of my thoughts . . . My door has not been continually creaking on its hinges nor will my curtain be pulled aside; my thoughts may march safely on.[21]

Saints Matthew and John are sometimes shown working behind a partly drawn curtain in illuminated gospels (Figure 5.2); and pictures of Saints Augustine and Jerome also use the trope (Figure 5.3). Perhaps, then, engravings that similarly depict both Martin Luther and John Calvin (Figure 5.4) deploy the same iconography to suggest that these men had replaced the thinkers of the old religion.[22] The same arrangement of figure, properties, and curtain occurs on the title page of Francis Bacon's *The Advancement of Learning*.[23] We cannot know if such pictures had a direct influence on how study scenes in plays were staged, but they all share the common idea of the study as a private space containing secret knowledge, into which the viewer or playgoer is being permitted to see.

The idea that the study was a place of both its occupant's privacy and vulnerability is conveyed in several plays in which a figure is discovered there. In Armin's *The Valiant Welshman* (1612), "*The Generall drawes the*

---

[21] Seneca, Letter LXXX, "On Worldly Deceptions" (*Seneca Six Pack 2*, 1). I am grateful to Michael Hendry of Staunton VA for bringing this to my attention.

[22] For Saint John, see http://digi.vatlib.it/view/MSS_Pal.lat.50, 67v; Botticelli's *Saint Augustine in His Cell* is in the Uffizi collection; and for Martin Luther, see http://objektkatalog.gnm.de/objekt/HB24592.

[23] See http://luna.folger.edu/luna/servlet/s/38r80k.

Figure 5.2 Saint Matthew, *Stockholm Codex Aureus*, mid-eighth century

Curtaines, and finds Caradoc a reading" (H4v) in his "chamber" and he attacks him: "Now Caradoc, thy life is in our hands: / Behold, thou art ingirt with a whole hoste" (H4v). Indeed, as the use of "behold" here indicates, this is a discovery for Caradoc too. In *Henry VIII* (1613), "*the King drawes the Curtaine and sits reading pensively*" and when Norfolk enters,

Figure 5.3 *Saint Jerome in his Cell*, Albrecht Dürer, 1511

Henry demands, "How dare you thrust your selves / Into my private Meditations?" (TLN 1100–1, 1105–6). In Marlowe's *The Massacre at Paris* (1593) the idea that "*Enter Ramus in his studie*" signals a discovery is supported by his statement that he is "sitting at his book" (B2v) when

Figure 5.4 *John Calvin*, seventeenth century

the Guise comes to murder him. The use of a study-discovery to dramatize privacy invaded can also be found in *Alphonsus, Emperor of Germany*, when Alphonsus says, "Within this Chamber lyes my Secretary" and "This Key commands all Chambers in the Court," then "*He opens the door and finds Lorenzo sleep a loft*" (B1v).[24] It then seems that having opened the "door," Alphonsus is in the study and that it is furnished with props, because he says, "What's this? *Plato*? *Aristotle*? tush these are ordinary, / It seems this is a note but newly written" (B1v; original italics). As Alphonsus reads the note, "*Lorenzo Riseth, and snatches at his sword which hung by his Bed side*," saying, "What are there thieves within the Emperour's Court? / Villain thou dy'st; what mak'st thou in my Chamber?" Alphonsus responds, "Ly down Lorenzo, I will sit by thee" (B2r) and during the ensuing scene Alphonsus first gives Lorenzo a drug to make him sleep and then poisons him.[25] Not only has Alphonsus invaded Lorenzo's private space, but he has used Lorenzo's own secret potions and instructions to murder him.

The convention of using a discovery for scenes set in the privacy of a study is well represented in Marlowe's *Doctor Faustus* (1588). The first Chorus concludes its introduction of Faustus by bringing his career to the present, then discovering him:

> For falling to a devilish exercise,
> And glutted more with learnings golden gifts,
> He surffets upon cursed Negromancy,
> Nothing so sweete as magicke is to him
> Which he preferres before his chiefest blisse,
> And this the man that in his study sits.   (A2r–v)

In the 1604 quarto (quoted here) the initial direction is "*Enter Faustus in his Study*" (A2v); in the 1616 quarto it is "*Faustus in his study*" (A2v).[26] As the scene develops it becomes clear that the "study" contains a number of books and that, as the Chorus says, its occupant is misusing the knowledge they contain. This discovery scene is thus part of a small but significant subset in which a figure engaged in "cursed necromancy" is presented in his private space. As the play proceeds, several more such discovery scenes symbolically chart the consequences of Faustus's misuse of learning and

---

[24] The phrase "sleep a loft" is almost certainly an error; perhaps "a loft" is a conflation of "aloof off": at a distance.

[25] Although it might be expected that the two figures would move forward out of the "study," if the text is to be believed, it seems that Lorenzo lies on the bed and Alphonsus sits beside him until Lorenzo dies and Alphonsus exits, at which point presumably the "door" or curtains are shut and the study disappears.

[26] Citations are of the 1604 quarto unless otherwise indicated.

practice of magic. At the start of Act 2 both versions have "*Enter Faustus in his Study*," where his first words are, "Now Faustus must thou needes be damnd, / And canst thou not be saved?" (B4r). In this scene he conjures and makes his deal with the devil. The consequence of that deal is conveyed in the 1616 quarto by a third discovery: "*Enter Faustus in his Study, and Mephostophilis*" (C1v). In this pivotal scene the two "dispute" and Faustus presses Mephistopheles for forbidden knowledge. In each case the effect of the staging is to give playgoers the impression that they are seeing the reality of Faustus's corruption. No directions describe how the 1604 version of the final scene was staged, but Faustus's last words are "Ugly hell gape not, come not Lucifer, / Ile burne my bookes, ah Mephostophilis," then the devils "*exeunt with him*" (F3r). In the 1616 quarto the Good Angel tells Faustus, "The jawes of hell are open to receive thee," after which "*Hell is discovered*" (H2r), implying the use of an opening in the tiring house wall.[27] If Faustus were taken away into the same space in which he was repeatedly discovered it would have visually conflated his study with hell. Indeed, it would be surprising if, in this overtly emblematic play, the links between the events that culminate in this denouement had not been made explicit by Faustus's exit into a property "Hell mought" such as that owned by the Admiral's Men.[28]

Another play in which a study and its occupant are linked to magic is Peele's *The Old Wives Tale* (1590), in which "*Enter Sacrapant in his studie*" (C2r) near the start signals a discovery (as in *Doctor Faustus*). Sacrapant's first speech helps to define him and the space when he describes how he has used "enchanting spells" (C2v) to capture Delia. Later two Furies enter "*out of the Conjurers Cell*" (D4v), further helping to create a sense of the supernatural practices within. Thus at the end of the play when Sacrapant has been defeated and Jack says to Eumenidies, "And now maister to the Lady that you have so long looked for," then "*draweth a curten, and there Delia sitteth asleep*" (F1v), we can safely assume that he discovers her in the "study" where Sacrapant first appeared. It is commonly observed that this playtext is very short and thus probably incomplete, and that might be so; but it is worth noting how its "tale" begins with one discovery scene and ends with another in the same space, thus giving the inner plot an obvious and satisfying symmetry.

Interestingly, three Red Bull plays from 1619 to 1622 include study scenes that almost certainly allude to *Doctor Faustus*. *The Two Merry Milkmaids*

---

[27] To my knowledge, *discover* is never used to describe the opening of a trap door in the stage.
[28] See *Henslowe's Diary*, ed. R. A. Foakes and R. T. Rickert, 319, line 56.

(1619) begins with "*Enter Bernard in his Studie, Candle and Bookes about him*" (B1r). The study is actually that of Landoffe, Bernard's tutor. Bernard comments to himself,

> Never before my warie Tutor did
> Leave this doore open, which he well might call
> His private Studie; for here Secrets lye
> Were worth mans labour to arrive to 'hem:
> Here are the Names, Shapes, Powers, and Government
> Of every severall Spirit, their Degrees,
> Their great Effects, particular Seigniories.   (B1v)

A later scene begins, "*Enter Landoffe in his study, a spirit to him*" (I1v), followed by echoes of both *Doctor Faustus* and *The Tempest*:

LANDOFFE	Thanks my industrious spirit.
SPIRIT	What else is thy command?
LANDOFFE	Nought else at this time, but on all occasions
	Thou in a thought be ready to attend.
SPIRIT	I shall. (I1v)

The last act of Dekker and Massinger's *The Virgin Martyr* (1620) begins, "*Enter Theophilus in his study, Bookes about him*" (K3r). He quotes from several of the books, then Harpax, an "evil spirit," enters "*in a fearefull shape, fire flashing out of the study*" (L1r). And an episode in *The Two Noble Ladies* (1622) begins with Bare-Bones saying, "Ile runne into my masters studdy," followed by "*Ciprian discovered at his booke*" (82–3). Ciprian is a conjurer who is finally redeemed and throws his books away.

In a few plays the discovery is specifically of a counting house, another secluded space in the real world. Marlowe's *The Jew of Malta* (1589) begins very much like *Doctor Faustus*, with a speech introducing the protagonist. In this case Machevil says he has come "to present the Tragedy of a Jew, / Who smiles to see how full his bags are cramb'd, / Which mony was not got without my meanes" (B1v). The direction "*Enter Barabas in his Counting-house, with heapes of gold before him*" (B1v) then signals the discovery[29] of the space that defines him, and that he defines in the speech that follows:

---

[29] In his edition of the play, N. W. Bawcutt says, "it is unlikely that Barabas was in full view of the audience while the prologue was being spoken, and probably at the end of the prologue 'Machevil' drew a curtain which disclosed Barabas sitting at a table with his ledgers and piles of coin in front of him" (199). In this and other scenes that begin with a discovery of a figure and props in an enclosed upstage space, it is probable that, for practical reasons, once the staging had served its thematic

> This is the ware wherein consists my wealth:
> And thus me thinks should men of judgement frame
> Their meanes of traffique from the vulgar trade,
> And as their wealth increaseth, so inclose
> Infinite riches in a little roome. (B2r)

The use of this stage space for Barabas's Machiavellian plotting at the start is completed in the final scene. The phrasing of "*A Cauldron discovered*" (K2r) almost certainly indicates that this property was revealed in the same defining space where Barabas first appeared.[30] Thus as at the end of *Doctor Faustus*, here the visual and verbal combine to evoke a hell-mouth: from the cauldron Barabas cries, "But now begins the extremity of heat / To pinch me with intolerable pangs" (K2r).[31] The events of *Arden of Faversham* (1591) culminate when Alice and Susan "*open the countinghouse doore, and looke uppon Arden*" (E2v), revealing the truth of what they have done. Alice's description – "See Susan where thy quondam Maister lyes, / Sweet Arden smeard in bloode and filthy gore" (I2v) – may be unnecessary for Susan, but it is typical of discovery scenes that use dialogue not only to heighten the effect but also to supply what might be difficult for some playgoers to see. In this case, Arden lying murdered in his counting house symbolizes Alice's violation of domestic ideals.

Middleton and Rowley's *The Changeling* (1622) probably includes two ironically linked discovery scenes that use a "closet." Although neither the stage directions nor the dialogue are specific enough to be certain, both scenes could be staged as discoveries, and given the thematic relationship between the two, if one scene is a discovery the other is even more likely to be. Early in Act 4, no sooner has Beatrice-Joanna married Alsemero than she begins to worry about what will happen when he realizes she is not a virgin. Looking for a way to escape detection she says,

> here's his closet,
> The key left in't, and he abroad i'th Park,
> Sure 'twas forgot, I'le be so bold as look in't.
> Bless me! A right Physicians closet 'tis,
> Set round with viols, every one her mark too. (F2r)

---

purpose, the action moved forward on the stage as the scene progressed, although the fictional location is still the study.

[30] David Hard Zuker also notes the symmetry of the play's initial and final discoveries (*Stage and Image*, 83).

[31] Among Philip Henslowe's properties was a "cauderm for the Jewe" (*Henslowe's Diary*, ed. R. A. Foakes and R. T. Rickert, 321, line 93).

Her words indicate that she opens the "closet" and that it contains the paraphernalia of a "physician," including vials and a "manuscript" called the "Secrets in Nature," where she finds "How to know whether a woman be a maid, or not" (F2v) – to see within, as it were. Armed with this knowledge, when Alsemero gives her the test, Beatrice-Joanna – in a *tour de force* of false appearance – is able to deceive him by reacting as she would if she were a virgin. The final consequences of this deception are staged using the same space at the end of the play when Alsemero learns the truth about Beatrice-Joanna and De Flores. Having accused her of adultery, Alsemero says, "you shall / Be my prisoner onely, enter my Closet" (I1r–v), and Beatrice-Joanna exits, presumably into the same space where she has found his secrets earlier. When De Flores then enters, Alsemero confronts him, and Beatrice-Joanna calls out from "*within*." Alsemero tells De Flores, "get you into hir" (I1v) and De Flores enters that same "closet," thus setting up the play's second and completing discovery scene. Thinking he has found the killers of Alonzo, Vermandero tells Alsemero, "I have a wonder for you"; but the cuckolded husband replies, "'tis I, have a wonder for you" before he opens the closet, saying, "Come forth you twins of mischief" (I2r). The truth-telling that typically accompanies a fifth-act discovery then follows, with De Flores and Beatrice-Joanna confessing before they die. By staging the scene in this way, Middleton and Rowley were able to encapsulate visually how the secrets that Beatrice-Joanna found when she entered that private space earlier have led inexorably to Alsemero imprisoning and then discovering her there with De Flores.

Chairs

The idea that scenes set in hidden or secret locations such as studies and closets were staged as discoveries to emulate such secluded locations in the real world is given further support by approximately thirty-five additional directions for the action. Some of these are not specific about location, but privacy is typically a factor. More particularly, these discoveries are of figures who are somehow immobile – most are seated, sometimes asleep, sometimes dead. And it might be significant that a "chair" is usually specified in the directions or dialogue of these discovered scenes, whereas smaller and more portable stools are typically used in banquet scenes, for which, as I have already noted, the necessary properties are put out on the main stage. So it seems that there were both practical and aesthetic reasons for discoveries of stationary, usually seated figures in private spaces. In Ford's *The Lover's Melancholy* (1628), for example, "*Drawes the Arras,*

Melander discovered in a chaire sleeping" (E4r) signals the revelation of a man who is depressed and living in seclusion. In *The Trial of Chivalry* a figure "turns a key" to *"Discover her sitting in a chayre asleepe"* (D1r). A direction in Ford's *The Broken Heart* (1630) – *"Ithocles discovered in a Chayre, and Penthea"* (E4r) – is preceded by the information that Ithocles "would be private" for the ensuing conversation with his sister. *The Two Noble Ladies* has a figure *"discovered in a chaire asleep, in her hands a prayer book, divells about her"* (1752–4).

In other examples the chair is implied by the information that figures are sitting, again in secluded locations. Marston, Barkstead and Machin's *The Insatiate Countess* (1607) has *"The Countess of Swevia discovered sitting at a Table covered with blacke, on which stands two blacke Tapers lighted, she in mourning"* (A2r); and Henry Shirley's *The Martyred Soldier* (1613) has *"Eugenius discovered sitting loaden with many Irons, a Lampe burning by him"* (E1v). In several instances the discovery is of a tableau with several seated figures, as in Fletcher's *The Faithful Shepherdess* (1608): *"The Curtayne is drawne, Clorin appears sitting in the Cabin, Amoret sitting on the on side of her, Allexis and Cloe on the other, the Satyre standing by"* (K1v); Marston's *What You Will* (1601): *"Enter a Schole-maister, draws the curtains behind with, Battus Nows, Slip, Nathaniell and Holifernes Pippo, schole-boyes, sitting with bookes in their hands"* (C4r); and *The Wisdom of Doctor Dodypoll* (1600): *"A Curtaine drawne, Earle Lassingbergh is discovered (like a Painter) painting Lucilia, who sits working on a piece of Cushion worke"* (A3r). Sometimes when the discovery is of a sleeping figure the property is not specified but other details again imply a chair, as in Tourneur's *The Atheist's Tragedy* (1611): *"A Clozet discover'd. A Servant sleeping with lights and money before him"* (K1v) and Davenant's *The Distresses* (1639): *"He steps to the Arras softly, draws it. Charamante is discovered sleeping on her Book, her Glas by"* (4G3r). In *The Fatal Contract* the Eunuch *"draws the Canopie, where the Queen sits at one end bound with Landrey at the other, both as asleep"* (H3r). The Eunuch murders Landry and the Queen, then again *"shews Landrey and the Queen"* (I4r; see Chapter 6).

Other situations differ in particulars but share the elements of seclusion and immobility, as in Munday's *The Downfall of Robert, Earl of Huntington* (1598): *"Curtaines open, Robin Hoode sleepes on a greene banke, and Marian strewing flowers on him"* (F3v) and Dekker's *Old Fortunatus* (1599): *"A curtaine being drawne, where Andelocia lies sleeping in Agripines lap"* (G2v). In *Henry IV, part 1* (1597) there are no stage directions when Falstaff is asleep out of sight and Hal tells Peto to "goe call him forth," but Peto's description of Falstaff "fast asleepe behinde the Arras, and snorting like a Horse" (E4r) pretty clearly signals a similar staging. In this scene, furthermore, the essential purpose and function of discoveries – the revelation of truth – is apparent and emphasized (see Chapter 6).

Beds

A bed is almost by definition a private place, so it is not surprising that beds are sometimes described as being discovered – although there are many more calls for the property than those specifying a discovery or curtains, and often it is difficult or impossible to know what kind of staging is being signalled. In what follows, therefore, I have included only those bed scenes with stage directions or dialogue that actually call for a discovery or refer to curtains.[32] But even then the staging of bed scenes can be difficult to interpret because references to curtains are ambiguous. A discovery might be effected by drawing curtains in front of the tiring house wall to reveal a bed in an imagined bed chamber, the same way a study is staged. Alternatively, a curtained bed might have been put out on stage, and its curtains opened for the discovery. Both kinds of scene exist, but some scenes might be one kind or the other. Although these ambiguities cannot be completely ignored, my focus here is primarily on the action of discovery, the reasons why the device is used, and its effects.[33] By my count forty-two plays have discovery scenes involving a bed; in these, six directions call for a bed to be discovered; sixteen have a figure discovered on a bed; twenty-five call for curtains to be opened to reveal a bed; and there are fifteen dialogue references to curtains in relation to a bed. Whatever the particular staging, however, the device of discovery again gives playgoers the impression of looking into what would be a place of restricted entry in the real world. Such scenes can intrigue or titillate, surprise or satisfy. In addition, as with many other discoveries the revelation is typically of a truth that, for good or ill, is essential to the plot and meaning of the play.

Sometimes the discovery of a bed is explicitly an action of invasion or exposure. For example, in *The First Part of the Contention* (1591) the murder of Duke Humphrey is staged as a violation of this private space: "*Then the Curtaines being drawne, Duke Humphrey is discovered in his bed, and two men lying on his brest and smothering him in his bed*" (E2r). Suffolk tells the

---

[32] If there is no reference to curtains and no other clear indication that they are needed, I assume that there are none, or if a bed has them, they are tied up and not used.

[33] For a consideration of all bed scenes, see Leslie Thomson, "Beds on the Early Modern Stage."

murderers to "see the cloathes laid smooth about him still, / That when the King comes, he may perceive / No other, but that he dide of his owne accord," and after this is done, he says, "draw the Curtaines againe and get you gone" (E2r). When Henry speaks of not knowing how Humphrey died, Warwick says, "Enter his privie chamber my Lord and view the bodie" and "*Warwicke drawes the curtaines and showes Duke Humphrey in his bed*" (E2v–E3r). This second discovery is ostensibly of the truth that Humphrey died of natural causes, but the playgoers know otherwise. As to the staging of the bed, in the Folio version, *Henry VI, part 2*, these directions are absent, but just before Warwick shows Henry the body, there is "*Bed put forth*" (TLN 1849). Therefore, when Warwick says, "Come hither, gracious Soveraigne, view this body" (TLN 1852–3), he must open bed curtains to make the discovery, so perhaps this is how to interpret the Quarto directions. That a similar discovery is used – with no small irony – to stage the death of Winchester, the man who arranged Humphrey's murder, is made clear in the Quarto: "*Enter the King and Salsbury, and then the Curtaines be drawne, and the Cardinall is discovered in his bed, raving and staring as if he were madde*" (F1v). In the Folio this direction is absent, but Henry's "draw the Curtaine close" (TLN 2166) at the end of the scene seems to indicate a similar staging. Significantly, when Winchester is discovered here, he as much as confesses to the murder of Humphrey – who was discovered dead in, presumably, the same property bed.

In Peele's *Edward I* (1591) the discovered bed is one of birth, not murder: "*the Queenes Tent opens, she is discovered in her bed, attended by Mary Dutches of Lancaster, Jone of Acon her daughter, & the Queen dandles his young sonne*" (F4r). At the end of the scene "*They close the Tent*" (G1r) so the queen can sleep, emphasizing the idea of privacy. This also prepares for the next discovery when "*The Queens Tent opens*" (G2v), after which "*The Nurse closeth the Tent*" (G4r). Given this repeated action it is likely that the direction for the queen's final appearance – "*Elinor in child-bed with her daughter Jone, and other Ladies*" (K3v) – again signals a discovery. Now, however, the queen is dying. Besides this use of the discovery device as a way to signpost Elinor's progress through the play, this staging also helps to create a sense of the secret world where she has deceived Edward.

In *Tamburlaine, part 2* (1588) Marlowe deployed a substantial discovery scene to stage the death of Zenocrate. The directions leave little doubt about how the scene was to be performed: it begins, "*The Arras is drawen and Zenocrate lies in her bed of state, Tamburlaine sitting by her: three Phisitians about her bed, tempering potions. Theridamas, Techelles,*

Usumcasane, and the three sonnes" (C6r) and ends, "*The Arras is drawen*" (D8v). This indicates that the event crucial to the career of Tamburlaine and pivotal in the structure of the whole play was located in a doorway or a curtained space. Possibly the bed was thrust forward on stage and back again at the scene's end, but nothing indicates this. And the advantage of staging it at a distance, as a spectacle, is how the event would have been set apart for playgoers, emphasizing significance that the dialogue confirms.

Always with Shakespeare's discoveries, what is revealed and how it is revealed are directly relevant to the concerns of the particular play, and in none is this more effectively so than *Othello* (1602?), in which the idea that truth will be revealed in time and the dramatic action of discovery are given tragic specificity. In making possible first Emilia's then Othello's realization of the truth about both Iago and Desdemona, Emilia's fifth-act discovery of Desdemona on her bed is the structural and thematic culmination of a process of deception initiated by Iago as the play began. Not surprisingly, therefore, the discovery is unique in how it is set up and executed. As Othello is smothering Desdemona, Emilia calls repeatedly to be let in to speak with him. Having convinced himself that Desdemona is dead, Othello finally pays attention to Emilia's cries; but before letting her in he says to himself, "let me the Curtaines draw" (TLN 3368), and in doing so hides Desdemona from view. As Emilia tells Othello about the deaths that have occurred outside the room, Desdemona is heard from behind the curtains: "O falsely, falsely murder'd" (TLN 3384). Presumably she is referring to Emilia's news about Cassio, but her words will soon apply to herself, and they prompt Emilia to open the curtains and find Desdemona dying on the bed. What Emilia exposes is a paradigm of truth destroyed by deception, as the ensuing exchange between her and Iago makes clear. Furthermore, during Emilia's repeated insistence that Desdemona was "true" and Iago's that she was "false," Emilia finally sees – or can no longer not see – the truth of Iago's evil. When Iago orders his wife to keep silent, she replies, "I will not charme my Tongue; / I am bound to speake"; and she tells the truths she has discovered: "My Mistris heere lyes murthered in her bed. / ... / And your reports have set the Murder on" (TLN 3466–8, 3470). To this Othello says, "Nay stare not Masters, / It is true, indeede" and Gratiano responds, "'Tis a strange Truth" (TLN 3471–3).

In Marston's *Sophonisba* (1605) a bed features in a thematic sequence of three titillating discoveries. First, "*The Ladies lay the Princes in a faire bed, and close the curtaines whil'st Massinissa Enters*" (B1v). The bride and groom are about to consummate their marriage. When he enters, "*the boyes draw the Curtaines discovering Sophonisba*" (B1v).[34] At the end of this scene, "*The Ladies draw the curtaines about Sophonisba, the rest accompany Massinissa forth*" (B4v), phrasing that suggests curtains on the bed. This discovery of the bride on her wedding night is then contrasted with two subsequent discoveries. In Act 3 Massinissa's rival for Sophonisba is about to come to bed. She and her maid drug her guard, Vangue, and "*They lay Vangue in Syphax bed & draw the curtaines*" (D4v). Sophonisba and her maid escape before Syphax enters and "*Offering to leape into bed, he discovers Vangue*" (E1r), then kills him on the bed. This property is not needed again until Act 4, when the enchantress Erictho enters "*in the shape of Sophonisba, her face vailed and hasteth in the bed of Syphax*" (F1v). Then "*Syphax hasteneth within the Canopy, as to Sophonisbas bed*" (F2r), setting up a bed-trick. This is the end of Act 4, and when Act 5 begins the implication is that Syphax thinks he has had sex with Sophonisba until he "*drawes the curtaines and discovers Erichtho lying with him*" on the bed and realizes the horrible truth: "Thou rotten scum of Hell – / O my abhorred heat! O loath'd delusion!" (F2r).

Discovered-bed scenes usually include descriptive dialogue from the figure performing the discovery and/or the one responding to it. These reactions express their responses to the revelation; but, as I have noted, they probably also served the practical function of describing to playgoers what they could not see because of the staging. This combination of visual and verbal is characteristic of most of these scenes, but several provide especially good examples. In the last act of Tourner's *The Atheist's Tragedy* D'Amville is forced to accept a sad truth. When a servant tells him, "Never you will see your Sonne alive," D'Amville responds, "Nature forbid I e'er should see him dead." But then "*A Bed drawne forth with Rousard*" and D'Amville says, "Withdraw the Curtaines. O how does my Sonne?" (K2v). When a servant says that Rousard is dying, the grieving father comments on what he sees: "Destruction take thee and thy fatall tongue. Death . . . – Art not thou the face of that prodigious apparition star'd upon me in my dreame?" (K2v). D'Amville sees that his son is dying, but also recognizes Death from the vision he had in 4.3. Contrasting discoveries occur in *Brennoralt* when the stage direction "*Francelia (as in a Bed.)*" is immediately followed by the entrance of Brennoralt who "*drawes the curtaines*" (C2v) to reveal her, saying:

---

[34] If this bed was "thrust out" the stage would have been very full, with a canopied bed and nine players, four of whom needed space to dance. But if the bed was in an opening in the tiring house wall, the ability of playgoers to see the action on the bed would have been seriously restricted.

So Misers looke upon their gold,
Which while they joy to see, they feare to loose:
The pleasure of the sight scarse equalling,
The jealousie of being dispossest by others;
Her face is like the milky way i'th' skie,
A meeting of gentle lights without name.   (C2v)

The play ends with a parallel scene when Brennoralt returns and *"drawes the curtain,"* thinking he will see Francelia sleeping; but playgoers have just watched her die and will wait for his realization of the truth: "Awake fair Saint and blesse thy poore Idolator / Ha! – pale? – and cold? – dead" (D2v).

Tom a Lincoln (1611?) includes four dumb shows, all introduced and summarized by a figure named Time. For the first two shows Time not only explicates what is shown but also performs a discovery, in both cases of a bed with a figure on it. Time introduces the first dumb show by providing context: "king Arthure did Angellica embrace / within the Cloyster with unlawfull sports / and wanton dalliance" (137–9); she became pregnant and the abbess delivered the child. He ends, "what afterward befell / mark what ensues and yt will plainly tell" (147–8) and the "Dumbe shew" begins:

> *Time drawes a curtaine & discovers Angellica in her bed a sleep, the infant lying by her, then enters the kinge & the Abbesse whispering together the Abbesse takes the childe out of the bed & departs, the kinge alsoe after a litle viwinge of Angelica at an other doore departs, Angell: still sleepinge he being gone [Time] drawes the Curtaynes & speaks.* (150–5)

Time reports that Angelica fell asleep and when she awoke the child had been taken by the king and abbess: "whither twas Convayd / observe the sequel and yow shall perceave / an Aunciant sheaphard did the babe receave" (162–4). This is presented in the second "Dumb shew," which ends, *"then time discovers Angell: In her bed awake, weepinge & lamentinge, wth the kinge strivinge to comfort her, wch done time drawes ye curtayne"* (169–71).

Tombs, Caves, Tents and Canopies

Discovered scenes are not accidental (or incidental); they are specifically signalled by stage directions and/or dialogue, and they require extra effort to stage. This is certainly true for a small group of scenes that use a tomb, cave, tent or canopy for a discovery. And as with the other kinds of discoveries included in this chapter, these are of places that are private, secluded, even mysterious.

Tombs bring their own atmosphere of the unknown and usually include bodies or ghosts.[35] I have discussed *Romeo and Juliet* already (see Chapter 4), but it is worth returning to the tomb scene for the moment of discovery. When "*Romeo opens the tombe*" (Q1, K1r), playgoers anticipate what he (and they) will see; but his action is interrupted by Paris. Only after Romeo has killed Paris and is putting the body into the tomb does he see inside: "O my Love, my wife"; "Tybalt lyest thou there in thy bloodie sheet?" (Q2, L3r). A seemingly dead woman is also found in two plays that do not explicitly call for a tomb to be opened or discovered (the two verbs are interchangeable), but do include dialogue that seems to signal a discovery that is followed by descriptive commentary. In *How a Man May Choose a Good Wife from a Bad* (1602) a man comes to a churchyard to see the body of a woman he thinks is dead. He seems to describe the action of opening a vault and finding a coffin within: "This is the Church, this hollow is the Vault, / Where the dead bodie of my Saint remaines, / And this the Coffin that inshrines her bodie" (H2r). In *Law Tricks*, the direction "*Countesse in the Tombe*" signals the last of the play's discovery scenes.[36] The reactions of the surprised onlookers complete the effect: "*Duke.* Sister? *Polymetes.* Aunt? *Emilia.* Madam? / *Lurdo.* My much wronged wife?" (I3v). Other examples, including the much more spectacular version in *The Second Maiden's Tragedy/Lady's Tragedy* (see Chapter 3), suggest that the discovery of a female figure in a tomb became a minor dramatic trope.

The most extensive use of a tomb for such discoveries is in Chapman's *The Widow's Tears* (1604), in which the last two acts feature a "tomb" being repeatedly opened to reveal its occupants, especially Cynthia, the widow of the title. This sequence begins when Lysander "*discovers the Tombe, lookes in and wonders, &c.*" Since Lysander soon says to Ero, who is inside the tomb, "ope, or Ile force it open" (H1v), he evidently first discovers the tomb, then opens it and sees Cynthia. As the playgoer knows, she is mourning Lysander, her husband, who has arranged for her to be told he is dead, then has returned in disguise to see if she will keep her vow to be true to him if he died. Indeed, the inevitable result of his testing her is probably prepared for by the staging of this scene, because she is discovered in the seclusion of the tomb but then moves out to join Lysander on the main stage, before returning to the tomb. At the end of a discovery scene it

---

[35] In addition to the tomb scenes discussed here, other examples are included in the discussion about lighting in Chapter 4.

[36] This direction is the same idiom as discoveries signalled by *X in his study*, as in this play: "*Polymetes in his study*" (H3r).

is rare to find a signal to close whatever was opened, although this must normally have been done; at the end of this scene, however, Ero "*shuts up the Tomb*" (H4r). This and subsequent similar directions to close the tomb (I1v, I4v, K2r) are required because the action of Acts 4 and 5 is essentially, and uniquely, a series of six discovery scenes for which the tomb must be closed before it can be reopened.[37] Clearly Chapman wanted to emphasize these repeated actions, and in performance they would certainly make visual the numerous invasions of the mourning woman's seclusion. This point is underlined both by figures outside the tomb who look in and describe what the playgoer cannot easily see, and by having parts of several scenes evidently occur inside the tomb itself, including when the "*Tomb opens, and Lysander within lies along*" (I3v) and, after the tomb has been shut again, "*Ero opens, and hee sees her* [Cynthia's] *head layd on the coffin, &c.*" (K1v). From inside the space at the end of this scene, Cynthia says, "Shut up the tomb" (K2r). Chapman's desire to give a physical, literal dimension both to Lysander's jealous testing of his wife and to the gradual weakening of her vow seems to have trumped any difficulties posed by the extensive use of the discoverable space seemingly called for by the text.

Marlowe seems to have understood well how strategically placed discovery scenes can have cumulative thematic significance.[38] The Marlowe–Nash collaboration *Dido, Queen of Carthage* (1588) begins strikingly with an emblematic tableau: "*Here the Curtains draw, there is discovered Jupiter dandling Ganimed upon his knee, and Mercury lying asleepe*" (A2r).[39] This discovery of Jupiter with Ganymede as a love object on his knee and Mercury sleeping, combined with Jupiter's and the play's first words – "Come gentle Ganimed and play with me" – vividly introduces the play's central motif of secret, obsessive, misdirected love and consequent neglect of responsibility. It is therefore thematically fitting that at mid-play a door or opening in the tiring house wall is probably required again for the "cave" where Dido and Aeneas meet during the storm. At the end of Act 3 they "*Exeunt to the Cave*" (E1r), and almost certainly curtains would have been drawn closed over the opening between acts. Neither of the lovers is visible when shortly into Act 4 Iarbus asks, "where have ye left the Queene?" (E1r),

---

[37] For a discussion of problems with and possible stagings of these tomb scenes see Akihiro Yamada's introduction to the play (*The Widow's Tears*, lxvii–lxx) and Dessen, *Recovering Shakespeare's Theatrical Vocabulary*, 182–3.

[38] For a detailed discussion see Leslie Thomson, "Marlowe's Staging of Meaning."

[39] The *OED* gives this as the first example of I.4.c. "*Theatre*. To reveal or present (a character, group of characters, etc.) in a particular position or state when the curtain rises. (Esp. as a stage direction.)" ("discover, v." *OED Online*, Oxford University Press, September 2016). *Reveal* and its other forms are not used in early modern stage directions.

and Cupid (disguised as Ascanius) asks, "where is my warlike father, can you tell?" Anna's response, "Behold where both of them come forth the Cave," together with Iarbus's surprised "Come forth the Cave: can heaven endure this sight?" (E1r), likely signal the reopening of curtains (or a door) to effect the discovery of Dido and Aeneas in the same location where Jupiter and Ganymede were revealed at the start. If this is an accurate interpretation of the staging, the same stage space was used to create visual links among characters and events. Very possibly, then, the play's final action of first Dido then Anna immolating themselves used the same space to complete the thematic sequence.

Three other uses of a cave seem intended to allude to emblems of discovered Truth discussed in Chapter 2. As we have already seen, *Hoffman* begins when the protagonist *"strikes ope a curtain where appeares a body"* (B1r) to show playgoers his dead father hanging in what seems to be the same "cave" as the one Hoffman opens in the last scene to realize he has been tricked: "S'death who stands here? / What's that? Lorriques pale ghost? / I am amaz'd" (L1v). In *The Whore of Babylon* the emblematic element is emphasized by the use of a dumb show that begins with an ironic inversion: *"A cave suddenly breakes open, and out of it comes Falshood, (attir'd as Truth is) her face spotted, she stickes vp her banner on the top of the Cave"* (G2v). And in *The Jews' Tragedy* (1627) Josephus *"Opens the Cave"* to show himself to Valerio, his enemy:

> Lo I am [t]he brave Roman that have stood
> The furious shock of my distressed fate;
> Behold me now, and whilst thou lookst upon
> This lump of earth captivd to thee and Rome,
> Know then that Joseph dares, but cannot dye,
> Our sacred Law forbids such cruelty.   (D4r)

In the context of discovery scenes, "tent," "canopy," and "pavilion" all seem to refer to the same kind of property – one in which a figure is enclosed then revealed. In *A Looking-Glass for London and England* Rasni prepares for one kind of discovery when he signals the opening of a "tent" to reveal Romelia: "Now ope ye foldes where Queene of favour sits"; but *"He drawes the Curtaines and findes her stroken with Thunder, blacke"* (C2v). By contrast, in *The Devil's Charter* Katherine thinks her sons are dead when Caesar *"discovereth his Tent where her two sonnes were at Cardes,"* saying "Behold thy children living in my Tent" (I1v) and "Lady behold thy treasure in my Tent" (I2r). And in Heywood's *The Iron Age, part 1* (1612) the action displays an iconic Homeric event: *"Achilles discovered in his Tent, about him his bleeding Mermidons, himselfe wounded, and with him Ulisses"* (H4v).

Two of Peele's plays include similar directions, one for a "tent," the other for a "pavilion." In *Edward I "the Queenes Tent opens, she is discovered in her bed, attended by Mary Dutches of Lancaster, Jone of Acon her daughter"* (F4r); at the end of the scene, *"They close the Tent"* (G1r). Later, *"The Queens Tent opens"* and at the end of the scene, *"The Nurse closeth the Tent"* (G2v, G4r). In *David and Bethsabe* the same kind of enclosure seems to be signalled when David, mourning the death of Absalom, *"goes to his pavillion, and sits close a while"*; then he *"lookes forth"* and *"sits close againe."* Then Joab *"unfolds the pavillion"* where the king is "sitting" (H4v).

Three late plays call for a "canopy" to be opened to reveal secret or private actions. In Davenant's *Albovine* (1628), *"A Canopy is drawne, the King is discover'd sleeping over papers"* (L2v) and vulnerable when Paradine enters with an unsheathed sword. In *The Fatal Contract*, the Eunuch *"solemnly draws the Canopie, where the Queen sits at one end bound with Landrey at the other, both as asleep"* (H3r); this is his handiwork and at the end of the scene he *"draws the Curtain again"* (I1r). And as already noted, another sleeping figure is discovered in Davenant's *The Platonic Lovers* (1635) when Theander *"Drawes a Canopie; Eurithea is found sleeping on a Couch, a vaile on, with her Lute"*; he comments that "shee lies as in a shady Monument" (D2v).

Shops

Unlike studies, beds, tombs, etc., shops are public places; but shops are also typically staged as discovery scenes, which raises a number of related questions: what was "discovered"? why? and how? Ralph Treswell's survey of 16 Cornhill (Figure 5.5) illustrates a common shop configuration, with an outside counter or stall, a front room designated "a shop," and (sometimes) a warehouse and other spaces behind it. One might therefore assume that when a shop is discovered the interior space is shown; in fact, however, the evidence of dialogue and stage directions indicates that it is the exterior, the street-front of the shop, that suddenly appears. A contemporary illustration of Cheapside (Figure 5.6) gives a sense of how such shop-fronts looked. Although the stage directions for a shop-discovery repeatedly call for the shopkeeper to appear *in* his shop, which might seem to mean that he is inside it, these same shopkeepers also call out "What d'ye lack?" to passers by, which tells us that they are standing or sitting at the outside counter – as they did in reality. Instead of exposing an

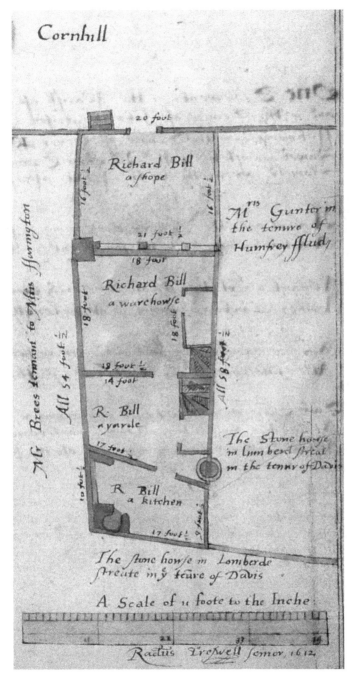

Figure 5.5 Survey of 16 Cornhill, detail, Ralph Treswell, 1612

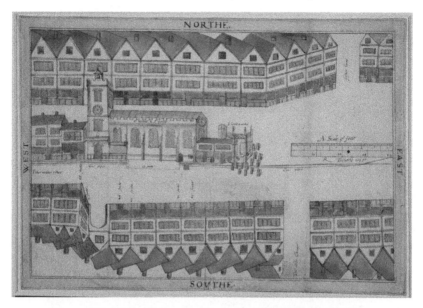

Figure 5.6 St Michael le Querne, Cheapside shops, Ralph Treswell, 1585

enclosed place, therefore, when a shop is discovered, it is a representation of what playgoers saw as they walked the streets of London: a shopkeeper in front of an interior, unseen space. Furthermore, these stage shops typically require only a few properties – a stool, merchandise and something to display it on – which might easily have been put out on stage like banquets. That this did not happen but that shops were discovered suggests that perhaps one aim of this minor staging convention was to surprise and impress playgoers with its realism and topicality. By my count seventeen plays include twenty-three shops that are certainly or probably discovered.[40] These plays were written and performed between 1597 and 1639 – but eleven of them appeared in the much shorter period between 1602 and 1613, which doubtless reflects the growing number and variety of shops on the streets of early Jacobean London. And the kinds of stage shop – haberdasher, draper, goldsmith, shoemaker – were the most common in the world of the playgoers.

---

[40] About thirty-three extant plays include stage directions that refer to a shop or include dialogue, action and properties that establish the location as a shop, whether or not it was discovered. For a discussion of shop scenes that addresses many of the same matters, see Dessen, *Recovering Shakespeare's Theatrical Vocabulary*, 155–9.

In the seventeen plays with discovered shop scenes, seven stage directions specify the discovery of a shop or shopkeeper in a shop; four directions refer to shops "open" or "opened"; one has a figure "appear" in a shop; seven call for figures to "enter in" a shop, and one has a figure "enter at" a shopboard. My premise, as with study scenes, is that a direction for a figure to "enter in" a shop signals a discovery, in this case of a figure at a table or other property representing the counter at the front of a shop. That shops were discovered is certain and in none of these scenes is there a direction to bring the necessary properties out on stage as there usually is for banquets. It is therefore reasonable to conclude that these shop scenes all used basically the same staging convention; indeed, perhaps it was also used for other shop scenes but not signalled in stage directions. As to where shops were discovered, it could have been at a doorway in the tiring house wall, or at a central opening in the wall, if there was one.[41] But specifics are few; for example, unlike other discoveries, shop scenes have no references to opening a curtain or door to effect the revelation. Perhaps playwrights knew that implementation of their directions would depend on the particular venue. Some examples will help to illustrate these general points.

The discovery of a shop typically comes at the start of an act or scene. In some cases it begins the play, as in Cooke's *Greene's Tu Quoque* (1611): "*A Mercers Shop discovered, Gartred working in it, Spendall walking by the Shop: M Ballance walking over the Stage: after him Longfield and Geraldine.*" Adding to the realism is the first line, from Spendall, the apprentice: "What lacke you sir? faire stuffes, or velvets?" (B1r). And 2.2 of Middleton and Webster's *Anything for a Quiet Life* (1619) begins: "*Enter (a Shop being discover'd) Walter Chamlet, ... two Prentices, George and Ralph*" (C3r). George's cry indicates the kinds of merchandise on display:

> What ist you lack, you lack, you lack?
> Stuffs for the Belly, or the Back?
> Silk-Grograns, Sattins, Velvet fine,
> The Rosie-colour'd Carnadine;
> Your Nutmeg hue, or Gingerline,
> Cloth of Tissue, or Tobine,
> That like beaten Gold will shine
> In your Amarous Ladies eyne,
> Whilest you their softer Silks do twine:
> What ist you lack, you lack, you lack? (C3r)

---

[41] See the Appendix.

Similarly, the discovery of a shop at the start of Massinger's *The Renegado* (1624) is accompanied by a description of the tempting merchandise it contains and which, presumably, playgoers could see:

> What doe you lacke, your choyce China dishes, your pure Venetian Christall, of all sorts, of all neate and new fashions, from the mirror of the madam, to the private utensile of her chamber-maide, and curious Pictures of the rarest beauties of Europa: what doe you lacke? (C2r)

William Rowley's *A Shoemaker, a Gentleman* (1607–9) includes a scene that begins with the discovery of a tableau: "*Enter discover'd in a Shop a Shoo-maker, his Wife spinning, Barnaby, two Journimen*" (B4r). In Dekker's *Match Me in London* (1611–13) a slightly different stage direction – "*A shop opened, Enter Bilbo and Lazarillo*" (C3v) – seems to indicate the same staging, and when two gallants enter, the apprentices call to them "What is't you lacke Gentlemen, rich garters, spangled roses, silke stockins, embroidered gloves or girdles" (C3v–4r) and "Don sweet Don, see here rich Tuscan hatbands, Venetian ventoyes, or Barbarian shoo-strings – no poynt" (C4r).

The direction at the start of *Greene's Tu Quoque* calls for the discovery of a figure "working" in the shop, which would seem to indicate that the player was in the shop before the discovery; so too in Jonson's *The Case Is Altered* (1597): "*Juniper a Cobler is discovered, sitting at worke in his shoppe and singing*" (A2r). Much later this play, after several changes of location, comes a less detailed direction, probably for an identical discovery: "*Enter Juniper in his shop singing: to him Onion*" (F4r). The shop scene in Dekker's *A Shoemakers' Holiday* (1599) begins: "*Enter Jane in a Sempsters shop working, and Hamond muffled at another doore, he stands aloofe*" (F3r). This direction combines the same conventional elements of a figure working in a shop and another outside the shop, to whom Jane says, "Sir, what ist you buy? / What ist you lacke sir? callico, or lawne, fine cambricke shirts, or bands, what will you buy?" (F3v), which implies that these goods are on display. These similarities lead me to conclude that, like the others, this scene was discovered. And if it was, the same is probably true for other "*enter in*" directions, such as this in Heywood's *A Fair Maid of the Exchange* (1602): "*Enter Boy in a Shop cutting of square parchments, to him enter Phillis*" (E4v), and another in Dekker and Middleton's *The Honest Whore, part 1* (1604): "*Enter Candido, his wife, George, and two Prentices in the shop: Fustigo enters, walking by*" (E2r). In each of these examples, first the occupied shop is discovered, then a figure comes to it.

The scene in *The Honest Whore* is among a group in which the discovery is not just of a shop but also of the shopkeeper's wife or daughter. Indeed, perhaps this combination is what led to the use of a discovery, because it was certainly topical. Discussing the increasing materialism of Londoners in this period, Ian Archer says that conspicuous consumption "contributed to the anxieties about the position of women and the young [i.e. apprentices] in the capital," which was "at odds with elements of the prevailing patriarchal ideology."[42] Furthermore, "Consumption was a moral problem because the desire for goods was linked with sexual desire. The Christian tradition had conflated luxuria and lust: luxury was equated with desire, and desire with disobedience." More particularly, Archer argues that "The drama suggests that shopping expeditions by court gallants were as much occasions for sexual aggression against citizens' wives as for the purchasing of goods." Noting the common belief that shopkeepers put their wives in prominent positions as bait, Archer observes, "Thus shopping became a locus for anxieties about the gender order: the apparent availability of women in the shops and the desire of city women for consumer goods threatened the patriarchal order on which the authority of citizen husbands rested."[43] These ideas are evident in Heywood's *The Wise Woman of Hogsdon* (1604) at the start of 1.2 – "*Enter Luce in a Sempsters shop, at worke upon a lac'd Handkercher, and Joseph a Prentice*" (A4v) – where again the visual and verbal similarities suggest the conventional discovery staging. Luce says, "I doe not love to sit thus publikely"; and when Boyster comes to the shop and she asks, "what ist you lack" (A4v), he makes it clear that what he wants is her. The same ideas about women shopkeepers are also central to the plot and expressed in the title of *A Chaste Maid in Cheapside*, which begins, "*Enter Maudline and Moll, a Shop being discovered*" (B1r). This shop scene is particularly noteworthy because the title page tells us that the play was performed at the Swan playhouse, which according to van Buchel's copy of de Witt's drawing had no central opening in the tiring house wall (see the Appendix). If this was the case, the direction must mean that the shop was set either in one of the two doorways or in a temporary fixture – perhaps a curtained area located between the two doors. By whatever means this and other shop

---

[42] Ian W. Archer, "Material Londoners?" 184.
[43] Ibid., 186. And see Leslie Thomson, "'As proper a woman as any in Cheap'."

discoveries were effected, though, it seems the aim was to give playgoers a realistic picture of a London shop.

The discovery scenes that are the focus of this chapter create "a local habitation and a name" and provide real-world contexts for the action. Typically these discovered places would have had moral – or amoral or immoral – values associated with them in the world of the playgoer, values which would have been brought with them into the play. Such scenes were probably worth the staging effort because of the thematic work they did – analogous to that of a curtained altar in early Christian church performances, discussed in Chapter 3. In a secular rather than religious context, discovered studies, tombs, caves and shops had iconographic qualities and therefore could be used to create and convey meaning instantly to early modern playgoers.

CHAPTER 6

Invention and Artifice

In the hands of inventive playwrights, the action of discovery is used in ways that depend on the basic idea of the revelation of truth, but is also reworked or adapted to the thematic concerns and generic requirements of the particular play. The more unusual or innovative examples demonstrate both how entrenched the convention was and how it could be a means of creating and manipulating playgoer expectations in such a way as to surprise, enlighten and satisfy. More particularly, because the action of discovery is explicitly, inherently "theatrical" – non-realistic, contrived – it heightens the sense of artifice and allows playgoers to enjoy revelations of a sort that rarely occur in real life. Jeremy Lopez describes "the kind of drama Renaissance drama is":

> a drama where conventions and the narratives they order strain and crack under the weight of plots that make utterly free use of these conventions as they move with relentless energy toward a state where everything is merely theatrical; where language, character, action become, rather than the subject of representation, sites for admiring the act of representation itself. Playwrights are so successful in casually acknowledging to their audiences the potential absurdities of their favorite devices, even as they use these devices to more and more hyperbolic ends, because to a tremendous degree they share the audience's position: inside and outside the theatrical space.[1]

Certainly, each of the plays discussed below uses the convention of discovery in ways that highlight rather than downplay its essential theatricality; but in some cases, at least, the discoveries work as reminders of fundamental ideas – appearance vs reality; the relationship between time, truth and justice; the possibility of repentance and renewal – and invite playgoers to think about their implications.

Mucedorus is often dismissed as being simple and silly; but this assessment ignores the complexities and significance of the layers of disguise and

---

[1] Jeremy Lopez, *Theatrical Convention and Audience Response*, 128.

discovery present as both thematic elements and stage business. The first known quarto is dated 1598, but the play was probably written as much as a decade before that and therefore offers one of the earliest examples of an extended disguise that leads to not one but two performed discoveries. Furthermore, the third quarto of 1610 includes non-authorial "new additions" that alter the basic premise and treatment of this disguise plot.[2] The main difference between the two versions is that in the first two quartos Mucedorus is in disguise as a shepherd from his first appearance, but in the third and subsequent fifteen quartos he initially appears as the prince he is before donning that disguise. Other Q3 additions support this revision. Moreover, the original version withholds the revelation of the shepherd's true identity until late in the play, whereas the revised version explicitly provides that information at the start.[3] Certainly, the original playwright's use of the device was notably innovative and demonstrates an awareness of how to create the conditions for a discovery that would include playgoers in the surprise; in this it anticipates later plays that keep the playgoer in the dark about a disguise until the moment of discovery.

The Q3 reviser's addition at the beginning of Act 1 is clearly intended to establish Mucedorus's real identity, his reason for adopting a disguise, and why he chooses the disguise he does. The audience learns that Mucedorus is the prince of Valencia, who has heard praise of Amadine, princess of Aragon, and wants to go there in disguise to see for himself. Mucedorus and his friend Anselmo discuss possible disguises and Anselmo offers a "Cassocke," saying, "t'was a Shepheards, / Which I presented in Lord Julio's Maske" (Q3, A4v). As this added scene ends, Mucedorus puts on this cloak for his entrance *"like a Shepheard"* (A3v), which is his first appearance in Q1. Then at the beginning of Act 4 the revised version has a scene in which the King of Valencia, Mucedorus's father, wonders where his son has gone and Anselmo tells him, providing a mid-play reminder of the disguise and the reasons for it. These changes make it easy for playgoers to enjoy the disguise while also expecting its discovery, and they also give a context for Mucedorus's noble actions while looking like a shepherd.

Regardless of the changes, the disguise – or rather disguises – of Mucedorus are at the centre of the plot, and his final self-discovery makes possible its resolution. In both versions, the second time Mucedorus

---

[2] The phrase is from the title page. For publication details, see Arvin Jupin, *"Mucedorus": A Contextual Study and Modern Spelling Edition*, 1–12.

[3] There are reasons to think that although the truth is withheld in the first version, playgoers might well have suspected a disguise. See Leslie Thomson, *"Mucedorus: From Revision to Nostalgia."*

disguises himself the playgoer watches him do so, as signalled by two stage directions: "*Enter Mucedorus to disguise himselfe*" and "*he disguiseth himselfe*" (D4r, D4v).[4] Before this, he and Amadine had arranged to meet in the woods and escape, but she arrived early and was captured by Bremo, a wild man. Ignorant of this, Mucedorus thinks Amadine has changed her mind, but hoping to see her again decides to disguise himself as a hermit and remain in the woods. He says, "No shepheard now, a hermit I must be" (D4v), and puts on a white gown and hat. In this second disguise Mucedorus encounters Bremo and the captive Amadine, which provides him with an opportunity to demonstrate his worth by killing the wild man and freeing her.

Having rescued Amadine, Mucedorus, still disguised as a hermit, asks what she will do, and when she replies that she will search for the shepherd she loves, "*He discovers himselfe*"[5] by removing the hermit costume. He asks, "Say Ladie doe you know your shepheard well?" and Amadine responds, "My Mucedorus" (F1r). Thus the hermit disguise leads to a discovery that returns Mucedorus to his shepherd disguise and sets the plot in motion again. When Mouse (the Clown figure) and Segasto, Amadine's courtly suitor, try to force her to return to court, Mucedorus tells her to "make thy choice of three, / There stands Segasto, here a shepheard stands, / There stands the third" and, emphasizing the nature of her choice, Mouse adds, "A lord at the least I am" (F1v–2r). When Amadine quickly chooses Mucedorus, he reminds her that as a shepherd he has no lands and her life will be one of drudgery: "No princes then but plaine a shepheards wife" (F2r). But she dismisses that possibility, because as her husband he will be "crowned king of Arragon." This finally brings Mucedorus to declare:

> Then know that which nere tofore was known
> I am no shepheard, no Arragonian I,
> But borne of Royall blood, my fathers of Valentia
> King, my mother queene.   (F2r)

But the play is not over and another discovery is still to come; for whether or not Mucedorus actually removes his shepherd disguise as he identifies himself to Amadine and Segasto, he is wearing it when he returns to Aragon with them. When her father refers to him as an "accursed wretch," he insists "I do deserve the daughter of a king" and the King

---

[4] All subsequent quotations from *Mucedorus* are from the first (1598) quarto.
[5] "*He disguiseth himself*" in the first quarto is clearly an error.

responds "Oh, impudent, a shepheard and so insolent" (F3r–v). When Mucedorus then verbally identifies himself – "No shepheard I, but a worthy prince" – the King, still seeing a shepherd, again rejects him: "In farre conceit, not princelie borne." Mucedorus replies, "Yes princely borne my father is a king. / My mother Queene, and of Valentia both" and this time the king responds, "What, Mucedorus, welcome to our court, / What cause hadst thou to come to me disguised?" (F3v). This change to immediate recognition suggests that as Mucedorus speaks he also physically discovers himself.[6]

Other early plays also use discoveries in ways that call attention to the device. *Edmond Ironside* (c. 1595) includes a brief but noteworthy use of disguise to effect a switch of social roles when Edricus, a lord, and Stich, his servant, "*shifte apparell*" (1226). Commenting on the contrast between his appearance and true self, Edricus says, "well this plaine suite doth now Contayne more witt / then for soe meane a peece of Cloth is fitt" (1241–2). And Stich says, "oh what a foole is my mr to Change his nobillitie for my worshipe" (1257–8). In the next scene Ironside becomes suspicious that "yon plaine fellow should bee Edricus" and "*pulls of the velvet patch of his face*" (1310, 1313). When Ironside asks why he "Came this disguisde," Edricus vows to tell the "trewth" (1316–17), saying, "I came thus plainely to yor majestye / disguised in clownes attire to sound the truth / what oppinion yf good or bad / You had of me" (1321–4). With this discovery, an unusual role reversal has served its purpose and when Stich next enters, he is wearing his own clothes again.

In Yarington's *Two Lamentable Tragedies* (1594), one plot uses the disguise–discovery–recognition–resolution formula quite self-consciously. The two disguises are those of Fallerio and Alenso, a father and son. Fallerio tells Alenso he intends to have his nephew and Alenso's cousin, young Petrillo, murdered so as to inherit his estate. Alenso refuses to go along with the plan, and when the murder is done he wants to die because he did not do more to save Petrillo. The two murderers fall out and fight, each fatally wounding the other; but one lives long enough to confess to the Duke. Alenso sees an opportunity to save his father and ensure his own death by disguising himself as Fallerio. When his father protests that Alenso does not have a beard or grey hair as he does, Alenso says he has bought a beard "at Padua / Such as our common actors use to weare: / When youth would put on ages countenaunce," and tells Fallerio that to disguise him he will shave

---

[6] The absence of a stage direction means little; indeed, it might indicate that the dialogue was considered sufficient to cue the action.

off his hair and dress him "in a lowlie shepheardes weede" (H2v). When they appear, "*Alenso in Falleriaes apparrell and berd, Falleri[o] shaven in shepheards habilliments*" (H4r), Vesuvio is fooled, identifies the disguised Alenso as Fallerio, and has him arrested. In the trial scene, Fallerio, still disguised as a shepherd, watches as Alenso, disguised as Fallerio, is accused and, as planned, denies the charge. He answers in what seem to be riddles; but playgoers know the truth, and the scene builds anticipation until Alenso "*Puls off his disguise.*" The Duke exclaims, "How now my Lords, this is a myracle, / To shake off thirtie yeares so sodeinlie, / And turne from feeble age to flourishing youth" (I3v); but once his identity is known, Alenso is sentenced to death for the deception. This brings Fallerio to identify himself verbally, but he is not believed, setting up his self-discovery. He says, "Oh still I see these weedes do seare your eyes: / I am Fallerio, make no doubt of me" and physically reveals himself: "*Put off*" (I4r). Both father and son are sentenced to death and have long speeches of truth-telling confession before being taken away.

Marston's *Antonio and Mellida* (1599) begins with an Induction that focuses not only on the use of disguise in the play about to be performed, but also on the convention of a male character disguised as a female. When asked what role he plays, "Antonio" replies:

> Faith, I know not what: an Hermaphrodite; two parts in one: my true person being Antonio, son to the Duke of Genoa; though for the love of Mellida, Pieros daughter, I take this fained presence of an Amazon, calling my selfe Florizell, and I know not what. I a voice to play a lady! I shall nere doe it. (A4r)

But "Albert" disagrees:

> O, an Amazon should have such a voice, virago-like. Not play two parts in one? away, away; 'tis common fashion. Nay if you cannot bear two subtle fronts under one hood, Ideot goe by, goe by; off this worlds stage. O times impuritie! (A4r)

Thus as well as inserting a reminder of how disguise on the stage is a commentary on duplicity in real life, this exchange makes playgoers aware of Antonio's disguise from the start. He next appears "*disguised like an Amazon*"[7] (B2r). In this disguise to protect himself from Piero, he tells Mellida that Antonio has drowned; but knowing the truth, playgoers will await his revelation to her that he is alive. When that moment comes in

---

[7] To my knowledge this is the first use of the Amazon disguise in an early modern play, long before it occurs in *Swetnam the Woman Hater*, discussed later in this chapter.

Act 2, it is not clear if Antonio actually sheds his disguise, although when he tells Mellida to "Looke but behinde thee" and she finally recognizes him – "O, Antonio; my Lord, my Love" (D4r) – it seems likely that he removes the Amazon disguise here. When next he appears he is dressed as a sailor in a "*sea gowne*" (F4r). To evade her father, Mellida is disguised in a "*Pages suite*" (G2v) when she meets him and others searching for her. Because she fails to remove her cap as a sign of respect, Ballurdo says, "stand bare," then exclaims in recognition, "Whogh! heavens blesse me: Mellida, Mellida" (G4v). The most obvious explanation is that he has knocked off her cap and in doing so has released her hair.[8]

The next figure to appear in disguise is Andrugio "*in armour*"; he is announced as "a knight, hath brought Andrugio's head" (I2r) to Piero, who has set a price on it. When Andrugio is promised the reward, he says, "Then, here, Piero, is Andrugios head, / Royally casked in a helme of steele" (I2v), which probably cues Andrugio's removal of his helmet – in response Piero recognizes him and relinquishes power. Then a "*cofin*" is brought on, ostensibly containing "the breathlesse trunke of young Antonio" (I3r). When last seen at the end of Act 4, Antonio was in despair upon learning that Mellida had been taken away by her father Piero, so playgoers would probably be prepared to accept his death, and certainly the other characters do. And whether his body is visible to the audience or not, this is effectively another disguise – Balurdo says, "he lookes as pittifully, as a poore John"[9] (I3v). But after a remorseful Piero says that he would let Mellida marry Antonio if he were alive, the latter comes out of the coffin: "Stand not amaz'd, great states: / I rise from death, that never liv'd till now" (I3v). Mellida's surprised response captures her ready acceptance of what she sees: "Can breath depaint my unconceived thoughts? / Can words describe my infinite delight, / Of seeing thee, my Lord Antonio?" (I3v). As the Induction indicated, disguise-discovery is capitalized on as a theatrical device in *Antonio and Mellida*, and the ways it is deployed in the action highlight the artifice and contrivance. Moreover, each disguise and subsequent discovery is different from the others, but all suggest that Marston knew his audience would recognize his inventive uses of the convention and be both amused and satisfied by the comic conclusion they make possible.

---

[8] Perhaps the boy player had long hair or he was wearing a woman's wig under the cap in preparation for this moment.

[9] "Poor John, *n*." 1.a. Fish, usually hake, salted and dried for food; a fish preserved in this way (*OED Online*, Oxford University Press, June 2017).

Early in *The Wise Woman of Hogsdon* Heywood introduces "*2d Luce, a yong Countrey Gentlewoman, in the habit of a Page*" (B2v) under circumstances that encourage playgoers to sympathize with her and be complicit with her disguise: "2 Luce" is looking for Chartley, who fled to London on their wedding day. She has heard him mention the wise woman of Hogsdon and decides to become her servant, Jack. In the many comic plot twists that follow, 2 Luce-as-Jack is disguised as a woman for a while, and at one point enters "*halfe ready and maskt*" (D4v) and is asked, "what art thou? Girle or Boy?" She replies, "Both, and neither; I was a Ladd last night, but in the morning I was conjured into a Lasse: And being a Girle now, I shall be translated to a Boy anon. Here's all I can at this time say for my selfe" (D4v). Only she and the playgoers know what she means. In the last scene, after all the other complications have been resolved and Chartley is ready to accept the truth that they have been married without his knowing it, 2 Luce reappears in what has been referred to as "*her boyes shape*" (G2v). She sets up her self-discovery, telling him, "perhaps I have more in mee, then you expect from mee" and "You and I have bin better acquainted and yet search mee not too farre least you shame mee, looke on mee well, nay better, better yet, ile assure you I left of a petticoate when I put on these breeches, What say you now," and "*shee skatters her hayre*"[10] (I3v). As the play ends, the surprised Chartley recognizes his "First love, and best beloved" and the Wise(er) Woman comments ironically, "My boy turn'd girle … ile never entertaine any servant but ile have her searcht" (I4r).

In *Epicoene* (1609) Jonson notoriously used the convention of boys playing women to foster the belief that Epicoene is a female. Since "epicoene" could refer to either sex,[11] playgoers might smugly have assumed that the name was a sly metatheatrical reference to the boy actor playing a female; in addition, they could have registered the name as a hint about how, once married to Morose, Epicoene takes over, like a man. Certainly the process by which Jonson controls the deception of characters on one level and playgoers on another is ingenious.[12] For example, when

---

[10] The quarto reads "*fayre*" but clearly *hayre* is intended. This direction provides clear evidence of an action implied in several other plays. See the discussions of *The Two Gentlemen of Verona* and Q1 *Philaster* in Chapter 4 and of *Antonio and Mellida*, above.

[11] The term is an adjective "designating nouns and pronouns which may denote individuals of either sex" ("epicene, adj." *OED Online*, Oxford University Press, September 2016).

[12] According to Hyland, "The tricks played in *Epicoene* and *Philaster* deprive disguise of any possible metatheatrical meaning insofar as they sacrifice dramatic irony in the course of the play. However, the dramatists were manipulating their spectators in a different way, forcing upon them a radical revision of their understanding of what they have seen: a metatheatrical climax that exposes the

Morose first meets Epicoene she is masked, so that when she unmasks he thinks he is seeing the real Epicoene (as does the playgoer). And the play has so many deceptions, each dependent on the assumption that Epicoene is a female, that this central premise is likely to be unconsciously accepted. Once Dauphine has got Morose to sign over his estate to him, he says, "Then here is your release, sir" and *"He takes of Epicoenes perruke"* (3D5v). This surprises even Dauphine's co-conspirators, because only he knew that Epicoene was "a gentlemans son, that I have brought up this halfe yeere, at my great charges" (3D5v) for the specific purpose of deceiving his uncle. Immediately after this discovery, Dauphine stages a second when *"He pulls of their beardes, and disguise"* (3D6r) to reveal Otter and Cutbeard who, pretending to be learned clerics, have judged Morose's case against Epicoene. Both Dauphine and Jonson capitalize on the difficulty of seeing below a persuasive and plausible exterior.

The treatment of the disguised page in *The Honest Man's Fortune* (1613) indicates both how ubiquitous and popular the girl-as-page convention was by the time this play was written and the influence of Jonson's earlier play. Field, Fletcher and Massinger seem to have deliberately encouraged their audience to think the usual convention was being deployed yet again in order to set up a surprise discovery. Probably the mere existence of a page would have encouraged playgoers to suspect a conventional disguise, and these suspicions would have been strengthened by the relationship between Montaigne and his page Veramour, who clearly dotes on his master from their first appearance in Act 1. When Veramour next appears in Act 3, a dissolute courtier, Laverdine, assumes that Veramour is actually a "disguisd whore" (5V4r). Veramour rejects Lavardine's advances but not his assumption, thereby confirming his belief. Probably this would also have helped to persuade playgoers further that the typical set up of a boy actor playing a woman disguised as a boy was being deployed. This is followed at the start of Act 4 by a scene between Montaigne and Veramour in which the page expresses affection for his master, which again seems intended to foster the belief that Veramour is actually a female. Thus when near the end of the play Veramour enters dressed *"like a Woman"* (5X4r), the expectations of Laverdine and the playgoers seem to be confirmed – so no surprise, but some complacent satisfaction. Indeed, Veramour admits

fraudulence of theatre" (*Disguise on the Early Modern Stage*, 105). For Lloyd Davis, however, "With the recurring treatment of the processes and dilemmas of cross-dressing, even for plays like *Epicoene* and *Philaster* where the cross-dresser is disguised from the start, the impact seems to reside less in startling revelations than in a gradual guild-up and complication of familiar issues and theatrical tropes" (*Guise and Disguise*, 130).

to Montaigne, "I am a poor disguis'd Lady / That like a Page have followed you full long for love god-wot," and when asked why she wore boy's clothes explains, "I took example by 2 or 3 playes, that methought / Concernd me." But when Montaigne asks why she kept it a secret from him she replies, "I knew it not my selfe, / Untill this Gentleman [Laverdine] opend my dull eyes, / And by perswasion made me see it." One of the onlookers asks, "Could his power in words make such a change?" (5X4r) and the surprise is sprung when Veramour lifts the skirts of the woman's dress to discover the boy's breeches underneath:

VERAMOUR	Yes, as truly woman as your selfe my Lord.
LAVERDINE	Why but hark you, are not you a woman?
VERAMOUR	If hands and face make it not evident, you shall see more.
MALLYCORN	Breeches, breeches, Laverdine. (5X4r)[13]

Veramour's reference to the "2 or 3 playes," in which female characters adopt a page disguise, heightens the metatheatricality of the deception of Laverdine and also of the playgoers, who would have thought they knew more than the characters but found themselves equally gulled. The trick is also a reminder to us that only when boys played female roles was such a metatheatrical deception possible.

As we have repeatedly seen, when Shakespeare used a discovery, he reworked the convention in ways that exemplify or dramatize an idea. Some additional examples demonstrate the range of his inventiveness. In 5.4 of *Much Ado About Nothing*, Beatrice and Hero enter wearing masks to hide their identity from Benedict and Claudio, as they have been instructed to do by Leonato (I3r). But in the case of Hero this disguise also hides the fact that she is alive, not dead as Claudio thinks. Believing that he is about to wed Hero's cousin, Claudio says, "sweet, let me see your face," but Leonato replies that Claudio must first "take her hand, / Before this Frier, and sweare to marry hir." When Claudio complies, Hero finally speaks: "And when I liv'd I was your other wife; / And when you loved, you were my other husband." There is no stage direction, but this seems a clear signal for her to unmask: Claudio says, "Another Hero." Shortly afterward, Benedict asks, "which is Beatrice?" and she replies, "I answer to that name" (I3v), as she too cues her self-discovery. Given that *Much Ado* was probably written in

---

[13] In response to Laverdine's question in the manuscript version of the play, Veramour signals the discovery by saying, "I'll open all"; then the MS is damaged and what remains reads: "th is," and "am no other then that I seem'd / at first to bee, a boy" (ll. 2896–8). I suggest that this begins, "The truth is, I."

1598, Shakespeare was perhaps the first to use a mask for a disguise-discovery, which is noteworthy in itself and also because Hero enters as a bride, so one might expect her face to be hidden by a veil (as is Mariana's in *Measure for Measure*). As to reasons why Shakespeare might have chosen masks as the form of disguise here, some points are worth noting. First, the events of 5.4 are prepared for in 2.1, the so-called masked ball scene, when probably only the men are masked.[14] If she is not masked in 2.1, Hero's natural simplicity and inability to dissemble are emphasized by the visual. By contrast, in 5.4, which completes the betrothal begun in 2.1, Hero's wearing a mask emblematizes her acceptance of the necessity of duplicity (even if to undo duplicity). She insists she is the same Hero, but a comparison of these two "mask" scenes suggests otherwise.

A short but telling sequence of novel thematic discoveries occurs in *Henry IV, part 1*. They are set up when Hal tells Falstaff, "Go hide thee behind the Arras" (E3v; see Chapter 5) to escape capture by the sheriff; then after the sheriff has left, Hal tells Peto, "goe call him forth," at which Peto discovers Falstaff "fast asleepe behind the Arras, and snorting like a horse" (E4r). Hal tells Peto to "search his pockets" and the result is a second discovery of a kind, when Peto "*findeth certaine papers*" (E4r); the one Peto reads aloud is an unpaid bill. This symbolic, even emblematic dual discovery captures the reasons why Hal must distance himself from Falstaff. In particular, it echoes the imagery of discovery and payment used by Hal earlier when, using the language of self-discovery, he vows to redeem the time: "when this loose behaviour I throw off / And pay the debt I never promised" (B1v). In addition, the discovery of the bill for what Hal calls "an intollerable deale of sack" (E4r) is echoed and developed in Act 5 on the battlefield when the Prince opens Falstaff's case looking for a pistol but finds a bottle of sack. These two "pocket-discoveries" are particular to the process by which Shakespeare brings Hal and the playgoer to see and accept that if he is to fulfill his vow, the Prince must separate himself from Falstaff.

Perhaps not surprisingly, the one Shakespearean romance without a miraculous revelation is *Cymbeline* (1610). But the play does include two discoveries, without either of which there would be no plot. When asking Innogen if she will keep a "Trunke" (TLN 819) for him, Iacomo tells her it contains gifts for the Emperor. This sets up the moment in 2.2 when

---

[14] Most editors are strangely silent about whether or not the women are masked; an exception is A. R. Humphreys, who says, "It seems from what follows that only the men mask" (*Much Ado About Nothing*, 2.1.78 note). The dialogue between the men and women during the scene strongly supports this view.

Iacomo comes "*from the Trunke*" (TLN 917) in a combined disguise-discovery and discovery scene wherein his methods of disguise and self-revelation exemplify his duplicity. And the bracelet Iacomo takes from the sleeping Innogen here he later tauntingly shows to Posthumus, saying, "I begge but leave to ayre this Jewell: See, / And now 'tis up againe" (TLN 1264–5). This brief discovery of false evidence helps Iacomo to persuade Posthumus that his lie about Innogen's fidelity is true.

Law Tricks is subtitled "who would have thought it" and, indeed, the intertwined plots are replete with surprises (at least for the characters), many effected by discoveries, each of which capitalizes on and reworks the convention. Perhaps unsurprisingly, this is one of those plays that has never been modernized and therefore is rarely read and never performed, so some contextualizing description is necessary. One plot-line focuses on the Countess. As the play begins, her husband, Count Lurdo, is divorcing her because Horatio, who wants her for himself, has convinced Lurdo that she has been unfaithful. Duke Ferneze, the Countess's brother, also believes this falsehood and laments her "shame" (A4r). In the second plotline, the Duke's daughter, Emilia, who was sent to a convent as a child and later taken prisoner by the Turks, arrives in Genoa with her page. Wanting to test the world she has returned to before identifying herself, she takes the name of Tristella. The Duke also has a son, Polymetes, who worries his father because he spends his time in "strict contemplation" rather than "knightly exercise" (B1r). The complications begin when the Duke leaves Genoa to search for Emilia and in his absence Polymetes is attracted to "Tristella" and turns "absolute prodigall" (C1v). Lurdo, fearing that Tristella is after Polymetes's fortune, persuades her to stay with him. At the same time, Horatio woos the Countess and when rejected turns against her; but his page takes pity on her and gives her a place to hide. Tristella/Emilia convinces Lurdo she wants to marry him; but the Countess must be got rid of and he decides to kill her.

The first discovery scene is set up when Tristella's plotting with Lurdo is about to be interrupted by the arrival of Polymetes and Julio. Not wanting to be found with her, Lurdo hides behind an arras until Polymetes asks, "has the Arras an ague, it trembles so?" (E1r). As Polymetes is about to expose Lurdo, Tristella says it is a "Picture" (i.e., a statue[15]) and tells him not to "deface it with your weapon, nor

---

[15] "A three-dimensional representation of something, esp. as a work of art; a statue, a sculpture. Now *rare*" ("picture, n." *OED Online*, Oxford University Press, September 2016).

soile it with your breath." Then they "*discover Lurdo behind the Arras*"[16] (E1r). Whether or not Polymetes and Julio actually believe it is a statue of Lurdo, they comment on it as if they do, at Lurdo's expense. Thinking he has the upper hand in the contest for Tristella, however, Lurdo is not bothered. But the Countess must be eliminated, so he and the vengeful Horatio decide to poison her. This plotting is followed immediately by what is probably a discovery of seated figures: "*Enter Countesse, three or foure young Gentlewomen, sowing by an houre-glasse*" (E3r). This discovery initiates an emblematic scene that puts the Countess and her misery at the centre of the action. In addition, if both the Countess in this scene and Lurdo in the previous one were discovered in the same space, the staging would have underlined the contrast between the foolish husband and his suffering wife. In this play that veers repeatedly between comedy and tragedy, the third act ends with Horatio telling the grateful Countess that he will poison her.

Act 4 begins with Polymetes, Julio, Tristella/Emilia and Horatio about to enjoy a costly meal when Duke Ferneze enters in disguise as a messenger to bring Polymetes news of his father's (Ferneze's) death. Ferneze watches and listens as his son celebrates his new status and talks about how he will spend his inheritance. Having learned the truth, Ferneze leaves but soon reappears as himself to confront his son. Hearing that his father is not dead but has returned, Polymetes knows his prodigality will be found out and devises a plan to avoid punishment. When the Duke asks about his son, Joculo says he is "lunatique" and that he "found him in his study, and a company of botlnos'd Devils dauncing the Irish hay about him, which on the sudden so startled the poore boy, as a cleane lost his wittes" (G1v). When the Duke asks, "may wee without danger / Go neere his study?" Joculo "*Discover[s] Polymetes in his study,*" saying, "See where a sits, be Patient and observe" (G1v), and they watch and listen as Polymetes pretends to conjure and spouts astrological mumbo-jumbo. In an aside before he exits, the Duke makes it clear that he knows the truth but will wait to confront his son. As Polymetes and Julio are congratulating themselves on the success of their "jest" (G2v), Horatio's page enters with the news that the Countess is dead. But when Polymetes asks how she died, the page says, "Ile tell your honor that hereafter and give you the ground of an admirable jest" (G3r), providing playgoers with a clear hint that his news should not be taken too seriously.

---

[16] In the quarto "discover Lurdo behind the Arras" is in roman, thus it misleadingly seems to be part of Polymetes's response.

The last act returns to the Duke and his wayward son. "*Polimetes in his study*" (H3r) almost certainly signals a repeat of the earlier discovery scene, with Polymetes again playing a role to deceive his father. His pseudo-conjuring brings on "*Julio like a Marchant, and Joculo like a Lady*" (H3v). Having been told to expect Emilia, the Duke immediately recognizes the disguised Joculo as his long-lost daughter. He calls for the "Wench" who "borrow'd thy habit and Usurpes thy name" (H4r) to confront her with the "real" Emilia. But Tristella/Emilia challenges the disguised Joculo with a series of questions about her life, until it comes to her age and Joculo falters:

EMILIA   Come your reply, nay quick your certen age.
JOCULO   I am just as old as – true Emilaes page.
DUKE   A page?
ANGELO   Disguisde?
ADAM   Wrapt in a womans smock?   (I1v)

Clearly this exchange signals a disguise-discovery, and must have provided special amusement to playgoers by reworking the convention of the lost child found and identified. Rather than having Tristella remove a disguise to show that she is Emilia, Day shifted the discovery so that Emilia exposes her imposter. And this process of discovery is not finished. Still suspicious, Lurdo says to Emilia, "ile but see your brest" and she responds "Go to, reade your errors," signalling yet another kind of discovery. Lurdo says "Brother, embrace your childe, your second heire, / I found firme witnes in her bosome bare" (I1v–2r). Day plays with another convention here, because of course the actor playing Emilia was a bosom-less boy.[17]

With this plotline complete, the resolution of the Countess–Horatio–Lurdo plot is initiated when Horatio's page whispers to Polymetes that the Countess is alive, then pretends to "raise up" (I2v) her ghost. This "shadow" (I2v) enters, writes on a paper and exits; her message is that Horatio poisoned her and she wants the Duke to avenge her. Horatio implicates Lurdo and the Duke sentences both to be "clos'de alive in her dead tombe" (i.e., in the tomb where she is dead; I3r). The next stage direction – "*Countesse in the Tombe*"[18] (I3v) – signals the last of the play's discovery scenes. When Horatio's page explains that the Countess is alive because he

---

17 This might be the first time in an early modern play that breasts are discovered to expose a female-as-male disguise; the ironic business is used again in Middleton's *No Wit, No Help Like a Woman's* (1611), G8v–H1r; Killigrew's *The Prisoners* (1635), C9v; and Suckling's *Brennoralt* (1639), D1v.

18 This is the same idiom as discoveries signalled by *X in his study* or *Y in his shop* or, in this play, "*Polymetes in his study*" (H3r).

gave her a sleeping potion rather than poison, Lurdo is reprieved and the Countess forgives him; but Horatio is banished from the court. The comic conclusion is given metadramatic emphasis when the Duke says to the page, "Lastly, thy merrit is not triviall, / That turnd to mirth a Sceane so tragicall" (I3v).

Law Tricks uses the discovery device to reveal a sequence of five overtly contrived scenes characterized by conscious artifice: Lurdo as a statue, the Countess and her women sewing, Polymetes in his study, Polymetes in his study again and the Countess in her tomb. Each scene is visually and structurally a focal point. Furthermore, elements of each scene depict and explore the relationship between appearance and reality, or art and life. In the first, Lurdo pretends to be a statue[19] behind an arras decorated with "a Poeticall fiction" (D4v); in the second, the tableau of the Countess and her women is explicitly emblematic in its focus on embroidery and time;[20] in the third, the Duke is deceived by Polymetes's performance as a lunatic conjurer; in the fourth, Polymetes seems to conjure up the disguised Julio and Joculo, then the "shadow" of the Countess; and in the fifth, what seems to be the Duchess's ghost is actually the living woman. In this context the play's disguise-discoveries might seem minor, but Emilia's disguise as Tristella at the start and the discoveries at the end create an ironic frame, implicitly commenting on and heightening the more obvious artifice of the discovery scenes.

The Revenger's Tragedy (1606) is a play with many self-referentially metadramatic elements, including multiple discoveries of both kinds. Indeed, it seems that Middleton, like Day, wanted to use this staging device in ways that called attention to it as a theatrical convention being put to thematic use. After Vindice, the play's serial disguiser, appears briefly as himself at the start, in 1.3 he takes on the disguise of Piato, a malcontent and pander, until 4.2 when he reappears as Vindice. On the one hand, this disguise should not be relevant here because it does not end with an onstage discovery; on the other hand, one might speculate that Middleton omitted that expected action in order to emphasize what happens instead. While Vindice is disguised as Piato, he devises a plot to murder the Duke by poisoning the disguised skull of Gloriana. The bizarre scene (3.5) is a theatrical *tour de force* of disguise and discovery at several levels, involving the deception of, first, Hippolito (and probably also the

---

[19] Commenting on the "statue" Polymetes says, "'tis so like him I doubt wether it be the shadow or his substance" (D4v).

[20] Using the artifice of rhymed couplets, the women talk about how to render flowers in art.

playgoer) and then of the Duke. The direction for Vindice (as Piato) to enter with "*the skull of his love drest up in Tires*" (F1r) is not precise enough to be certain, but probably "tires" means not just a head covering but also some kind of dress, to make it seem as if this is a real masked woman.[21] Vindice seems to engage in conversation with her, and he evidently fools Hippolito, who reacts in surprise when Vindice uncovers the skull – "ile unmask you" (F1v). But as Vindici tells his brother, "I have not fashiond this only for show / And uselesse property, no, it shall beare a part / E'en in it owne Revenge" (F2r). So the disguised and poisoned skull deceives the Duke, who kisses it. As the Duke is dying, Vindice says, "dost knowe / Yon dreadfull vizard, view it well, tis the skull / Of Gloriana" (F2v). "Vizard" clearly refers to the skull here, but also to the mask that Vindice then removes from it, saying, "Looke monster, what a Lady hast thou made me, / My once betrothed wife" (F3r).[22] It has been plausibly suggested that Vindice also discovers himself here,[23] and certainly the dialogue seems to signal such an action: the Duke asks "Is it thou, villaine" and Vindice responds, "T'is I, 'tis Vindici, tis I" (F3r).[24] But if Vindice removes some or all of the Piato disguise at this point, he is wearing it again in 4.1 when Lussurioso accuses him of being a "false knave" (G1v) and dismisses him in what seems an anticlimactic end to the Piato disguise. But then in 5.1 Vindice and Hippolito enter with the dead Duke dressed in that same disguise and Vindice, now as himself, seems to kill Piato at Lussurioso's command. Only then does Lussurioso discover the truth: "ha? oh, villaines, murderers, / Tis the old Duke my father" (H4v). Possibly Lussurioso merely looks closely at the body, but a literal disguise-discovery would be an ironic and fitting replacement for the more conventional one that never happened earlier.

In the scene immediately following Vindice's discovery of the poisoned skull to the Duke, the action shifts to Ambitioso and Supervacuo, who think they have arranged both the release from prison of their younger brother and the beheading of Lussurioso. But a mixup of which the brothers are unaware has resulted instead in the execution of the younger brother and release of Lussurioso. As is the case elsewhere in this playtext, neither the stage directions nor the dialogue are specific enough to be

---

[21] See Alan C. Dessen, "Editing and Staging *The Revenger's Tragedy*," 69.

[22] R. A. Foakes glosses "made me" as "made for me" and says, "It seems that Vindice should here hold the skull by him, as if he were with his 'lady'" (*The Revenger's Tragedy*, 3.5.166 note).

[23] Foakes adds the direction, "*Throwing off his disguise*" (3.5.167).

[24] For a discussion of this scene and whether or not Vindice removes his disguise here, see Hyland, *Disguise on the Early Modern English Stage*, 57.

certain, but possibly when the officer enters with the head, it is concealed.[25] This could explain why neither Ambitioso nor Supervacuo recognizes it immediately. Certainly they pay no attention to the head until Lussurioso appears and they realize it cannot be his. The exchange that follows also leaves the staging unclear, but if the officer removes the head from a bag or unwraps it, the parallel with the earlier discovery of the skull would be emphasized visually:

SUPERVACUO   where's this head now?
OFFICER   Why heere my Lord,
           Just after his delivery, you both came
           With warrant from the Duke to be-head your brother.
AMBITIOSO   I, our brother, the Dukes sonne.
OFFICER   The Dukes sonne my Lord, had his release before you
           came.
AMBITIOSO   Whose head's that then?
OFFICER   His whom you left command for, your owne
           brother's?
AMBITIOSO   Our brothers? oh furies –.   (F4v)

Moreover, Ambitioso and Supervacuo's belief that their younger brother is alive until his head is discovered by the officer can be likened to Lussurioso's belief that the corpse of his father disguised as Piato is alive until he discovers it is his dead father. These are both analogous to the Duke's belief that the disguised skull is a living woman until Vindice discovers the truth to him. Is this an inversion of the conventional discovery in which a person thought to be dead is found to be alive? This ironic treatment and the parallels among the three scenes would obviously be highlighted if each involved the action of revelation.

The Revenger's Tragedy also includes certainly one and probably two discovery scenes. The first is, in its way, as much a theatrical set-piece as the discovery of the poisoned skull, and it too involves a dead woman. The detailed direction is partly fictional, partly theatrical: "*Enter the discontented Lord Antonio, whose wife the Duchesses youngest Sonne ravisht; he Discovering the body of her dead to certaine Lords*" (C1v). Antonio tells them to "Draw neerer Lords and be sad witnesses" and "behold my Lords, / A sight that strikes man out of me" (C1v). As they look at the body, Antonio finds "A prayer Booke the pillow to her cheeke" (C1v), indicating that this scene includes a couch or bed on which the body lies.

---

[25] In his edition MacDonald P. Jackson adds two directions, first for the officer to enter "*carrying the head in a bag*" (3.6.29.1) and later, "*He takes the head from the bag and displays it*" (3.6.73.1).

The existence and details of this discovery scene make it more likely that a second scene is also discovered. At the start of 2.3 Vindice (as Piato) and Lussurioso arrive expecting to catch the Duchess in bed with Spurio, but they actually surprise an innocent Duchess and frightened Duke. No stage directions describe this action and the dialogue signals are vague, but very probably the same location and property used for the earlier discovery scene are used again for this one.[26] Certainly Lussurioso is surprised by what he sees: "I am amazde to death" (E1r).

Given that virtually every early modern playwriting convention is present (and parodied) in Beaumont's *The Knight of the Burning Pestle* (1607), it is unsurprising to find it includes several discoveries. In "The London Merchant" plot, Venturewell forbids his daughter Luce to marry Jasper, his apprentice, so after numerous plot twists Jasper decides to deceive Venturewell into thinking he is dead. He sends Venturewell a request that his body be brought in its coffin to Luce, and her father agrees. When Luce is alone with the coffin, she decides to join Jasper in death. There is no stage direction, but since the boy who delivers the coffin tells her that Jasper's body is "here enclos'd" (H4r), Luce must first open the coffin before she says, "Thou sable cloth, sad cover of my joies, / I lift thee up, and thus I meete with death" (H4v). When he is thus discovered, Jasper rises up and reassures the surprised Luce, "I am no spirit, / Looke better on me, do you know me yet?" (H4v). This use of a coffin to discover life rather than death is not unusual, but the play's technique of comic exaggeration is evident when the property appears a second time. To escape Venturewell's house, Luce gets in the coffin and Jasper has it sent to his father, Merrythought. The last act begins with Jasper appearing to Venturewell disguised as his own ghost with "*his face mealed*" (I3r). He reports that Luce is dead and Venturewell repents. When the coffin arrives at Merrythought's house, he thinks it contains Jasper, but the disguised Jasper says, "Marie looke you sir," and "*Heaves up the Coffin*" (K1v) to discover Luce. But as Luce's father is arriving, the two lovers depart unseen, setting up a final revelation. Venturewell tells Merrythought how he is haunted by Jasper's ghost and Luce's death and asks forgiveness, which Merrythought readily grants. The comic conclusion is confirmed with a final discovery when Merrythought sings, "With that came out his Paramoure" and "With that came out her owne deere Knight" (K2v) to

---

[26] Supplementary directions for some version of a discovery scene here can be found in the *Complete Works*, Regents Renaissance, New Mermaids and Norton *English Renaissance Drama* editions of the play.

signal the entrance of Luce and Jasper from the "inward roome" (K2r) where they have been hiding.

The title *Swetnam the Woman Hater* (1618) would have been topical, but it is misleading in suggesting that the play focuses on that one figure.[27] In fact, this tragicomedy also includes a disguised prince and two disguised lovers in a plot structure that consists of a series of tests that progress to a denouement replete with satisfying discoveries of truth. By the time this play was written, the disguise convention was well enough entrenched that it invited both metadramatic acknowledgement and inventive reworking. Playgoers could be relied on to get the allusions and appreciate the ironies. In the first act Lorenzo enters "*disguised*" (B2v), although this is not known to playgoers or to Iago, his servant. When Lorenzo inquires about "Prince Lorenzo" and Iago answers that he is feared dead, Lorenzo says, "You know him, if you see him" and Iago's "My Lord Lorenzo!" indicates that the prince has removed his disguise; he explains that he has been testing Iago's "unfayned love" (B3v–4r). Lorenzo also tells him, "I intend a while in some disguise / To observe the times and humors of the Court," because he wants to know where the "chiefe errors" of his state "grow" (B4r) before he becomes king. This lets playgoers in on a disguise that will not be discovered until the final scene.

Swetnam the Woman Hater also includes two lovers – the king's daughter Leonida and Lisandro – whose relationship the king has forbidden. To get access to her, Lisandro decides to disguise himself as Friar Anthony, Leonida's confessor. Lisandro (and probably also his anonymous creator) acknowledges the usefulness of this disguise:

> Godamercy Cowle;
> It is no marvell tho' the credulous World
> Thought themselves safe from danger, when they were
> Invested with this habit, 'tis the best,
> To cover, or to gaine a free accesse,
> That can be possible in any project.   (C2v–3r)

Another test ensues when Lisandro-as-friar tells Leonida she should marry someone else, but she replies that she loves Lisandro. He responds, "Then here the Frier concludes: my taske is done"; presumably he removes his hood here, because Leonida exclaims, "Lisandro, my deare Love!" (C4v). Act 3 begins with a literal trial of Leonida and Lisandro, who have been found out. When each takes the blame so the other can escape the penalty

---

[27] For details about the controversy of which this play is a part, see chapter 1 of Coryl Crandall's edition.

of death, the frustrated king's reaction uses the language of deception and
discovery in relation to justice, while also initiating the next test:

> It is impossible
> That sacred Justice should be hudwink't still,
> Though she be falsly painted so; Her eyes
> Are cleare, and so perspicuous, that no cryme
> Can maske it selfe in any borrowed shape,
> But shee'le discover it. Let um be returnd
> Back to their severall Wards, till we devise
> Some better course for the discovery.   (D4r–v)

The judges decide that the only way to get at the truth is to find one male
and one female advocate to debate whether man or woman is the first cause
of sin.

Here at the play's centre the two plots come together. Lorenzo enters
"disguised like an Amazon" (E1r) named Atlanta (a rare disguise of an adult
male as a female) to argue that man was the cause; and the figure designated
in the Dramatis Personae as "Swetnam, alias, Misogynos, The Woman-
hater" (π2v) argues that woman was the cause. Atlanta loses the debate, so
Leonida is sentenced to be executed. But another consequence is that
Misogynos has fallen in love with "Atlanta." In Act 4, following a dumb
show of Leonida being led to execution and dialogue describing her death,
a guard enters with her "herse" (H1r) and reveals the body to Lisandro:
"Then here you may behold, / All that is left of faire Leonida" (G4r).
In response to this discovery Lisandro tries to kill himself, but Atlanta takes
him away to recover. Then the queen laments over Leonida's body and
Atlanta re-enters with the news that Lisandro is dying. Thus the last scene
begins with characters and playgoers fearing the worst.

The use of a masque as a context for final revelations is yet another
disguise-related convention deployed in this play. This pastoral masque
allows for heightened symbolism in the form of Repentance, at whose
appearance the evil Nicanor realizes that his plots to gain the throne will be
found out: "now I see, / Truth will discover all mens Trecherie" (K4r).
Lorenzo, disguised as an old shepherd for the masque, tricks the king into
agreeing to the marriage of two other masque figures, a shepherd (Lisandro
in disguise) and a sylvan nymph (Leonida in disguise). Once the king has
blessed their union, Lorenzo says, "Princes, discover: Here are witnesses /
I now to testifie this royall match" (K4v). The surprised king says,
"My daughter, and Lisandro, living?" and the queen adds, "Oh, I am
made immortall with this sight: / My daughter, and Lisandro, both alive?"
(K4v). Calling attention to the *deus ex machina* quality of the revelation,

the queen asks, "What happie accident preserv'd your lives? / Whose was the project?" whereupon Lorenzo, disguised for the masque as an old shepherd, answers, "Madam, 'twas mine" (K4v) and removes that disguise to reveal Atlanta; when he is praised as Atlanta, he finally removes that disguise too. His father exclaims, "My Sonne Lorenzo!" and "Welcome from death, from bands, captivitie." As both masque and play end, the king voices his new ability to see the truth: "Now we can discerne / Our friends from flatt'rers" (L1r).[28]

The manipulation of playgoer expectation and surprise is part of the recipe that produces successful discoveries, and by the 1620s some play-wrights can be seen reworking the convention in ways probably intended to keep playgoers off-balance and interested. William Rowley's *A Match at Midnight* (1622) is certainly not the first play to include a character whose disguise is kept from playgoers until the denouement (or even the first that provides that information to readers in the Dramatis Personae); but at this play's end this version of the disguise-to-discovery plot is given an extra twist. The list of characters includes "Jarvis, the Widdowes Husband disguised like her servant" (A3r). When Jarvis first appears in 2.1, nothing suggests he is other than what he seems – a servant helping his widow-mistress to evade the suitors seeking to marry her. Then in Act 3 he tells the Widow about a gentleman who has loved her for a long time and now waits to see her; she agrees to meet him, whereupon Jarvis exits, only to return "*like a Gentleman very brave with Jarvis cloathes in's hand*" (F1r). He explains that, having heard of her beauty, he took the position of her servant and now he loves her and wants to marry her. Nothing indicates that she recognizes him as anyone other than the man she (and playgoers) knew as Jarvis. She accepts his proposal, but tells him to return to being Jarvis until the next day. In subsequent scenes he is again Jarvis the witty servant, tricking the Widow's suitors – and encouraging playgoers to enjoy their superior knowledge about him. Finally, though, in the last moments of the play Jarvis again enters "*brave*" (I4v) and the Widow, thinking she is springing her surprise, says, "Know all, this Gentleman has to obtaine his Lust, and loose desires, serv'd me this seven moneths, under the shape and name of Jarvis." When everyone reacts with surprise – "Possible?" – she continues, "Looke well, doe ye not know him?" Probably some action of

[28] This realization might have had particular resonance for contemporary playgoers: in 1615 King James had fallen out with his favourite Robert Carr after the murder of Thomas Overbury; then in 1617 George Villiers, Carr's successor in James's affections, was made an Earl and in 1618 he was made a Marquess. In October 1618, Sir Walter Raleigh was beheaded for allegedly conspiring against James.

discovery occurs here, because one of the other characters says, "The very face of Jarvis" (K1r).[29] Having taken charge, the Widow continues,

> Come y'are cozened,
> And with a Noble craft, he tempted mee
> In mine owne house, and I bid him keep's disguise
> But till this morning and he shoo'd perceive,
> I loved him truely, intending here before ye,
> To let him know't.   (K1r)

But, she says, this was only to discourage her other suitors; the "truth" is "I meane never to marry" (K1r); instead she will stay married to the memory of her husband. When one of her suitors comments that her husband was a "madman" and another that he is dead, Jarvis says, "He is not dead Sir, hee had it spread a purpose, he is in England, and in your house, and looke: doe ye not see him?" (K1v). The surprised Widow asks, "Where, where?" and Jarvis finally confesses the truth:

> Here, here hee is that hath found rash jealousie,
> Loves joyes, and a wife whose discreet carriage
> Can intimate to all men a faire freedome.
> And to one be faithfull, such a wife I prove,
> Her husbands glory worth a wealthy Love.   (K1v)

Nothing indicates that playgoers should even suspect that the figure who was a gentleman pretending to be Jarvis is actually the Widow's husband, although her failure to recognize him even when he is dressed as a gentleman is a greater than usual challenge to a playgoer's willing suspension of disbelief. How the original audience responded is impossible to say; but what seems clear is that Rowley wanted a surprise denouement-by-discovery and was willing to risk alienating playgoers to achieve it.

Massinger's *The Renegado* (1624) includes three different kinds of discovery, each used inventively in a plot centred on a Christian/Muslim conflict. The Dramatis Personae lists "Vitelli, A Gentelman of Venice disguis'd" (A2v); he has come to Tunis to rescue his sister Paulina, who was captured by Grimaldi, a pirate and the "renegado" of the title. Vitelli is disguised as a merchant, and part of that disguise is his shop (see Chapter 5). This shop attracts the attention of Donusa, an appropriately veiled Turkish princess, to whom Vitelli describes the goods on offer, including several paintings. Perhaps these are covered by curtains which

---

[29] Jarvis says, "I must cast my skinne, and am catcht" (K1r), which perhaps indicates that he removes one layer of clothes to reveal those of "Jarvis" underneath.

he lifts, because she says, "I instantly could shew you one, to theirs / Not much inferior." When he replies, "With your pardon Madame / I am incredulous," she asks, "Can you match me this!" and "*Unvailes her selfe*," causing Vitelli to exclaim, "What wonder looke I on!" (C4r–v). Thus a discovered shop is not only inventively used as part of Vitelli's shopkeeper disguise, but the merchandise is used to represent "the rarest beauties of the Christian world" (C4r). Then the common analogy between drawing open a curtain on a painting and lifting a woman's veil is given a novel twist when Donusa lifts her Muslim veil. Not surprisingly, the relationship between Vitelli and Donusa that begins here, ends in Act 5 with her conversion to Christianity and escape with him back to Venice. But before that conclusion is reached, there are two more discovery variations. One involves Paulina, held captive by the lustful Asambeg. Her first appearance in the play comes when Asambeg takes a key and "*opens a doore, Paulina discoverd comes forth.*" His language conveys an idolatrous worship of this woman who has been protected from his advances by a magic charm: "Appeare bright sparke / Of all perfection" (E3v). Then in the Vitelli-Donusa plot, when Asambeg catches the two of them together, he arrests both and sentences them to death. But, setting up a unique discovery, Donusa smuggles a "*Bak't-meate*" (M1r) to Vitelli. Entering with the pie, he describes what he does and finds:

> There's something more in this then meanes to cloy
> A hungry appetite, which I must discover.
> Shee, will'd me search the midst. Thus, thus I pierce it:
> Ha! what is this? a scrole bound up in packthread?
> What may the misterie be?
> *The Scrole.*
> Sonne, let downe this packethread, at the West window of the Castle. By it you shall draw up a Ladder of ropes, by which you may descend, your deerest Donusa with the rest of your friends, below attend you. Heaven prosper you. Francisco. (M1v)

In James Shirley's *The Humorous Courtier* (1631) the device of keeping a disguise secret from both characters and playgoers is used from the start, with the figure listed in the Dramatis Personae as "Giotto, a cunning Court favourite" (A4v). In this role he is a favourite of the Duchess of Mantua, who is ostensibly looking for a husband. Only in the play's final moments, after the Duchess has rejected her other suitors, is the truth revealed when she cues a discovery: "Beehold (Lords) your Prince Foscari, Duke of / Parma, and of Mantua, now our Lover, / Whom lately you supposed dismissed our Court" (K1r). One onlooker comments, "Indeed we see the Golden Fleece his order, / And a face like his, but yet his chinne wants / Part of his beard," to which Giotto/Foscari replies, "I left that naked, more to disguise me / From your knowledge" (K1r–v). He explains that he adopted the disguise

> to helpe us in discovery
> Of all your soules and hearts; the better to
> Inable us; how to dispose of each
> Beneath our governement. (K1v)

This late version of a disguised-ruler plot has a play-long buildup to the revelation of a disguise unknown even to playgoers, and the denouement is further emphasized by the Duke's use of the language of discovery to summarize the truths he has learned.

By the time Richard Brome was writing plays, the use of a discovery to effect a turn in the plot or to make a significant revelation was a long-established practice. Nevertheless, he often used discoveries of both kinds, sometimes formulaically but sometimes inventively. In *The Queen and Concubine* (1635) one disguise-discovery occurs when the Doctor and midwife enter disguised as pilgrims, intending to murder Eulalia, the deposed "queen" of the title. But she immediately recognizes them and tells one of her followers, "Now take off his false Beard: see if you know him, / And let the woman be unmuffled" (G5r). In recognition one exclaims, "O Divels!" (G5r). There is also the disguise of Sforza, a general who is believed dead but returns, and when it seems safe to do so "*Discovers himself*" (H4r). The king, who had been his enemy, says, "I am all wonder" and, in language that acts as a reminder of the ideas behind the discovery device, adds, "Shew me, shew me yet the face of glorious Truth; where I may read / If I have err'd, which way I was misled" (H4r). Not surprisingly, this moment in Act 4 is the turn that makes the play a tragicomedy. Then near the end of Act 5, Alinda, the "concubine" of the title, is brought on "*in a Chayre, veyl'd*" (I8r). When last seen she had gone mad and fallen into a trance, so everyone wonders if she has recovered. As "*Eulalia unvailes Alinda*" she speaks for all those watching: "Bless'd Heaven! she lives and wakes I hope in health" (I8v). Sure enough, Alinda has repented and asks for forgiveness. Once Eulalia has reassured Alinda's father that his daughter is speaking the truth – not metaphorically veiling her motives as before – he forgives her. She then announces she wants to enter a nunnery and puts the veil back on (K1r). By reversing the action of unveiling in this way, Brome injected new meaning into an old device.

Written near the end of the period, Mayne's *The City Match* (1637) is a play about "City" matters: prodigal sons, finances, inheritance and marriage between merchants' daughters and Inns of Court men. The play's concerns, topical references and jokes would have been readily understood by audiences at both Whitehall and Blackfriars where, according to the title page, it was performed. But this is one of those plays that has not escaped the past. Its complex intertwined plots might be easy to follow in performance; but in print centuries later the description is unavoidably convoluted and therefore probably confusing. But the action revolves around a series of disguises and subsequent discoveries that nevertheless show how the formula could still be effective after fifty years of use. In particular, Mayne's deployment of the discovery convention rests on the idea that (as in the real world of the London audience) costume determines how characters perceive and classify each other.[30] As with disguises in most plays since *Mucedorus*, the deceptions are successful partly because disguised characters wear clothing that signals a social class or a trade different from the one to which they actually belong. That is, although Mayne was not a career playwright, he clearly was familiar with how disguise-discovery had been used in other plays, and he understood its potential for exploring the appearance–reality dichotomy while also weaving together interrelated plots. Indeed, the seven disguises that progress toward onstage discoveries in *The City Match* are the basis of its plot complications and resolutions. Furthermore, despite their number, which might seem to indicate parody of the device, these multiple disguises and subsequent discoveries are used conventionally and without apparent irony.

The Persons of the Play in the first edition gave readers information that was not available to playgoers: Bannswright is "Old Plotwell disguised" (B1v).[31] And Bannswright's actual identity is kept from both playgoers and characters until he discovers himself in the play's last moments.[32] This trick, used as early as the first quarto of *Mucedorus* and continuously through the period, as we have seen, was still evidently effective; certainly nothing indicates that Mayne intended the disguise to be subverted by knowing hints or winks.

Besides this play-long disguise, others are donned and discovered as each plot develops. Two prodigals, Frank Plotwell and Timothy Seathrift, have

---

[30] The play is full of in-jokes about clothes and how they convey social status, or not; see, for example, 1.4, where the difference between the costume of Inns of Court men and merchants (or "Fleet Street" and "Cheapside") is the focus of the discussion and action. The beginning of 2.2 is an argument about clothing between Aurelia dressed as a lady and Dorcas dressed in Puritan garb as her waiting woman.

[31] Throughout the playtext Bannswright's speech-headings maintain the deception.

[32] Act 1 has a reference to Frank Plotwell's absent father, but nothing links him to Bannswright here or later.

respectively an uncle, Warehouse, and a father, Old Seathrift, who decide to test their young heirs' morals by pretending they (the older men) have been drowned at sea. They have Cypher disguise himself as a waterman and report the drowning to the two young men; then Warehouse and Old Seathrift return in disguise to see how Frank and Tim react to the news. Unsurprisingly, when the old men see the delight of the young, "*They undisguise*" (Kir). Warehouse asks his nephew, "D'you know me, sir?" and Frank exclaims, "My uncle!"; Old Seathrift asks his son, "And doe you know me, Sir?" and Tim exclaims, "My father!"; then Warehouse says, "We'll open all the plot," telling Cypher to "reveal yourself," and Frank exclaims, "Cypher, the waterman!" (Kiv). In each case the playgoers know of the deceptions and disguises and therefore have the satisfaction of seeing three anticipated revelations and recognitions come to pass.

These mid-play events trigger subsequent plots led by Frank Plotwell and his seamstress sister Penelope (disguised as Aurelia, a rich lady), that involve Tim Seathrift and his sister Susan (disguised as a Puritan seamstress, Dorcas), and culminate in the comic revelations and recognitions of Act 5. Playgoers will watch the unfolding of these plots knowing that at one time Frank Plotwell was to marry Susan Seathrift, and Penelope Plotwell was to marry Tim Seathrift. In response to what the old men have learned about Frank and Tim while disguised and pretending to be dead, and to the way the young men responded to news of the old men's death, Warehouse vows to marry and disinherit Frank, while Old Seathrift tells Tim he will disown him and make Susan his heir. To find a wife quickly, Warehouse turns to Bannswright, who provides the services his (false) name suggests. To thwart this plan, Frank also enlists Bannswright to match his uncle with "Madam Aurelia," and then arranges for his friend Salewit to perform the fake ceremony disguised as a French curate. At the same time, Aurelia and Frank plot to trick Tim into marrying her (in ignorance of the fact that she is actually Penelope Plotwell, to whom he was once betrothed). Aurelia arranges with Dorcas for her to take Aurelia's place in the fake marriage to Warehouse and then to make him want an annulment, after which Aurelia will help Dorcas marry Frank (to whom she was once betrothed). Aurelia clearly has the upper hand in these plots, and knowledge of her and Dorcas's true identities as Warehouse's niece and Seathrift's daughter would keep an audience complicit with them while building anticipation for the complications and revelations to come.

The final elements of the now interdependent plots are set in motion by the fake marriage of Warehouse and Dorcas. As soon as that ceremony is done, Dorcas makes Warehouse regret it: she rejects him on account of his age, refuses to kiss him, demands separate bedrooms, tells him she will find younger men to satisfy her, and admits that she married him for his money. As Warehouse laments his situation Frank Plotwell arrives to play his part in the trick that he and Aurelia have planned. He adds to the bad news, telling Warehouse that Dorcas has three illegitimate children by three different fathers. Then Cypher, who is also part of the trick and now disguised as a sailor, comes to tell Warehouse that two of his ships have sunk, with a great loss of cargo and crew. When Warehouse starts to despair and talk about suicide, Frank is ready with solutions to both problems. He regains his uncle's favour by offering to get two insurance men to guarantee the safe return of the ships if Warehouse will give up three quarters of their value. Frank also tells him that he can prove the marriage to Dorcas is not legal. The two insurance men, actually Bannswright and Quarterfield in disguise, bring forms for Warehouse, who signs them, happy that he has saved a quarter of the ships' value. Then Salewit arrives in the curate disguise he wore to marry Warehouse and Dorcas, and Cypher returns in the sailor disguise he wore when announcing the sinking of Warehouse's ships. Having used trickery and disguise to manipulate his uncle into reinstating him as his heir, Frank confesses the truth that the ships have not sunk, and Cypher "*undisguises.*" Frank then admits that the insurance men are actually "two friends"; "*they undisguise*" and Warehouse exclaims, "Bannswright and Captain Quarterfield!" (R2v). This trick has got Frank the money Warehouse signed over in the insurance scam. When Warehouse then accuses Bannswright of having matched him with a whore, the latter admits that the marriage was "but in jest" and Salewit "*undisguises*" (R2v). Frank confesses that he has married Dorcas and says he hopes they can keep the jointure Warehouse made her. When his uncle agrees, Frank's plot to regain his inheritance is complete.

But the play is not over; two disguises remain and their treatment says a lot about how Mayne used the device throughout this late City comedy. Although playgoers are made aware from 2.4 that Dorcas is actually Susan Seathrift, the only characters who know the truth are Frank and Aurelia, so that when Frank says who he has married, Seathrift reminds Frank that he was "Betrotht once to my daughter" and asks why "have you match'd this woman?" Frank replies, "because this is your Daughter, Sir" and Seathrift wonders how he could "Be out in my own child so" (R2v–S1r). Then it is revealed that Timothy Seathrift has married Frank's sister, having taken her for "a Ladie." Warehouse tells Seathrift that "things / Are just fallen out as we contriv'd 'em" (S1r). He gives the conventional signal of closure,

"Let's in" and Seathrift replies, "Lead the way, Sir." But Bannswright intervenes with "Pray stay a litle," prompting Warehouse's surprised "More Revelations yet?" (S1r). Using a metaphor of theatrical discovery, Bannswright says, "I all this while have stood behind the Curtaine," and once he is assured by Seathrift that his debts have been paid, he too "*undisguises*," saying of his "unworthy shape," "Now I can cast it off, / And be my true selfe" (S1r–v). Because Old Plotwell's disguise and self-discovery are also a surprise to playgoers, Warehouse's response includes them in the play's thoroughly comic conclusion:

> Well what was wanting
> Unto our joyes and made these Nuptials
> Imperfect, Brother you by your discovery
> Have fully added.   (S1v)

Hemings's *The Fatal Contract* comes near the end of a long period of revenge tragedies, so its excesses are not surprising. But two extreme uses of the discovery scene in this play also demonstrate how effectively staging could be used to convey a figure's obsession with and delight in revenge. The play's principal revengers are Queen Fredigond and the figure referred to as Castrato – ostensibly a eunuch Moor, until the end of the play when she identifies herself as Chrotilda. For the first part of the action Castrato pretends to be Fredigond's helper in revenge. The queen's intended victims and reasons for revenge are many, as a set-piece discovery early in the play literally illustrates. The episode begins with the direction for Fredigond to "*Draw the curtain and shew the picture*" (B3v), after which she describes it to Castrato – and to the theatre audience. Probably this discovery was of a property painting, toward which Fredigond evidently gestures as she explicates:

> This picture drawn by an Italian
> (Which still I keep to whet mine anger)
> Does represent the murder of my brother,
> For ravishing this beautious piece of ill;
> A bloody and a terrible mistake,
> To murder Clodimir for Clotarrs fact,
> For which behold how Fredigond's reveng'd,
> This old Dumaine and father to this maid,
> With all his kindred, sociates and alies,
> (These brace of wicked ones, and that ravisht whore,
> The fair and fatall cause of these events
> Onely excepted) are here, here in this picture:
> Is't not a brave sight, how doth the object like thee?

> How prettily that babie hangs by th' heels,
> Sprawling his Armes about his mothers wombe,
> As if againe he sought for shelter there?
> Here's one bereft of hands, and this of tongue,
> Finger thy Lute Maria, sing out Isabel:
> . . .
> And here's the Granddam with her glares out;
> . . .
> Tow horie Gray-berds in this angle lyes,
> Will find their way to Hell without their eyes,
> Villaines that kil'd my Brother; how does this like thee?
> To execute men in picture, is't not rare?   (B3v–4r)

By using a work of art for Fredigond to describe her reasons for wanting revenge and to identify her actual and potential victims, Hemings also calls attention to the artifice that characterizes the play at every level. When this show elicits an enthusiastic response from Castrato, the queen says, "I find thee Eunuch apt for my imployments" (B4r). But in fact Castrato is the play's chief revenger and before long Fredigond becomes one of the eunuch's victims. It is probably significant, therefore, that an overtly artificial combination of discovery and description is used again when Castrato displays Fredigond and her lover Landrey in Act 5. The last scene begins, "*Enter the Eunuch, whilst the waits play softly, and solemnly draws the Canopie, where the Queen sits at one end bound with Landrey at the other, both as asleep*" (H3r). The only viewers of this show are the playgoers, to whom Castrato speaks directly:

> Here sits our Beldam dieted for Venerie,
> And by her, her Landrey not surfeited;
> Her Ladyship's allou'd a mouldie crust,
> He stinking water to peece out his life,
> Between them both they banquet like one slave,
> Condemn'd perpetually to the Burdello;
> They think I know not that they thus are us'd,
> When it is onely I that use them thus.
> How wickedly they look, oh I could laugh
> To hear them rail at others misery;
> He curses her, and she sooth curses him,
> And both each other damn for their offences.
> Learn ye that pamper up your flesh for lust,
> The Eunuch in his wickedness is just.   (H3r–v)

This description makes clear that Castrato is the creator of this scene of misery. Furthermore, the staging probably had the effect of distancing

Castrato and the playgoers from the two bound figures on display. After taunting Fredigond and Landrey, Castrato poisons both and *"draws the Curtain again"* (I1r) in preparation for the next discovery. This show-and-tell is for Clothair, the queen's son, on whom Castrato wreaks her final vengeance. At the direction *"shews Landrey and the Queen"* (I4r), Castrato says, "Look here my cousin'd fool I do not bungle" and when Clothair asks, "Are these dead then?" Castrato responds, "As sure as you live, pray ask them else" (I4r). But this is also a discovery for the dying queen on the other side of the curtain, as indicated by Castrato's words to her: "Look Queen, here's the top-branch of all thy Family, / Mark but how kindly for thy sake I'l use him." Seeing Castrato about to stab her son, the queen cries, "Oh, oh, oh" and *"dyes"* (I4v). Having accomplished this revenge, instead of killing Clothair, the eunuch taunts him until Clothair stabs him. Only then, dying, does the eunuch reveal that he is actually Chrotilda and that she has fallen in love with Clothair. Nothing indicates that she actually removes her eunuch disguise, but this is probably for practical reasons (it includes a blackened face). In any case, here in one of the last plays to use both discovery scenes and disguise-discoveries, we can see the inevitable exhaustion of a long- and well-used staging convention.

For those of us attempting to interpret both disguise-discoveries and discovery scenes in these plays, difficulties arise in relation to their original meaning and performance. In this study I have provided reasons to think that the emblematic concept of Truth as the Daughter of Time, together with the rituals of Catholic liturgy, informed both the actions and language of discovery on the early modern stage. Furthermore, I have shown how real-world enclosed spaces familiar to playgoers were probably the basis for like locations discovered on the stage. But even an awareness of these original contexts, I would argue, cannot ensure our full understanding of such business four centuries later. To this caveat I would add another: performance conditions then were very different from those today.

I have referred several times to how performed discoveries typically have two audiences – characters watching in the play, and playgoers – and to how the reactions of the former might influence those of the latter. But in a system that had each player memorize his part on his own and offered little opportunity for rehearsal, how (or how well) did the interconnected business of discovery-and-response get staged?[33] The playtexts often provide minimal or no help for the players. As we have seen, disguise-

---

[33] For a summary and discussion of the evidence related to part-based rehearsal and performance practices, see Tiffany Stern, "Actors' Parts."

discoveries are sometimes only signalled obliquely in dialogue from the disguiser or those watching, or both. In many cases a player would have had to know or guess from what he said that he was also to perform a self-discovery, and other players would have had to know or guess what had elicited the exclamations of surprise in their parts. Under such conditions, the players might have been as surprised as the playgoers. Different but related questions arise about discovery scenes: when a tomb or smaller property is to be opened, the staging would have been relatively simple and easily managed. But with minimal time for rehearsal, how were actual discovery scenes prepared and, since such scenes typically include considerable action, how did the players know where to stand and what to do?[34] How were beds and other large properties managed, especially when there were playgoers seated on the stage?[35] Were plays with such discovery scenes staged in provincial venues?[36] To ask such questions is not to imply that answers can be found, but to emphasize what we do not know. My hope is that the contexts and discoveries I have discussed in this study, together with the many additional examples gathered in my online database, will encourage further investigations into all aspects of discoveries performed on the early modern stage.

[34] For a consideration of this problem in relation to silent action, see Leslie Thomson, "Dumb Shows in Performance on the Early Modern Stage."

[35] See Leslie Thomson, "Blackfriars Stage Sitters and the Staging of *The Tempest, The Maid's Tragedy* and *The Two Noble Kinsmen.*"

[36] See Leslie Thomson, "Staging on the Road, 1586–1594: A New Look at Some Old Assumptions."

Was There a Central Opening in the Tiring House Wall?

Although my principal concern in this study is the thematic and dramatic significance of discoveries of figures and properties wherever or however they were staged, since all such events depended for their meaning and effect partly on the action itself, the matter of where discovered scenes were located and how they were performed cannot be ignored. That such scenes were included in plays written throughout the period is an indication that they could be – and surely were – staged effectively and successfully. But in the absence of authoritative illustrations, detailed stage directions or explicit dialogue it is possible to interpret what evidence we do have in different ways and impossible to know for certain which, if any, theories are the most accurate. The most vexing and intractable questions have to do with whether or not most playhouses had a wide opening in the centre of the tiring house wall, with curtains that could be opened to effect a discovery. Theatre historians have offered a range of answers, but in the absence of hard evidence all theories are necessarily premised on the actual or implied stage directions in the playtexts and "what seems to make sense." Such interpretations vary from critic to critic and over time.

That there was a central opening in the tiring house wall of early modern purpose-built London playing venues is the view long held by most theatre historians, including Glynne Wickham, G. F. Reynolds, Richard Southern, C. Walter Hodges, Bernard Beckerman, Richard Hosley, Andrew Gurr and Mariko Ichikawa. And for years I had no reason to question what I took to be a fact. But then I read the work of Tim Fitzpatrick, who has developed an approach to early modern stage movement that includes a detailed challenge to the established theory of a central opening. His position is that Aernout van Buchel's copy of Johannes de Witt's drawing of the Swan playhouse is accurate in showing a two-door tiring house wall and that such a configuration was practical and therefore typical. In particular, he argues that if there was a central feature for discoveries, it was a temporary "concealment space" with no access to the tiring house. Fitzpatrick's detailed presentation of this theory has seriously challenged my easy acceptance of the idea that there was a central opening into the space behind the stage. As the arguments for the opposing views demonstrate, the available evidence has been used to support both positions. But each interpretation also provides reasons to question the other, with the result that I find myself at an impasse, unable to agree fully with either. My purpose in this appendix, therefore, is first to look at how the prevailing theory of a central opening was developed, then to summarize the counter-theory and finally to offer my own suggestions, based on what seems to make most sense to me in the light of these opposing views and the discovery scenes themselves.

At the beginning of this study, I noted that *discovery scene* is not an early modern term; indeed, there was no contemporary word or phrase to describe or denote the event, either in stage directions or elsewhere. Even more significant in the context of a consideration of arguments for and against a central opening in the tiring house wall, however, is that *discovery space* – the most common modern term – is also anachronistic, having been coined by Richard Hosley in 1959. In the absence of an early modern term, other theatre historians have referred to an "enclosure," "discovery," "enclosed space," "curtained alcove" and "wide central opening," and "accessory space."[1] Hosley's term was devised to designate a shallow opening in the centre of the tiring house wall, and to replace the idea of an actual "inner stage" or "rear stage" that had been imagined by earlier historians. But it is important to remember that all these terms are premised on the idea of a central opening (for which we have no indisputable proof) between two lateral doors (whose existence is certain). Indeed, we have the inescapable fact of the Swan drawing (Figure App. 1), which shows a tiring house wall with only two doors and a blank, seemingly uncurtained, wall between them. There have been various attempts to explain this drawing, but I think it fair to say that none has made it possible to dismiss it.

In his 1940 study of the Red Bull playhouse, G. F. Reynolds observes that although the Swan drawing provides no indication of a central opening, "reconstruction after reconstruction of the Elizabethan stage appears disregarding this fundamental evidence." And when doing his

---

[1] Terms used at one time or another by David Bevington, Walter Hodges, Scott McMillin, Andrew Gurr and Tom King respectively.

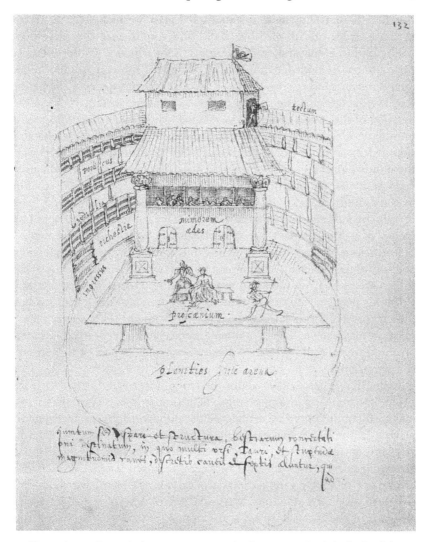

Figure App. 1 Swan playhouse interior, copy by Aernout van Buchel of a sketch by Johannes de Witt, c. 1596

own imaginary reconstruction of the Red Bull, he admits "the hard fact" that "the Swan picture permits no permanently curtained rear stage at all without drastic structural rearrangement."[2] But he also says that "since

[2] G. F. Reynolds, *The Staging of Elizabethan Plays at the Red Bull Theater*, 131.

the three door arrangement is so natural a plan, we may, I think, accept it … as a feature of the Red Bull."[3] This idea that the three-door configuration is "natural" is an assumption for which Reynolds provides no argument or evidence, but which governs his subsequent ideas about how discoveries were staged. When he turns to those scenes, he grants that even stage directions that specify a discovery seldom indicate the location of the action or how it was staged, while other directions might or might not have used what he calls a "discoverable space." Reynolds also acknowledges that even with a broad interpretation of such directions, the number and frequency of possible discovery scenes do not seem great enough to warrant a permanent fixture. In particular, he observes that in over six hundred scenes in Red Bull plays he finds only sixty-seven "uses of a discoverable space" and asks if it is likely that so little use would be made "of a discoverable space if it was always there ready to be used."[4] Nevertheless, because "there is no possible doubt that the Red Bull had a curtain, arras, traverse – different names, it would seem, for the same thing – and that this curtain was sometimes used for discoveries," Reynolds posits a "curtained framework easily removable" that was not present on the Swan stage when De Witt visited.[5] This seems a neat solution that resolves several problems at once, but it is nevertheless based on the unsupported premise of a centre opening as part of a "natural" configuration.

Richard Southern's ideas about the tiring house wall involve theories about its origins. He argues that the tiring house evolved from the medieval booth stage: "To explain its development into the Elizabethan playhouse one has to make only the simplest modifications; the slightly awkward entrances round the edges of the curtain may become regular doors; the curtain itself remains between them, but is capable, on particular (and relatively rare) dramatic occasions, of being parted in the centre to disclose a small discovery-space."[6] Southern's solution to the problem of the Swan drawing is to suppose that "De Witt visited the theatre when the play being performed was one (of the many) which do not happen to call for use of a discovery-space, and thus the central curtain or arras was never parted in his presence, with the result that he supposed it a mere decorative hanging against a solid wall."[7] In his later book, Southern says that "what De Witt shows is precisely reminiscent of a hall-screens. And thus it may well be that the blank centre to his

[3] Ibid., 109.   [4] Ibid., 161.   [5] Ibid., 131, 132.
[6] Richard Southern, "On Reconstructing a Practicable Elizabethan Public Playhouse," 32.   [7] Ibid.

tiring-house wall is equivalent to the centre screen of a hall set. In that case, a discovery space could easily have been rigged on the Swan stage for the (relatively rare) occasions when it was needed by setting up a traverse."[8] These explanations are consistent not only in accepting the evidence of the Swan drawing but also in citing the relative rarity of discovery scenes as reasons to posit a curtain that hung between the two doors and was used only when needed. The illustrations by Southern that accompany these points all show a two-door Swan configuration. His arguments, however, have not prevailed (although I shall return to the idea of a temporary fixture).

Long the best known and most influential study of the tiring house wall is Richard Hosley's 1959 article, "The Discovery-Space in Shakespeare's Globe." He begins by saying that the second Globe had "two (or three) double-hung stage-doors. (Probably there were three rather than two doors)."[9] He determines that the opening "need not have been deeper than 4 ft. or wider than 7 ft., for no discovery [of the twenty he analyzed] is of more than three players ... or of more or larger properties than a table and two seats or a day-bed and chair." Having itemized the requirements indicated by the discovered scenes he looked at, Hosley concludes, "These conditions would have been fulfilled if the Globe discovery-space was behind an open doorway in the tiring-house wall (usually, we may suppose, the middle doorway of three) essentially similar to the doorways in the Swan drawing and fitted with hangings as in the *Wits* frontispiece or the *Roxana* vignette."[10] Here, despite his reference to the Swan drawing with its two doors and blank space between them, Hosley assumes the presence of a centre opening that functioned as a "discovery-space."

In a 1964 study, however, Hosley fundamentally contradicts his earlier ideas, arguing: that "the [two-door] tiring-house of the Elizabethan public playhouse [Rose, Curtain, Theatre, Swan] originated in the Tudor hall screen";[11] that "since the plays assignable to later public playhouses have, in general, the same staging needs as those assignable to the earlier ones, we may suppose also that the tiring-houses of later public playhouses [Globe, Fortune, Red Bull, Hope, second Globe, second Fortune] were essentially similar to that of the Swan, the only difference being that one or two of the later public playhouses (like one or two of the earlier ones) may have had a three-door instead of a two-door tiring house";[12] that "the creators of the

[8] Richard Southern, *The Staging of Plays before Shakespeare*, 594.
[9] Richard Hosley, "The Discovery-Space in Shakespeare's Globe," 35.
[10] Ibid., 46. I discuss the *Roxana* and *Wits* illustrations below.
[11] Richard Hosley, "The Origins of the Shakespearian Playhouse," 35. [12] Ibid., 37.

earlier private playhouses [Paul's, First Blackfriars, Second Blackfriars and Whitefriars] either adapted an existing hall screen as a tiring-house or, if the room or hall converted into a playhouse was without a screen, built a tiring-house on the model of a hall screen, much as the builders of the first public playhouses did";[13] and that "Presumably (on evidence of the essentially unchanging staging requirements of private-theater plays) the later, new-built private playhouses [Porter's Hall, Cockpit or Phoenix and Salisbury Court] had tiring-houses generally similar to those of the earlier private playhouses. One or more of the private-theater tiring-houses may have been equipped with three doors, either through adaptation of a three-doorway hall screen or through construction of a tiring-house on the analogy of such a screen."[14]

Then in his 1975 survey of "The Playhouses," Hosley says that the first Globe probably had a two-door tiring house and that "Discoveries could have been accommodated within one of the tiring-house doorways."[15] But in direct contrast to his 1964 conclusions, here he says that "the two-door tiring-house of the Swan was probably *not* characteristic of the public playhouses of the period" (original emphasis).[16] He also argues that "a third, central doorway in the tiring-house façade would have been a great convenience in the management of discoveries, eavesdroppings and the putting forth from the tiring-house of large stage properties such as tables or beds, since during the preparation for and execution of such pieces of staging the use of a middle door would have left the two side doors free for regular entrances and exits by the players." He immediately qualifies this suggestion, however, when he adds that "a play designed for performance in a playhouse with a three-door tiring-house could readily be adapted for performance in a playhouse with a two-door tiring-house."[17] Note that for Hosley a "three-door tiring-house" has now become a fact. And while in a 1969 piece on a putative Blackfriars reconstruction he says that the venue could have had a two- or a three-door tiring house,[18] in his 1975 overview, after repeating these dual possibilities, he says that in his proposed reconstruction he has "*arbitrarily* preferred a theory of three doors" (my emphasis).[19] He then specifies that this tiring house "had three" doors and, moreover, that "The three-door tiring-house of the Blackfriars was apparently characteristic of the private playhouses of the period,"[20] again in direct contrast to his 1964 conclusions. To consider why Hosley's idea of a

---

[13] Ibid., 38.   [14] Ibid., 39.   [15] Richard Hosley, "The Playhouses," 195.   [16] Ibid., 228.
[17] Ibid., 229.   [18] Richard Hosley, "A Reconstruction of the Second Blackfriars," 79.
[19] Hosley, "The Playhouses," 209.   [20] Ibid., 228.

three-door configuration has prevailed is to become aware of how it conforms to what seems most "natural" to him (and to us); but Southern's conclusions (quoted earlier) show that the two-door Swan configuration might have been the one expected and seen by early modern playgoers.

Typically, as in the instances above, the Swan drawing is discussed in terms of what it shows, not how it shows it. The few detailed assessments of the quality of the drawing have produced inconclusive results, so that John Gleason concludes that if it is "'read' against the iconographic traditions of its own time" the drawing "conveys a clear and trustworthy message,"[21] while Jean Wilson comments that "the standard of drawing ... is not such as to produce absolute trust in de Witt as an accurate visual reporter, or in van Buchell as a copyist."[22] R. A. Foakes concludes that the details of the drawing "are hard to interpret,"[23] and that "It may be correct in the major features shown" – including "two doors to the stage" and "no inner stage" – "but if so, then these are features of the Swan, and not necessarily of other theatres of the period."[24] It might also be worth noting, though, that as Dutchmen both de Witt and van Buchel would have been familiar with the three-opening façade of Dutch street theatres, or *speeltanneel*, used by the *rederijker* (rhetorician) societies of the time, so de Witt would have been predisposed to include a middle opening to an inner stage, or *toog*, had there been one in the tiring house wall of the Swan, and van Buchel would hardly have omitted it if de Witt had drawn it.[25] But they pictured a *difference* from what they knew, rather than a similarity.

The idea that not all London playhouses were structurally alike, and especially that the Swan's tiring house wall might be unique or rare rather than representative, has frequently been advanced as a solution to the problem of its two doors and blank space between them. Evidence to support these views is drawn from the excavation of the Rose playhouse, from other contemporary illustrations and from stage directions in playtexts. But like the information in the Swan drawing, that evidence is open to a variety of interpretations.

In his archaeological study of the Rose, Julian Bowsher (Senior Archaeologist, Museum of London) notes that there is no evidence that the tiring house projected out from the rear wall of the structure, as the Swan's flat

---

[21] John B. Gleason, "The Dutch Humanist Origins of The De Witt Drawing of the Swan Theatre," 338.
[22] Jean Wilson, *The Archaeology of Shakespeare*, 73.
[23] R. A. Foakes, "Henslowe's Rose/Shakespeare's Globe," 18.
[24] R. A. Foakes, *Illustrations of the English Stage*, 54.
[25] For a discussion of these Dutch theatres see Martha Hollander, *An Entrance for the Eyes*, 32–3.

wall seems to have done. He says, "At the Rose, the tiring-house would appear to be integral to the main frame of the building. Given that the inner wall of the theatre also served as the back of the stage . . . The façade, or *scenae frons*, would therefore appear to be angled, although its line had been greatly disturbed by modern building activity."[26] With reference to the number of openings in the wall, Bowsher says that "the angled *scenae frons*, in both phases of the Rose, would suggest three," but he does not explain why.[27] Elsewhere he says: "The angled *scenae frons*, or back wall, of the first Rose stage clearly allowed for a central opening . . . as well as side doors."[28] Unfortunately, however, what remains of this area of the playhouse is not enough to move from "would suggest" and "allowed for" to certainty. I shall return to this idea of an angled tiring house wall when discussing the theories of Tim Fitzpatrick.

In addition to the Swan drawing, which is of an outdoor playhouse, four other contemporary illustrations (seemingly of indoor spaces) have been studied for evidence about tiring house wall configurations, although not only are they also difficult to interpret but the authority of each has been called into question. John Astington has done detailed analyses of the engraved title pages of *Roxana* (1632) and *Messallina* (1640), demonstrating that the playhouse in the *Roxana* engraving is derived from several non-theatrical sources, and that it is "the pattern for" the playhouse in the *Messallina* engraving (Figure App. 2). He adds that "the likelihood that the *Roxana* engraving represents *any* specific place is extremely slim" and that it is "a confection of iconographic conventions deriving from earlier engravings, etchings, and woodcuts" (original emphasis).[29] These may have included "illustrated editions of Terence, which provided the most widely known imaginative version of stage action in the *theatrum*," so that the purpose of the *Roxana* illustration was to invoke "the imagined theatre of classical humanism."[30] Astington also shows how figures in earlier title page illustrations were the basis for those in the *Roxana* illustration, which, in turn, were the source for those in the *Messallina* engraving, which therefore "has no independent authority as a depiction of a theatre, real or imagined."[31] Astington has also examined the engraved frontispiece of *The Wits* (1662) with similar results. His analysis of the figures and their costumes leads him to conclude that they "have more to do with iconographic and decorative conventions than with any specifically theatrical originals, of whatever chronological point in the twenty years between the closing of the theatres and the making of the

---

[26] Julian Bowsher, *The Rose Theatre*, 41.   [27] Ibid., 67.
[28] Julian Bowsher and Pat Miller, *The Rose and the Globe*, 119.
[29] John H. Astington, "The Origins of the *Roxana* and *Messalina* Illustrations," 152.
[30] Ibid., 158.   [31] Ibid., 167.

Figure App. 2 Title page detail, *The Tragedy of Messallina*, Nathaniel Richards,
engraved by Thomas Rawlins, 1640

[engraving] plate."[32] Furthermore, Astington says that "the theatre or temporary playing space the engraving depicts" is "an embarrassingly primitive
stage façade, bespeaking the rawest and most awkward of touring conditions,"
and that "the tiring-house end of the stage does not suggest a permanent
playhouse."[33] He concludes: "*The Wits* picture is merely a visual collage, a *jeu
d'esprit* showing a theatre that never was."[34]

---

[32] John H. Astington, "*The Wits* Illustration," 132.   [33] Ibid., 132–3.
[34] Ibid., 139. My summaries of Astington's points do not do justice to his arguments and supporting
 evidence, which are completely convincing and should be consulted.

The fourth piece of pictorial evidence sometimes adduced for early modern playhouse design in general and of the tiring house façade in particular is the group of neoclassical-style drawings found at Worcester College for an unidentified theatre. First thought to be the work of Inigo Jones and to date from 1616, these drawings have since been studied by Gordon Higgott, whose "careful investigation of the drawing style now places the Worcester College drawings at a much later date, the early 1660s, and convincingly ascribes the drawing work to John Webb, Jones's pupil who later became his assistant and collaborator."[35] Higgott says that "the drawings represent the earliest known example in England to design a public playhouse on classical principles, using the semi-circular auditorium and three-door *frons scenae* of the ancient Roman theatre, as described by Vitruvius in Book V of *De Architettura*." So although he concludes that the drawings represent "the final flowering of the Renaissance tradition in the design of the English indoor playhouse,"[36] Higgott does not explain how that design was based on "classical principles." In any case, the relationship between Webb's drawings and any pre-Restoration playhouse is rendered tenuous at best. Following on Higgott's research and conclusions, Jon Greenfield has acknowledged that "The drawings are not from 1616, and were not drawn by Inigo Jones."[37] And in the view of Oliver Jones, "While the drawings appear to share many of the features associated with Jacobean theatres, and may offer many useful clues for the organization of an indoor playhouse, we cannot rely on them as a true depiction of a playhouse of this period."[38]

Time and research have mostly lessened what we think we know about early modern playhouse design in general and the tiring house wall in particular. But premises and theories, which are necessary contexts for discussions of staging, continue to be developed and offered. Unquestionably the most influential of these are found in the work of Andrew Gurr, especially in the four editions of *The Shakespearean Stage*, but also in other books, chapters and articles. His working premise, which has remained essentially unchanged except gradually to expand and become more fixed over the years, is evident in what he sees as problems with the Swan drawing: "The two double entry doors onto the stage are at odds with the multitude of evidence that Elizabethan, Jacobean and Caroline plays all call for three stage entrances, one of them a *wide central opening*. There is certainly no 'inner stage', nor even a 'discovery-space'

---

[35] Jon Greenfield, with assistance from Peter McCurdy, "Practical Evidence for a Reimagined Indoor Jacobean Theatre," 35.
[36] Gordon Higgott, "Reassessing the drawings," 9.   [37] Greenfield, "Practical Evidence," 35.
[38] Oliver Jones, "Documentary Evidence," 71.

such as many plays require, and no hangings anywhere" (my emphasis).[39] As Gurr's theories about the tiring house openings have evolved, he has given increasing importance to the idea of a "wide central opening" and its uses. Although to my knowledge he never provides his reasons for these elaborations, they seem to grow at least partly out of a realization that he would find it difficult to argue for a central opening if it were used only for discoveries.

Indeed, as Reynolds and other critics have noted, the relative rarity of discovery scenes calls into question the need for a permanent "discovery space." His suggestion that there was a removable curtained structure at the Red Bull was an attempt to explain both the absence of a central opening in the Swan drawing and the fact that few plays actually required one. For his part, Hosley acknowledged that "the device of discovery was relatively infrequent, demonstrably occurring in only sixteen of the fifty plays considered [in his survey] . . . and, more important, in ten of those sixteen plays only once."[40] Thus he concludes that "the discovery-space was not designed for the purpose of effecting discoveries but was an occasional adaptation to that purpose of a tiring-house doorway together with the curtains or hangings which, fitted up within or in front of the doorway, masked the interior of the tiring-house while at the same time affording the players a convenient means of easy passage between tiring-house and stage."[41] Bernard Beckerman, in his study of Globe plays, argues for an "enclosure" in the tiring house wall, but he too notes that it was used "infrequently and briefly." This leads him to ask, "was the enclosure a permanent part of the stage, and if it was, why was it not used more frequently?" The answer, he says, "is that the enclosure *was* used more frequently, not to effect discovery, however, but to permit concealment" (original emphasis).[42]

In *The Shakespearean Stage* Gurr discusses what he refers to as "lesser uses" of the central opening, saying that "Most importantly it probably made a third entry-point."[43] In a chapter on the staging of Rose plays, Gurr

[39] This is from the fourth (2009) edition of *The Shakespearean Stage* (164); the first (1970), second (1980) and third (1991) editions are less insistent: "The two double doors are at odds with evidence that there were three or more stage entrances in many Elizabethan and Jacobean plays. There is certainly no 'inner stage' or 'discovery-space', as many plays require, and no hangings" (first edition, 90; second, 124; third, 132).

[40] Hosley, "The Playhouses," 233.

[41] Ibid. Note that a discovery does not necessarily require a central opening, although Hosley is thinking in terms of one.

[42] Bernard Beckerman, *Shakespeare at the Globe*, 73–4, 87–8.

[43] Andrew Gurr, *The Shakespearean Stage*. This is the phrasing in the first three editions (99, 138, 151), but in the fourth edition "probably" has been deleted (185).

says that "In both pre- and post-1592 plays it seems that at least two stage doors were expected, and possibly a third, though as usual that likelihood is confused by the question of the discovery space and its hangings being used for entries."[44] Elsewhere Gurr discusses the "discovery space" and theories about it at some length:

> Despite the absence of any central opening at all in De Witt's Swan drawing, the assumption that there was a wide central recess or discovery space has dominated all reconstructions of the *frons*, infecting calculations not only about the entry doors but about the balcony or "above" and the stage hangings. The long life of the inner stage theory reflects the two-dimensional thinking of earlier theatre historians. Its continuing life, transformed into a long and deep curtained alcove in the centre of the *frons*, dominates thinking about staging. The need to have it has called in doubt the strong evidence that there were lords' rooms over the stage, the location of which in a flat-walled *frons* would prevent the highest-paying customers from seeing any of the set-pieces uncovered in the central alcove. It has also, rather paradoxically, prevented the central opening in the *frons* from being used as an ordinary entry door and has consigned even royal and processional entrances to the flanking doors. It has been invoked as the only access big enough to be used for carrying large stage properties on and off the stage, an assumption that has allowed the two great double doors on each side of the Swan's stage to be replaced with single doors. It now operates as the fall-back position into which are pitched most of the unresolvable puzzles about routine Renaissance staging practices.[45]

In what might seem a critical summary of questionable theories, Gurr is actually preparing to insist on two other uses for that central opening: "One certain thing about the discovery space is that it must have been big enough not just to provide an entryway for ceremonial entrances, but also to carry on and off the largest properties. There was no other form of access to the stage platform."[46] But, to return to the Swan drawing, in his 1959 study Hosley calculates that the two doorways would have been "some 7 ft. or 8 ft. wide,"[47] which would have been wide enough to bring on large properties.

In a consideration of Globe staging, Gurr says that "the central opening was closed off by the stage hangings, or arras. They gave kings the dignity of making an entry heralded by the blue-coated stage hands who held the curtains back to admit the stately procession."[48] The most important aspect of Gurr's developing theory, it seems to me, is his certainty that

---

[44] Andrew Gurr, "The Rose Repertory," 124.   [45] Andrew Gurr, "The Bare Island," 31–2.
[46] Ibid., 33.   [47] Hosley, "The Discovery Space in Shakespeare's Globe," 35.
[48] Andrew Gurr, "Staging at the Globe," 161–2.

there *was* a "central opening," because once one is assumed to exist, uses must be found to justify its existence, and Gurr finds them.

In *The Oxford Handbook of Early Modern Theatre* Gurr explicitly states, without qualification, that at the Globe "The stage front, or *frons scenae*, had two doors on each side of a curtained central opening, known as the 'discovery space'."[49] This phrasing is ambiguous enough to suggest that the term was used by Shakespeare and his fellow playwrights, although as I noted above, it was first used by Hosley and Southern in 1959. Gurr also states his concomitant theory as fact: "The two flanking doors were used for oppositional entries . . . while the central opening was chiefly used for the entry of authority . . . and for the final exits in the comedies when the opposed parties are at last united."[50] It is important to keep in mind, however, that no stage direction (or dialogue) associated with such actions actually indicates the use of a central opening.

The assumption that such an opening existed also underlies the discussion in *Staging in Shakespeare's Theatres*, co-written by Gurr and Mariko Ichikawa. In a section titled "The Use of the Central Opening" they posit that "in addition to 'discoveries' and triple entrances and exits, several other kinds of situation might have benefited from the use of the central opening."[51] Their examples include "cave" and "cell" scenes, masques and shows, the appearance of ghosts and other supernatural figures, of chorus figures, and of performers in a play-within-a-play; also ceremonial entrances, the exit of funeral processions. In addition, "At the ends of the romantic comedies and some other plays, the central opening is fit for the joint departure of the two groups of characters who have achieved a harmonious relationship. Our final suggestion is that, whether regal or not, the general exits at the ends of these plays are made through the central opening."[52] Finally, though, Gurr and Ichikawa acknowledge that:

> We must admit that there are very few instances where we can claim with total confidence that the central opening was used for an entrance or exit. In the above-mentioned instances, it is not absolutely necessary for any enterer or exiter to use the central opening. If we took a minimalist attitude, we should have to abandon these speculations as unproven. However, since the central opening was available as a third entryway, it seems reasonable to speculate that, except when the company was on its travels and had to perform in a space with limited resources, the central opening would have served as the special and authoritative entry and exit point.[53]

---

[49] Andrew Gurr, "Why the Globe Is Famous," 195.   [50] Ibid.
[51] Andrew Gurr and Mariko Ichikawa, *Staging in Shakespeare's Theatres*, 105.   [52] Ibid., 112.
[53] Ibid., 113.

Again, the main premise – the existence of a "central opening" – remains unquestioned.

Not surprisingly, Gurr's repeated insistence on a central opening and his expansion of its uses have been echoed and broadly supported by Ichikawa in her own studies which, while very detailed, are nevertheless typically more qualified than Gurr's statements of seeming fact. For example, despite first stating that "Analysis of plays that we think may have been written principally for performance at these public playhouses shows that the stages of the Theatre, Globe, Fortune and most other public playhouses had two main entrance doors and a large opening for discoveries between them," Ichikawa is then more tentative when referring to three Fortune plays: "These plays *suggest* that the Fortune stage and *probably* its model, the Globe stage, had three doorways. Globe plays offer no conclusive proof for the existence of a third entry. However, as Bernard Beckerman argues, certain scenes do *suggest* the use of a middle entrance"[54] (my emphasis). Similarly, "Stage directions in plays performed at the second Blackfriars *suggest* that its stage had two doors, [and] a discovery space between them"[55] (my emphasis). I shall turn to the matter of the evidence provided by stage directions in due course.

Gurr's theories about the existence of a central opening and its uses have prevailed not simply because they have been repeated and embellished over time, but also because a centre opening fits how we imagine early modern plays were staged. But these "mind's eye" pictures are based on our experience of modern stagings, not only of modern plays but also of those written by Shakespeare and his contemporaries, which are influenced by the theories of theatre historians – of whom Gurr is the most prolific and influential – that there was a centre opening. This circularity is difficult to break out of even long enough to entertain contrary theories. Indeed, Gurr has defended and expanded on his theories in a series of exchanges with Tim Fitzpatrick, who explicitly and fundamentally differs with Gurr's basic premise of a central opening.

First in a series of articles, then, in *Playwright, Space and Place in Early Modern Performance*, Fitzpatrick has presented and defended his theory that there were only two openings in the tiring house wall, as in the Swan drawing. Like Gurr's theory of three openings, Fitzpatrick's is contingent on a broader theory of early modern stage management and performance. His detailed proposition (only summarized here) is that "the plays manifest a systemic division of the fictional world based on two and only

---

[54] Mariko Ichikawa, *Shakespearean Entrances*, 14.   [55] Ibid., 17.

two entry-points, and that this fictional division serves also as a stage-management system that assigns specific functions to those two doors."[56] This is a system of "spatial triangles" (created by two entry points and stage space) in which one of the two doors leads to fictional locations further outwards and the other to locations further inwards, and that these "might have been the spatial conventions the playwrights were working to and reinscribing in their texts so as to facilitate performance preparation by standardizing the spatial set-up"; as such, they would have constituted "a range of 'default settings'" that were "conventionally encoded as 'the usual way of doing things'" and that playgoers "would in turn decode these spatial patterns and use them to make meanings."[57] In "Hangings, Doors and Discoveries: Conflicting Evidence or Problematic Assumptions," Fitzpatrick and Wendy Millyard grant that a two-door configuration "may be distasteful to those who would prefer physical patterns of balance and symmetry on the Elizabethan stage," but they counter that "such 'frames' (possibly derived at least in part from an unconscious proscenium arch perspective) are not pertinent in a playhouse where two thirds of the audience were viewing the stage from oblique angles."[58] Acknowledging that their hypothesis "may be seen as a radical departure" and that "it does indeed have profound ramifications for our understanding of Elizabethan and Jacobean staging," Fitzpatrick and Millyard note that "in another sense it is merely a further evolution of our notions of what stood upstage centre on the Elizabethan stage. The old 'inner stage' was superseded by a 'discovery space', and this entity is now further curtailed in scope to become merely a 'concealment space'."[59]

Although Fitzpatrick's main purpose in *Playwright, Space and Place* is to set out his triangulation theory of early modern stage management, by the time he was writing the book there had been several published exchanges between him and Gurr about whether or not there was a central opening, which is perhaps why the book includes an appendix titled "'Three doors', 'Three ways' and 'In the midst': Inferring a Third Opening." Here Fitzpatrick's purpose is to look at "the limited and indirect iconographic evidence called on to argue for a three-door architecture" and then to "work systematically through the potentially relevant textual evidence to assess the extent to which its force and extent might have been over-stated."[60] On the one hand, he admits that "There are many indications

---

[56] Tim Fitzpatrick, *Playwright, Space and Place*, 288. [57] Ibid., 23, 4.
[58] Tim Fitzpatrick and Wendy Millyard, "Hangings, Doors and Discoveries," 11. [59] Ibid., 22.
[60] Fitzpatrick, *Playwright, Space and Place*, 249.

to suggest there was some sort of dramaturgical resource upstage centre between the two flanking doors: characters regularly hide themselves behind curtains at points where there is considerable stage traffic, suggesting something in addition to the two lateral doors shown in De Witt"; but on the other hand, "the textual evidence that it was a fully functioning third opening in the vast majority of playhouses is not as strong as some scholars would argue." Referring to his alternative, Fitzpatrick says he has "called this feature a 'concealment space' since it is generally used as a place where onstage characters can temporarily conceal themselves, to later return to the stage rather than disappear through an opening into the tiring house."[61] To rebut Gurr's (and Ichikawa's) counter-arguments, Fitzpatrick provides examples in which "a consideration of the broader logistical patterns around 'discoveries' suggests that a third entry-point is not required, and that the text seems to have been structured to enable fluid performance with just two entrance-points."[62] Citing Gurr's idea that "the central opening was substantially 'off limits' – reserved for a particularly restricted range of entrances, those of royalty and clowns," Fitzpatrick observes, "this would make of the central feature a deliberately under-utilized resource, and one could wonder how and for how long such a 'taboo' status imposed on an available entrance might survive pragmatic production pressures. An alternative and possibly more justifiable explanation for the massive textual lacuna is that this upstage central opening simply did not exist except perhaps in a few marginal playhouses."[63]

Fitzpatrick's detailed analyses of many of the same scenes used by Gurr and others to argue *for* a central opening show at least that his hypothesis can be supported by recourse to the same evidence. As a consequence, I find it difficult simply to reject his ideas in favour of the idea of a central opening, and they merit careful consideration. Here I want to focus on particular, and interrelated, aspects of both theories that seem to me especially relevant to matters of staging.

At the heart of Fitzpatrick's theory is a system of stage management that he argues would have facilitated the players' task under early modern performance conditions, especially minimal rehearsal time and various kinds of venues. One critic who shares his concern but from a different angle is Evelyn Tribble, who has considered Fitzpatrick's theory twice, first in an article, then in *Cognition in the Globe*. While in the article she rejected his theory, in the book she explains why she came to agree with it, and the reasons are significant. Tribble notes that "The fundamental features of

[61] Ibid., 261.   [62] Ibid., 271.   [63] Ibid., 248–9.

early modern playing spaces were extremely simple: some means of distinguishing on-stage from off-stage and the use of two flanking entrances" and that "It would be difficult to overestimate their importance in structuring, organizing, and simplifying the complex activity of the playing companies."[64] She then turns to "the long-standing debate about the use of – and the number of – stage doors" and the question, "How did actors know which door to use?" Tribble makes the important point that "the very paucity of written information about the use of stage doors is a powerful indication of the tacit, invisible, and deep understanding of the stage that must have underpinned the work of the companies" and she asks, "But how, in practice, did such conventions work?"[65] Tribble summarizes both sides of the issue, then uses "the principles of Distributed Cognition . . . to evaluate competing hypotheses," on the premise that "the hypothesis most likely to reduce cognitive demands upon individual agents [i.e., players] . . . would likely be correct."[66] Observing that "In an environment as cognitively demanding as the early modern playhouse, every incentive would have been to minimize any additional cognitive burdens," Tribble refers to the principles as a model of "cognitive thrift."[67] Her main reason for rejecting the three-door theory, therefore, is that it has a "long list" of exceptions, and "a 'rule of thumb' as complex as this becomes an impediment rather than an aid to fluid movement across the stage. Certainly this hypothesis violates the principles of cognitive thrift that Tribble has outlined. By contrast, "a common convention designating an inward/outward door binary [such as Fitzpatrick proposes] could have provided an important locus of attention and focus beneficial to both audience and player alike."[68]

Two other basic reasons for giving Fitzpatrick's theory serious consideration have been mentioned already: the relative rarity of discovery scenes and the absence of a contemporary term for a central opening. The various terms invented by modern theatre historians are evidence that such a space – if it existed – would have needed a name. Some scholars once thought that *study* was the contemporary term, but it is difficult to know why: when *study* is used in stage directions it designates a fictional location in the context of a plot (see Chapter 5).

The most likely sources of evidence about early modern performance spaces are the original stage directions, but while these might sometimes

---

[64] Evelyn B. Tribble, *Cognition at the Globe*, 29.   [65] Ibid., 30.
[66] Ibid., 31. The six "principles" Tribble uses to evaluate the different theories are set out on pages 31–2.
[67] Ibid., 32.   [68] Ibid., 35.

make it possible to speculate about a centre opening, they can be used to defend more than one interpretation, as the debate between Gurr and Fitzpatrick demonstrates. For example, Gurr tries to counter the arguments of Fitzpatrick and Millyard, stating that the *Dictionary of Stage Directions* "lists a collection of entrances by three doors."[69] He does not cite a *Dictionary* entry or page, but seems to be referring to the entry for *door* and especially for *midst, middle*, which gives examples of "directions for figures to enter/exit by the *middle door/in the midst*." Gurr seems to assume that these terms mean the same thing, but the equivalency is more apparent than real, as the examples indicate. There is only one occurrence of "the middle door" (to which I shall return), and although there are more examples of "in the midst," the phrase is used in a variety of ways that are open to different interpretations.

Gurr provides examples about which he says, "It is difficult to see how any of these events could have been staged without using a central opening."[70] These include stage directions in *The Maid's Metamorphosis* (1600) for a sequence of entrances:

> *Enter at one doore, Mopso singing.*
> *Enter at the other doore, Frisco singing.*
> *Enter Joculo in the midst singing.*   (C3r–v)

These figures reappear later: "*Enter Joculo, Frisco, and Mopso, at three severall doores*" (D4v). Fitzpatrick grants that the latter direction refers to three doors, but he also notes that the earlier group refers specifically to only two doors: "one" and "the other." He argues that "in the midst" here "specifies that the third character (wherever his point of entry) should end up between the other two." He therefore believes that the two directions "cannot both be right."[71] Fitzpatrick suggests that the reference to "*three severall doores,*" combined with the action, indicates a playwright who is aware that "some playhouses" have three doors but others do not. He notes, moreover, that in the second instance "Mopso and Ioculo have six [actually eight] lines of dialogue before Frisco is drawn into the conversation."[72] In fact, Mopso asks, "Frisco, where hast thou bene frisking" (E1r), suggesting that the third figure has only just entered. This would be similar to the first sequence, in which a pause occurs after the entrance of each figure, during which he sings a song, so Joculo could use either of the "several doors" through which the other two have entered when he arrives in the "midst."

---

[69] Andrew Gurr, "Doors at the Globe," 61.   [70] Ibid.
[71] Fitzpatrick, *Playwright, Space and Place*, 258.   [72] Ibid., 257.

Gurr also cites a direction in *The English Traveller* (1627) as evidence of a third door: "*Enter at one doore an Usurer and his Man, at the other, Old Lionell with his servant: In the midst Reignald*" (F1v).[73] But the reference to "*the other*" door indicates only two, and the dialogue makes it clear that Old Lionel's servant is Reginald, who comes on with him, then stands between (or "in the midst of") his master and the Usurer. Similarly, in *The Trial of Chivalry* warring factions enter "*at one dore*" and "*at the other dore*" to exchange thirteen lines of dialogue before three figures "*enter in the middest*" of the opponents (I3 v–4r). And in *Patient Grissil* (1600) the direction "*Enter Urcenze and Onophrio at severall doores, and Farnezie in the mid'st*" (E3r) might signal entrances from three different doors, as Gurr believes[74]; but it might also indicate that the first two enter through *separate* doors and Farneze follows one of them on; "in the midst" then indicates Farneze's location once he is on stage. A direction in *Appius and Virginia* (1624) is probably a longer and more explicit version of this idea: "*Enter Virginius . . . coming into the midst of the souldiers, he makes a stand*" (H1r). The combination of "at one door" with "at the other door" makes it difficult to insist that there was a third door; but many directions call for figures to enter "at one door" and "at another door," which might seem to indicate more than two. However, the first *OED* definition of *another* is "One more, one further; originally *a second* of two things" (original emphasis[75]), which makes it more likely that "another door" is merely a variant of "the other door."[76] *Nobody and Somebody* (1605) includes a sequence of directions that might seem to indicate three doors:

> *Alarum, they watch the doores, Enter at one doore Cornwell.*
> *Alarum Enter at another doore Martianus.*
> *Alarum, Enter at another doore Elydure, stopt by the Queene.*   (F4r)

But as with the serial entrances considered above, dialogue separates each of these entrances, so here too "another" can simply designate a door different from the immediately previous one.

Several unique directions seem to call for a third opening in the tiring house wall. At the start of *The Four Prentices of London* (1594) is "*Enter three in black clokes, at three doores*" (A4r), which might be thought unambiguous. But one of the three immediately asks the others, "What meane you,

---

[73] Gurr, "Doors at the Globe," 61.   [74] Ibid.

[75] "Another, adj. and pron. (and adv.)." *OED Online*, Oxford University Press, September 2016.

[76] This meaning of "another" is unambiguous in a direction in *Patient Grissil*: "*Enter Babulo with a bundle of Osiers in one arme and a childe in another*" (G4r). And *The Court Secret* includes one direction for "*one dore*" and "*another*" and two for "*the other dore*" (B1r, B5v, E6r).

my maisters, to appeare thus before your times? Doe you not know that I am the Prologue? . . . to what end come you to interrupt mee?" (A4r), which could be understood to mean that he entered first and was followed on – interrupted – by the other two. Directions in the rest of this play refer to entrances at "*two severall dores*" (I2v) and two groups "*at one doore/at another doore*" (I3r), as well as exits of "*two one way, and two another way*" (K4r). *The Travails of Three English Brothers* (1607) includes a direction for the entrance of three groups:

> *Enter three severall waies the three Brothers, Robert with the state of Persia as before, Sir Anthonie, with the king of Spaine and others where hee receives the order of Saint Iago, and other Offices, Sir Thomas in England with his Father and others.* (H4v)

This might seem to mean that the three enter simultaneously, but the speech preceding the direction suggests that here "several doors" probably means that they each enter separately and go to a particular location on the stage:

> But would your apprehensions helpe poore art
> Into three parts deviding this our stage:
> They all at once shall take their leaves of you,
> Thinke this England, this Spaine, this Persia.   (H4r–v)

In both of these cases, if there were a third, central way onto the stage it could or would have been used; but the directions could instead have been intended for a two-door configuration.

The most explicit and least ambiguous reference to a central "door" is in *Eastward Ho!* (1605), which begins. "*Enter Maister Touch-stone, and Quick-silver at Severall dores, . . . At the middle dore, Enter Golding discovering a Gold-smiths shoppe, and walking short turnes before it*" (A2r). Based on this single example, Hosley says. "this evidence suggests that the Blackfriars tiring-house had three doors";[77] similarly, Gurr says that this direction "is about as explicit as one could hope for" and that "This implies three doors, the central one large enough to conceal a shop. It suggests the possibility that the arrangement was for a broad doorway or set of double doors in the centre flanked by two single doorways. Some authors certainly expected one of the doors, presumably the middle one if it was used for discoveries, to be curtained."[78] Not surprisingly, this direction is the one on which both Gurr and Fitzpatrick focus to defend their opposing positions. But it

[77] Hosley, "The Playhouses," 218.   [78] Gurr, *The Shakespearean Stage*, fourth edition, 200.

is worth noting that this reference to a "middle door" is unique and as such it should more properly be doubted than used as evidence of anything.

Fitzpatrick offers that the reference to Golding "'*walking short turns*' before the shop might suggest that it is not a large feature" and that "This is confirmed in the second stage direction" which refers to it "merely as a 'stall', evidently so small that no-one can sit inside it" – three figures sit "*on either side*" of it. Fitzpatrick continues,

> More importantly, this feature need not provide access to and from the tiring house: Golding could be pre-positioned in the goldsmith's shop before the start of the performance and 'enter' from there at the start of the play, and the three characters who go into it at the end of I, ii clearly do not leave the stage before reappearing at the start of II, i.[79]

The "feature" to which Fitzpatrick refers is his proposed "concealment space"; he argues – and provides staging plans to demonstrate – that most discovery scenes could have been located at one of the two doors and scenes like this one could have been pre-set behind a curtain and therefore would not need access to or from the tiring house. Gurr counters that this "idea of a 'concealment space' had to be imported into the Fitzpatrick concept because we know from stage directions written for the Blackfriars and other indoor plays that the hall theatres had a *frons scenae* with a third opening."[80] Gurr also says, however, that the initial stage direction in *Eastward Ho!* "specifically places one shop in each doorway," but in fact there is only one shop. Based on this incorrect premise, he concludes that Touchstone's shop, "the most pretentious of the three sets of wares on display, had to be set in the most imposing location, the central opening."[81] As these statements demonstrate, the disagreements between Gurr and Fitzpatrick over whether or not there was such an opening are fundamental to how each imagines early modern performance. Fitzpatrick's theory is essentially practical and logical: two doors and a temporary concealment space would have provided the best conditions for the entrances and exits of the players in the context of the action. Gurr's theory, by contrast, is as much or more aesthetic and thematic: a centre opening would have been necessary to create and express meaning in the context of the plot.

---

[79] Fitzpatrick, *Playwright, Space and Place*, 255.   [80] Gurr, "Doors at the Globe," 61.

[81] Ibid. Gurr may be confusing the direction in *Eastward Ho!* with the one at the start of the second act of *The Roaring Girl*, which begins, "*Three shops open in a ranke*" (C3r) and is, to my knowledge, the only such direction.

As I have already noted, Gurr's belief that the central opening had an "iconic function"[82] has led him to posit more uses for it than just discoveries. In particular, he says that "The authority signified by using the central opening for formal entries in royal processions was matched by harmonious exits at the close of most comedies and all of the plays where two warring factions have been reconciled."[83] The problem again, though, is the absence of textual evidence to support his statement. As a rule, when a large group with a "train" enters, no doors are specified, probably because only one group is entering (from one door); but when there is the simultaneous entrance of another group, two doors are specified. Two examples involve processional entrances of different groups, which perhaps explains why one door and the other door are specified:

> *Enter Pericles at one doore, with all his trayne, Cleon and Dioniza at the other.* (*Pericles*, G3r)

> *Enter Astorax the King of Paphos, his Sister Calis, traine, and Cleanthe, Lucippe Gentlewomen, at one doore. At the other Eumenes a Souldier.* (*The Mad Lover*, B1r)

But another direction calls for the grand entrance of figures and a chariot through "one door"; and "met by" suggests that Aretinus et al. brought on the prisoners through the other door:

> *Enter at one doore Captaines with Lawrels, Domitian, in his Triumphant Chariot, Parthenius, Paris, Latinus, AEsopus met by Aretinus, Sura, Lamia, Rusticus, Fulcinius, and prisoners led by him.* (*The Roman Actor*, C3v)

And this next direction for opposite entrances of two large groups refers only to "*the other door*":

> *Enter six of the Guard, their Halberts reverst, then a Cardinal, Landrey, Old Brissac; then the Herse born by six youung men, then King, Queen, Eunuch holding up her train, two or three Ladies, these in mourning: at the other door, a Headsman, two Nuns in white singing, Aphelia with a Garland on her head, led by two little boyes in white; after these, more Virgins adorned like the rest; both Troops passe by each other; the song ended, the Herse is set down between both companies, Aphelia mourning at one end, and the King at the other.* (*The Fatal Contract*, E3v)

---

[82] Ibid., 65.

[83] Gurr, "Staging at the Globe," 161. In the first three editions of *The Shakespearean Stage*, Gurr says there was "a curtained alcove or discovery-space in the tiring-house wall which served as a shop, tomb, cell, study or closet" (first and second editions, 137; third edition, 149); in the fourth edition he adds "and as the entry-point and exit-point for major processions" (183).

Although, as in these examples, two doors are sometimes specified for the kinds of grand or important entrances Gurr describes, a phrase like "the middle door/way" is never used for such entrances, neither does any exit direction specify or even imply the use of a centre opening. And if large properties such as beds and banquet tables could have been brought on through one of the two doors, the absence of any playtext references to a central opening for such entrances is explained. The idea that bringing on such properties through a central opening was common practice so not specified is belied by the numerous directions that refer to the doors. Over time, as Gurr has repeated and elaborated his ideas about the multiple uses of a central opening, he has created a persuasive narrative of playhouse practice, so it is easy to forget that it is both premised on the existence of such an opening *and* an attempt to justify that existence.

Because Fitzpatrick's focus is the practical business of performance on the early modern stage, his argument is, essentially, that a third opening, for which we have little or no evidence, would have made performance more difficult by creating exceptions and inconsistencies that would not have existed with only two doors. In the article he co-wrote with Millyard, they take on Gurr's assumption that there was a wide central opening "used for special functions, in particular discoveries and beds." They address his belief in "the need for a third opening to enable such discoveries to be enacted without causing logistical problems at the lateral doors," arguing that "a third opening for discoveries can only be judged a necessity if both the doors are otherwise committed to accommodate entrances to the discovery." In the context of "entrances and exits in Elizabethan and Jacobean performance," they find "no cases in which a third opening to set up a discovery would relieve continuity problems between scenes. In fact discovery scenes often seem deliberately structured to enable two doors to suffice, and result in more logical movement patterns."[84]

Fitzpatrick nevertheless readily acknowledges that "There is no doubt that there was some upstage central feature":

> it might have been a concealment space for onstage characters, involving curtains hung against (or slightly forward of) the wall, but providing no access to and from the tiring house. As such, this feature might have been temporary, with the curtains hung only if required by a particular play – which might account for its absence from de Witt's sketch.[85]

---

[84] Fitzpatrick and Millyard, "Hangings, Doors and Discoveries," 7–8. See Fitzpatrick's *Playwright, Space and Place* for numerous detailed examples of discoveries that could have been set in one of the two lateral doors (261–80).

[85] Fitzpatrick, *Playwright, Space and Place*, 253.

Fitzpatrick is not alone in positing this kind of fixture; the key difference is that he envisions a concealment space with no access to the tiring house, whereas other theatre historians have explicitly or implicitly imagined a temporary fixture in front of a central opening through which figures and properties could and did enter and exit. Again, this difference is important because, as Fitzpatrick observes and Gurr's increasingly elaborate theories demonstrate, it is most unlikely that if there had been a central opening it would have been used only for discoveries, but we have no textual evidence of such an opening being regularly used for other purposes.

The need to reconcile the occasions when some kind of central fixture seems to be required for a discovery with the absence of anything between the two doors of the Swan drawing, has prompted a variety of suggestions, some more complex than others. In 1953 Walter Hodges asserted that "the Shakespearean public stage had its origin in the common scaffold stage of the street theatres" and that this evolved into a tiring house wall with a temporary "fit-up structure" projecting from it.[86] Reynolds's survey of the evidence from Red Bull plays led him to "the conclusion that the discoverable space was not a permanent feature of the stage."[87] In a later work he says, "I find I have been referred to as denying any rear stage in the Elizabethan theatre, but that is not true. I have questioned the existence, especially in the early years, of a built-in rear stage as a permanent part of the theatres. But I have supposed that there was always some way of making discoveries, suggesting that curtains may have been mounted on a movable framework, which, when desired, could have been put in place in front of the tiring-house wall."[88] Southern asks if it was possible that "the Elizabethan player was quite capable of rigging a 'discovery space' in circumstances like those shown by De Witt, if he wanted to," and answers, "Indeed, the whole history of the booth stage would seem to lead up to giving him just that knowledge."[89] William Armstrong posits that *canopy* could refer to "a curtained, roof-like projection from the rear wall of the stage" and he notes that

---

[86] C. Walter Hodges, *The Globe Restored*, 49–50, 60. Versions of this structure recur in Hodges's many drawings of scenes in early modern plays, especially in the Cambridge Shakespeare series, which has given them wide circulation. As attractive as they are, however, these drawings are problematic because although what they depict is almost completely imaginary, they have long provided realistic-seeming images that are difficult to forget and therefore very influential.

[87] G. F. Reynolds, *The Staging of Elizabethan Plays at the Red Bull*, 162.

[88] G. F. Reynolds, *On Shakespeare's Stage*, 107, note 21.

[89] Richard Southern, *Seven Ages of the Theatre*, 180.

the vignette on the title-page of N. Richards' *Messallina* depicts a wide ledge hung with curtains and projecting from the rear wall of a stage. In his definition of *scena* as "*properly the fore-part of a Theater where Plaiers make them ready, being trimmed with hangings, from out which they enter vpon the stage,*" John Florio may have been referring to a projecting canopy (*fore-part*) equipped with curtains (*hangings*) and enclosing an area to which the players had access via a door or opening in the tiring-house façade. In his inventory of the properties of the Admiral's Men, Henslowe lists "j wooden canepie." Hung with curtains and attached to the rear wall of a stage and supported with posts, this solid canopy may have been used for discoveries and interior scenes at the Rose and other public theatres.[90]

In his study of the *Messallina* title page illustration, discussed above, Astington notes that its engraver, Thomas Rawlins, was also a man of the theatre, and considers whether his "adaptations to [the *Roxana*] design were made to match what he knew of the [Salisbury Court] playhouse, or at least what he expected of it."[91] Astington says that "As a theatrical structure" what Rawlins "shows behind the stage is a far more likely arrangement." In particular, the *Messallina* illustration "shows the tiring house wall only at the upper level; on the stage a projecting curtained enclosure with a practical acting level forming its roof has been built out, possibly as a temporary arrangement for a particular play, in a fashion which has frequently been suggested by modern stage historians."[92] With reference to the Rose playhouse, Scott McMillin argues for a fixture he refers to as a "curtained pavilion" and a "special enclosure" used for "raised and enclosed scenes."[93] Gurr says that "McMillin thinks of a single demountable structure for the discovery space and the 'above', what he calls 'a removable pavilion, curtained below for discoveries and interiors, its roof affording ample space above.'" Gurr comments (rightly, I think) that "This does not seem very likely, given that, as we know from Henslowe's lists, a different play was staged each day, which meant dismantling the structure almost daily."[94] This objection cannot be made about J. L. Styan's more minimalist concept: "It is uncomplicated: an arras to sleep or to die behind, a space for an eavesdropper to hide in, a cloak to mask a special property . . . – these needs can be met by a curtain, one either permanently hung from the

---

[90] William Armstrong, "Actors and Theatres," 202–3, original emphasis.

[91] Astington, "The Origins of the *Roxana* and *Messalina* Illustrations," 168.

[92] However, Astington also provides reasons why "one is prepared to trust Rawlins's grasp of practicality only so far" ("Origins," 168).

[93] Scott McMillin, "The Rose and the Swan," 163. Jean Wilson notes how some tomb sculptures feature a projecting bay with curtains (*The Archaeology of Shakespeare*, 90–3).

[94] Andrew Gurr, "The Rose Repertory," 124.

projecting edge of the balcony between the doors or improvised for the production in hand." Styan adds that "There is a danger in making this curtain into a structure of timbers and hangings as immobile as the mythical inner stage itself."[95]

Significantly, unlike theories of a central opening, these repeated references to curtains in relation to discoveries are warranted by the stage directions themselves. Indeed, if we look for textual evidence of how discoveries were staged, the use of curtains is readily and repeatedly apparent. Moreover, of the approximately ninety references to curtains in stage directions (in about sixty plays), only nine refer to *a* curtain whereas the rest refer to *the* curtain(s), which could mean that they were a stock property always present or easily installed when needed. The use of curtains to effect a discovery would have been both practical and thematic; indeed, if the curtains were present only when they were going to be used, playgoers would have looked forward to a discovery.

As to how and where these curtains would have been hung, a purpose-built structure is a possibility but the evidence of one is sparse to non-existent and, as Gurr notes, such a structure would have had to be repeatedly set up and removed. But curtains that were simply suspended from an overhang projecting from the gallery level, as seems to be shown in the *Messallina* illustration, is an attractive idea. Discovered scenes are often shallow tableaux, as Hosley notes, so they could have fit behind a curtain hanging a couple of feet forward of the wall. If Fitzpatrick is correct that there would have been no access to this temporary space from the tiring house, discovery scenes that included large properties would have been set in one of the two doorways hung with curtains, as he says. Fitzpatrick refers several times to the probability that the tiring house wall at the round Rose playhouse was "angled" (Bowsher's term), arguing that if a curtain were hung in front of this concave wall, a concealment space would have been created naturally.[96] But even if the Rose had such a tiring house wall, the Swan did not, and it is unlikely that any rectangular playhouse had one either. Fitzpatrick also reluctantly allows the possibility that some playhouses had a centre opening in the tiring house wall, but it seems to me that this weakens his argument, a premise of which is the consistency and repeatability of performance practices. At the same time, however, companies such as the King's Men performed elsewhere than purpose-built playhouses – in the provinces and at court – so some degree of flexibility would have been necessary. Certainly the aesthetic appeal of a centrally

[95] J. L. Styan, *Shakespeare's Stagecraft*, 23.   [96] Fitzpatrick, *Playwright, Space and Place*, 36, 352.

located focal point is strong, and we have plenty of evidence of such a configuration in contemporaneous architecture and pictorial arts, in which a central framing arch, often within a triptych structure, is the basic motif. More particularly, many works of art – including a number of the illustrations used earlier in this study – depict a centrally placed revelation. This does not constitute evidence that discovery scenes were similarly staged, but it does raise the possibility that playwrights would have imagined the same configuration. Gurr argues that "the function of a central opening is ... far too potent a symbol in the concept of early staging, to be ignored."[97] He believes that there was a permanent central opening; but it is also possible that curtains were used to create a temporary discovery space. Fitzpatrick points out that because his concealment space did not have access to the tiring house, only scenes that could have been pre-set before the start of the play – such as the shop at the start of *Eastward Ho!* – would have been discovered there. But it is also possible that on the non-realistic early modern stage, players went into the concealment space during act-breaks or performance, giving playgoers reason to expect a discovery. If this was common practice, there would have been no need to signal it in a stage direction.

My purpose here has not been to insist that there was no central opening in any tiring house wall but rather, prompted by Fitzpatrick (with whom I do not always or necessarily agree), to look at the arguments and evidence for such a feature. As a result, for the reasons discussed above I have found myself with less and less confidence that such an opening existed in most playhouses. I want to agree with Gurr and others that it would seem to make sense aesthetically and practically for discoveries to have been staged in a central opening, for props to have been brought on and taken off through it, and even for formal entrances and exits to have been made through it. But these theories grow out of modern perspectives, and I keep returning to the same questions: why is there no early modern term for this fixture and why do no stage directions signal these uses for it, when directions do regularly signal the use of two doors, the area above and the trap? While the absence of evidence is not necessarily evidence of absence, it is surely significant that no unequivocal reference to a central opening exists in stage directions, which, after all, are not simply descriptions but prescriptions for performance by players in a physical space. If I could reconcile myself to this silence, I could more easily accept Gurr's theories and reject Fitzpatrick's; but even after (or perhaps because of)

---

[97] Gurr, "Doors at the Globe," 68.

having researched and written this appendix, I cannot. Consequently, my discussions of discovery scenes in the previous chapters assume only that the players knew how to stage them and that they did so successfully.

Opportunities to test theories about the configuration of the tiring house wall exist in the form of several modern "reconstructions" of early modern playhouses, notably Shakespeare's Globe in London (opened in 1997), the Blackfriars playhouse in Staunton, VA (2001), and the Sam Wanamaker playhouse in London (2014). All three venues ostensibly emulate the staging conditions for which Shakespeare and his contemporaries wrote their plays. But each of these playhouses has a central opening in the tiring house wall, and to my knowledge none has experimented with a two-door configuration in performance. This omission is particularly noteworthy in the case of the Wanamaker playhouse because, although – like the Staunton Blackfriars – it is based on the Worcester College drawings, those involved in the planning and construction of the Wanamaker knew of Higgott's 2005 conclusion that the drawings were made after the Restoration (discussed above).[98] Indeed, this new information should provide another reason for staging experiments that evaluate the two possible configurations equally. In any of the three venues, the central opening could be closed and hidden with a curtain to create something like what is represented in the de Witt/van Buchel drawing of the Swan. If nothing else, staging experiments that took Fitzpatrick's ideas seriously might show that they do not work and give support to Gurr's theories, not just about the existence of a central opening but also about the ways he believes it was used.[99] Or they might prove Fitzpatrick to be largely correct and to prompt the development of new staging practices for early modern plays.

In the conclusion of his 1975 overview of the playhouses, Hosley says that the "device of discovery was essentially a 'show' (usually for the benefit of characters on stage) of a character or object invested with some special interest or significance."[100] If discovery scenes exist primarily because of their thematic significance, which is based partly on extra-dramatic ideas and associations of the mysterious or private, then approaching them primarily as staging problems to be solved is the wrong place to start. To put it another way, if real-world associations determined the use of what might be called "place-discoveries" (of studies, shops, tombs, caves), perhaps playwrights called for them *despite* the staging requirements, even,

---

[98] See in particular Andrew Gurr and Farah Karim-Cooper, *Moving Shakespeare Indoors*, 1–2.
[99] Gurr was a consultant on all three projects.   [100] Hosley, "The Playhouses," 233.

paradoxically, because of the visual effects achieved by locating action in a space that was difficult to see into. Hosley also notes that a discovery scene "did not involve movement in depth within the discovery-space, for the discovered player (initially framed for a moment or two in the open doorway) usually leaves the discovery-space and comes forward upon the stage immediately or shortly after being discovered."[101] Thus the symbolic effect was achieved, but visibility was not inhibited for too long. Furthermore, as I have noted, viewers within the play typically respond to discovery scenes by talking about what they see, effectively describing what some playgoers could not see while also emphasizing the significance of what has been revealed.

[101] Ibid.

Bibliography

Primary Works – Dramatic

Unless otherwise indicated, the editions listed are at Early English Books Online and the place of publication is London. Play titles have been modernized.

Anon., *Alphonsus, Emperor of Germany* (1654), Wing C1952.

Anon., *Arden of Faversham* (1592), STC 733.

Anon., *The Bloody Banquet* (1639), STC 6181.

Anon., *Captain Thomas Stukeley* (1605), STC 23405.

Anon., *The Costly Whore* (1633), STC 25582a.

Anon., *Edmond Ironside*, ed. Eleanore Boswell (Oxford: The Malone Society, 1927).

Anon., *Faithful Friends*, ed. G. M. Pinciss and G. R. Proudfoot (Oxford: The Malone Society, 1975).

Anon., *The Family of Love* (1608), STC 17879.

Anon., *King Leir* (1605), STC 15343.

Anon., *A Knack to Know an Honest Man* (1596), STC 15028.

Anon., *London Prodigal* (1605), STC 22333.

Anon., *Ludus Coventriae*, ed. K. S. Block (London: Early English Text Society, Oxford University Press, 1922).

Anon., *The Maid's Metamorphosis* (1600), STC 17188.

Anon., *The Merry Devil of Edmonton* (1608), STC 7493.

Anon., *Mucedorus* (1598), STC 18230.

Anon., *Mucedorus* (1610), STC 18232.

Anon., *Nobody and Somebody* (1606), STC 18597.

Anon., *The Pride of Life* in *Two Moral Interludes*, ed. David Klausner (Kalamazoo, MI: Medieval Institute, 2008).

Anon., *The Second Shepherds' Pageant* in *Everyman and Medieval Miracle Plays*, ed. A. C. Cawley (London: J. M. Dent, 1974).

Anon., *Swetnam the Woman Hater* (1620), STC 23544.

Anon., *Thomas, Lord Cromwell* (1602), STC 21532.

Anon., *Tom a Lincoln*, ed. G. R. Proudfoot and H. R. Woudhuysen (Oxford: The Malone Society, 1991).

Anon., *The Trial of Chivalry* (1605), STC 13527.

Anon., *The Two Noble Ladies*, ed. R. G. Rhoads (Oxford: The Malone Society, 1930).

Anon., *The Wisdom of Doctor Dodypoll* (1600), STC 6991.

Armin, Robert, *The Two Maids of Moreclacke* (1609), STC 773.

The Valiant Welshman (1615), STC 16.

Barnes, Barnaby, *The Devil's Charter* (1607), STC 1466.

Beaumont, Francis, *The Knight of the Burning Pestle* (London, 1613), STC 1674.

The Woman Hater (1607), STC 1692.

Beaumont, Francis and John Fletcher, *Philaster* (1620), STC 1681.5.

Philaster (1622), STC 1682.

Berkeley, William, *The Lost Lady* (1638), STC 1901.5.

Brome, Richard, *The Antipodes* (1640), STC 3818.

A Jovial Crew (1652), Wing B4873.

The Queen and Concubine in *Five New Playes* (1659), Wing B4872.

The Sparagus Garden (1640), STC 3820.

Carlell, Lodowick, *The Deserving Favourite* (1629), STC 4628.

The Fool Would Be a Favourite (1657), Wing C580.

Osmond, the Great Turk (1657), Wing C579.

Chapman, George, *The Widow's Tears* (1612), STC 4994.

Chapman, George, Ben Jonson and John Marston, *Eastward Ho!* (1605), STC 4970

Chettle, Henry, *Hoffman* (1631), STC 5125.

Cooke, Jo., *Greene's Tu Quoque* (1614), STC 5673.

Davenant, William, *Albovine* (1629), STC 6307.

The Distresses in *The Works of Sr. William Davenant* (1673), Wing D320.

News from Plymouth in *The Works of Sr. William Davenant* (1673), Wing D320.

The Platonic Lovers (1636), STC 6305.

Davenant, William and Inigo Jones, *Britannia Triumphans* (1638), STC 14718.

Davenport, Robert, *The City Nightcap* (1661), Wing D369.

Day, John, *Law Tricks* (1608), STC 6416.

The Travails of Three English Brothers (1607), STC 6417.

Dekker, Thomas, *If It Be Not Good, the Devil Is in It* (1612), STC 6507.

Match Me in London (1631), STC 6529.

Old Fortunatus (1600), STC 6517.

Patient Grissel (1603), STC 6518.

Satiromastix (1602), STC 6521.

The Shoemakers' Holiday (1600), STC 6523.

The Whore of Babylon (1607), STC 6532.

Dekker, Thomas and Thomas Middleton, *The Honest Whore, part 1* (1604), STC 6501.

Field, Nathan, *Amends for Ladies* (1618), STC 10851.

Fletcher, John, *The Faithful Shepherdess* (1610), STC 11068.

The Lovers' Progress in *Comedies and Tragedies Written by Francis Beaumont and John Fletcher* (1647), Wing B1581.

The Mad Lover in *Comedies and Tragedies Written by Francis Beaumont and John Fletcher* (1647), Wing B1581.

Monsieur Thomas (1639), STC 11071.

Rule a Wife and Have a Wife (1640) STC 11073.

Fletcher, John and Philip Massinger, *The Custom of the Country* in *Comedies and Tragedies Written by Francis Beaumont and John Fletcher* (1647), Wing B1581.

Fletcher, John and Nathan Field, *Four Plays in One* (1647) in *Comedies and Tragedies Written by Francis Beaumont and John Fletcher* (1647), Wing B1581.

The Honest Man's Fortune in *Comedies and Tragedies Written by Francis Beaumont and John Fletcher* (1647), Wing B1581.

The Honest Man's Fortune, ed. Grace Ioppolo (Oxford: The Malone Society, 2011).

Fletcher, John, Nathan Field and Philip Massinger, *The Knight of Malta* in *Comedies and Tragedies Written by Francis Beaumont and John Fletcher* (1647), Wing B1581.

Fletcher, John and Philip Massinger, *Sir John van Olden Barnavelt*, ed. T. H. Howard-Hill (Oxford: The Malone Society, 1979).

Ford, John, *The Broken Heart* (1633), STC 11156.

The Lover's Melancholy (1629), STC 11163.

Love's Sacrifice (1633), STC 11164.

Garter, Thomas, *The Most Virtuous and Godly Susanna* (1578), STC 11632.5.

Glapthorne, Henry, *The Hollander* (1640), STC 11909.

Hemings, William, *The Fatal Contract* (1653), Wing H1422.

The Jews' Tragedy (1662), Wing H1425.

Heywood, Thomas, *The Brazen Age* (1613), STC 13310.

The English Traveller (1633), STC 13315.

The Fair Maid of the Exchange (1607), STC 13317.

The Fair Maid of the West, part 1 (1631), STC 13320.

The Four Prentices of London (1615), STC 13321.

The Golden Age (1611), STC 13325.

How a Man May Choose a Good Wife from a Bad (1602), STC 5594.

Love's Mistress (1636), STC 13352.

A Maidenhead Well Lost (1634), STC 13357.

The Iron Age, part 1 (1632), STC 13340.

The Rape of Lucrece (1608), STC 13360.

The Wise Woman of Hogsdon (1638), STC 13370.

J. C., *The Two Merry Milkmaids* (1620), STC 4281.

Jonson, Ben, *Bartholomew Fair* (1631), STC 14753.5.

The Case Is Altered (1609), STC 14757.

Catiline in *The Workes of Benjamin Jonson* (1616), STC 14751.

Epicoene in *The Workes of Benjamin Jonson* (1616), STC 14751.

Hymenaei (1606), STC 14774.

The Speeches at Prince Henry's Barriers in *The Workes of Benjamin Jonson* (1616), STC 14751.

The Staple of News (1631), STC 14753.5.

Volpone in *The Workes of Benjamin Jonson* (1616), STC 14751.

Killigrew, Thomas, *The Prisoners* (1641), STC 14959.

Kyd, Thomas, *The Spanish Tragedy* (1592), STC 15086.

Kyd, Thomas et al., *The Spanish Tragedy* (1602), STC 15089.

Lodge, Thomas and Robert Greene, *A Looking-Glass for London and England* (1594), STC 16679.

Marlowe, Christopher, *Dido, Queen of Carthage* (1594), STC 17441.

Doctor Faustus (1604), STC 17429.

Doctor Faustus (1616), STC 17432.

Edward II (1594), STC 17437.

The Jew of Malta (1633), STC 17412.

The Massacre at Paris (1594), STC 17423.

Tamburlaine, part 2 (1590), STC 17425.

Marston, John, *Antonio and Mellida* (1602), STC 17473.

The Malcontent (1604), STC 17481.

Sophonisba, or the Wonder of Women (1606), STC 17488.

What You Will (1607), STC 17487.

Marston, John, William Barkstead and Lewis Machin, *The Insatiate Countess* (1613), STC 17476.

Massinger, Philip, *The Bondman* (1624), STC 17632.

The Guardian in *Three New Playes* (1655), Wing M1050.

The Renegado (1630), STC 17641.

The Roman Actor (1629), STC 17642.

The Virgin Martyr (1622), STC 17644.

May, Thomas, *The Heir* (1622), STC 17713.

Mayne, Jasper, *The City Match* (1639), STC 17750.

Middleton, Thomas, *A Chaste Maid in Cheapside* (1630), STC 17877.

A Game at Chess (London? 1625?), STC 17884.

A Game at Chess (London? 1625), STC 17885.

Hengist, King of Kent, ed. Grace Ioppolo (Oxford: The Malone Society, 2003).

Michaelmas Term (1607), STC 17890.

No Wit, No Help Like a Woman's (1657), Wing M1985.

The Phoenix (1607), STC 17892.

The Revenger's Tragedy (1607), STC 24149.

The Roaring Girl (1611), STC 17908.

The Second Maiden's Tragedy, ed. Horace Hart (Oxford: The Malone Society, 1909).

The Sun in Aries (1621), STC 17895.

A Trick to Catch the Old One (1608), STC 17896.

The Triumphs of Truth (1615), STC 17904.

Your Five Gallants (1608), STC 17907.

Middleton, Thomas and William Rowley, *The Changeling* (1653), Wing M1980.

The World Tossed at Tennis (1620), STC 17909.

Middleton, Thomas and John Webster, *Anything for a Quiet Life* (1662), Wing M1979.

Munday, Anthony, *The Downfall of Robert, Earl of Huntington* (1601), STC 18271.

Peele, George, *David and Bethsabe* (1599), STC 19540.

    Edward I (1593), STC 19535.

    The Old Wives Tale (1595), STC 19545.

Rowley, William, *A Match at Midnight* (1633), STC 21421.

    A Shoemaker, a Gentleman (1638), STC 21422.

S. S., *The Honest Lawyer* (1616), STC 21519.

Shakespeare, William, *All's Well That Ends Well* in *Mr. William Shakespeares Comedies, Histories, & Tragedies* (1623), STC 22273.

    The Comedy of Errors in *Mr. William Shakespeares Comedies, Histories, & Tragedies* (1623), STC 22273.

    Cymbeline in *Mr. William Shakespeares Comedies, Histories, & Tragedies* (1623), STC 22273.

    The First Part of the Contention (1594), STC 26099.

    Hamlet (1604), STC 22276.

    Henry IV, part 1 (1598), STC 22280.

    Julius Caesar in *Mr. William Shakespeares Comedies, Histories, & Tragedies* (1623), STC 22273.

    King Lear (1608), STC 22292.

    Macbeth in *Mr. William Shakespeares Comedies, Histories, & Tragedies* (1623), STC 22273.

    Measure for Measure in *Mr. William Shakespeares Comedies, Histories, & Tragedies* (1623), STC 22273.

    The Merchant of Venice (1600), STC 22296.

    Much Ado About Nothing (1600), STC 22304.

    Othello (1622), STC 22305.

    Othello in *Mr. William Shakespeares Comedies, Histories, & Tragedies* (1623), STC 22273.

    Richard III (1597), STC 22314.

    Romeo and Juliet (1597), STC 22322.

    Romeo and Juliet (1599), STC 22323.

    The Tempest in *Mr. William Shakespeares Comedies, Histories, & Tragedies* (1623), STC 22273.

    Troilus and Cressida (1609), STC 22331.

    Twelfth Night in *Mr. William Shakespeares Comedies, Histories, & Tragedies* (1623), STC 22273.

    The Two Gentlemen of Verona in *Mr. William Shakespeares Comedies, Histories, & Tragedies* (1623), STC 22273.

    The Winter's Tale in *Mr. William Shakespeares Comedies, Histories, & Tragedies* (1623), STC 22273.

Shakespeare, William and John Fletcher, *Henry VIII* in *Mr. William Shakespeares Comedies, Histories, & Tragedies* (1623), STC 22273.

Shakespeare, William and George Wilkins, *Pericles* (1609), STC 22334.

Sharpham, Edward, *The Fleer* (1607), STC 22384.
Shirley, Henry, *The Martyred Soldier* (1638), STC 22435.
Shirley, James, *The Court Secret* (1653), Wing S3463.
　The Humorous Courtier (1640), STC 22447.
　The Sisters (1652), Wing S3485.
Suckling, John, *Brennoralt* (1646), Wing S6122.
Tourneur, Cyril, *The Atheist's Tragedy* (1611), STC 24146.
Townshend, Aurelian. *Albion's Triumph* (1632), STC 24155.
Udall, Nicholas, *Respublica*, ed. W. W. Greg (London: Early English Text Society, Oxford University Press, 1952).
Webster, John, *Appius and Virginia* (1654), Wing W1215.
　The Duchess of Malfi (1623), STC 25176.
Wilson, Arthur, *The Inconstant Lady: A Critical Edition*, ed. Linda V. Itzoe (New York, NY and London: Garland, 1980).
Yarington, Robert, *Two Lamentable Tragedies* (1601), STC 26076.

Primary Works – Non-Dramatic

Anon., *A Discoverie of the Treasons Practised and Attempted against the Queenes Majestie and the Realme, by Francis Throckemorton* (1584), STC 24051.
Badius, Conrad, *The Newe Testament* (Geneva, 1557).
Banister, John, *The Historie of Man Sucked from the Sappe of the Most Approved Anathomistes* (1578), STC 1359.
Berengarius, *Carpi commentaria cūm amplissimis additionibus super Anatomia Mūndini vna cum textu eiusdēm in pristinūm et verum nitorèm redacto* (Bologna, 1521).
Day, Angell, *The English Secretorie*, part II (1592), STC 6402.
Dekker, Thomas, *The Magnificent Entertainment Giuen to King Iames, Queene Anne his Wife, and Henry Frederick the Prince, vpon the Day of his Maiesties Tryumphant Passage (from the Tower) through his Honourable Citie (and Chamber) of London, being the 15. Of March. 1603* (1604), STC 6510.
de Montes, R. González, *A Discovery and Playne Declaration of the Sundry Subtill Practises of the Holy Inquisition of Spayne* (1569), STC 11997.
Durandus, William, *The Symbolism of Churches and Church Ornaments*: a translation of the first book of the *Rationale divinorum officiorum*, Introductory essay and notes by John Mason Neale and Benjamin Webb (Leeds: T. W. Green, 1843; third edition, Gibbings, 1906).
Dyke, Daniel, *The Mystery of Selfe-Deceiving. Or A Discourse and Discovery of the Deceitfullnesse of Mans Heart* (1614), STC 7398.
Greene, Robert, *Pandosto the Triumph of Time* (1588), STC 12285.
Harrison, Stephen, *The Arch's of Triumph Erected in Honor of the High and Mighty Prince James* (1604), STC 12863.

Hieron, Samuel, *The Discoverie of Hypocrisie in Two Sermons, upon Mathew. 3. verse. 10. And Three Other, Called the Perfect Patterne of True Conversion, upon Matth. 13. ver. 44* (1607), STC 13398.5.

The Holie Bible Conteynyng the Olde Testament and the Newe (1568), STC 2099.

Jonson, Ben, *B. Jon: His Part of King James His Royall and Magnificent Entertainement* (1604), STC 14756.

Junius, Hadrianus, *Hadriani Junii Medici Emblemata* (Antwerp, 1565).

Mainardi, Agostino, *An Anatomi: That Is to Say A Parting in Peeces of the Mass. Which Discovereth the Horrible Errors, and the Infinite Abuses Unknown to the People, Aswel of the Mass as of the Mass Book* (1556), STC 17200.

Marshall, William, *The Goodly Prymer in Englyshe* (1538), STC 15998.

Palmer, Thomas, *The Emblems of Thomas Palmer: Two Hundred Poosees, Sloane MS 3794*, ed. John Manning (New York: AMS Press, 1988).

Quarles, Francis, *Emblemes* (1535), STC 20540.

R. S., *Interiorum corporis humani partium* (1559), STC 564.6.

Robinson, Thomas, *The Anatomie of the English Nunnery at Lisbon in Portugall Dissected and Laid Open by One that Was Sometime a Yonger Brother of the Covent* (1623), STC 21126.

Scot, Reginald, *The Discoverie of Witchcraft* (1584), STC 21864.

Shakespeare, William, *Lucrece* (1594), STC 22345.

Sparke, Michael, *The Narrative History of King James, for the First Fourteen Years in Four Parts* (1561), Wing S4818.

Stanley, Sir William, *A Briefe Discoverie of Doctor Allens Seditious Drifts* (1588), STC 6166.

Wadsworth, James, *The English Spanish Pilgrime. Or, A New Discoverie of Spanish Popery, and Jesuiticall Stratagems* (1629), STC 24926.

Whitney, Geffrey, *A Choice of Emblemes and Other Devises* (Leyden, 1586).

Willis, Richard, *Mount Tabor. Or Private Exercises of a Penitent Sinner* (1639), STC 25752.

Secondary Works Consulted and Cited

Adams, John Cranford, *The Globe Playhouse: Its Design and Equipment* (Cambridge, MA: Harvard University Press, 1942).

Anderson, M. D., *Drama and Imagery in English Medieval Churches* (Cambridge University Press, 1963).

Anglo, Sydney, "The Evolution of the Early Tudor Disguising, Pageant, and Mask," *Renaissance Drama*, 1 (1968), 3–44.

Archer, Ian W., "Material Londoners?" in *Material London, ca. 1600*, ed. Lena Cowen Orlin (Philadelphia, PA: University of Pennsylvania Press, 2000).

Armstrong, William A., "Actors and Theatres," *Shakespeare Survey*, 17 (1964), 191–204, doi.org/10.1017/ccol0521064309.017.

Astington, John H., "The Origins of the *Roxana* and *Messalina* Illustrations," *Shakespeare Survey* 43 (1991), 149–69, doi.org/10.1017/ccol0521395291.014.

"*The Wits* Illustration, 1662," *Theatre Notebook*, 47 (1993), 122–40.

Aston, Margaret, *The King's Bedpost* (Cambridge University Press, 1993).

Augustine, *Concerning the City of God against the Pagans*, trans. and ed. Henry Bettenson (Harmsworth: Penguin, 1972).

Baker, Susan, "Personating Persons: Rethinking Shakespearean Disguises," *Shakespeare Quarterly*, 43 (1992), 303–16, doi.org/10.2307/2870530.

Barbour, Reid, *Deciphering Elizabethan Fiction* (Newark, DE: Delaware University Press; London and Toronto: Associated University Presses, 1993).

Barish, Jonas, "The Double Plot in *Volpone*," *Modern Philology*, 51 (1953), 83–92.

Bawcutt, N. W., ed., *The Jew of Malta* by Christopher Marlowe (Manchester: Manchester University Press; Baltimore, MD: Johns Hopkins University Press, 1978).

Beckerman, Bernard, *Shakespeare at the Globe, 1599–1609* (New York, NY: Macmillan, 1962).

"The Use and Management of the Elizabethan Stage," in *The Third Globe: Symposium for the Reconstruction of the Globe Playhouse*, ed. C. Walter Hodges, S. Schoenbaum and Leonard Leone (Detroit, MI: Wayne State University Press, 1981), 151–63.

Bergeron, David M., *English Civic Pageantry, 1558–1642*, rev. ed. (Tempe, AZ: Arizona Center for Medieval and Renaissance Studies, 2003).

Bevington, David, *Action Is Eloquence* (Cambridge, MA: Harvard University Press, 1984).

Bowers, Fredson, *Elizabethan Revenge Tragedy, 1587–1642* (Princeton University Press, 1940).

Bowsher, Julian, *The Rose Theatre* (Museum of London, 1998).

Bowsher, Julian and Pat Miller, *The Rose and the Globe – Playhouses of Shakespeare's Bankside, Southwark* (Museum of London, 2009).

Bradbrook, Muriel, "Shakespeare and the Use of Disguise in Elizabethan Drama," *Essays in Criticism*, 2 (1952), 159–68, doi.org/10.bradley1093/eic/ii.2.159.

Broude, Ronald, "Time, Truth, and Right in *The Spanish Tragedy*," *Studies in Philology*, 68 (1971), 130–45.

Brown, Keith, "More Light, More Kight," *Essays in Criticism*, 34 (1984), 1–13, doi.org/10.1093/eic/xxxiv.1.1.

Butler, Martin, "Private and Occasional Drama" in *The Cambridge Companion to English Renaissance Drama*, ed. A. R. Braunmuller and Michael Hattaway (Cambridge University Press, 1990).

Calvo, Clara and Jesús Tronch, ed., *The Spanish Tragedy* (London: Bloomsbury, 2015).

Campbell, Lily B., *Scenes and Machines on the English Stage during the Renaissance* (Cambridge University Press, 1923; rpt. New York, NY: Barnes and Noble, 1960).

Campbell, Thomas P., "Liturgy and Drama: Recent Approaches to Medieval Theatre," *Theatre Journal*, 33 (1981), 289–301, doi.org/10.2307/3207028.

Carroll, William C., *The Metamorphoses of Shakespearean Comedy* (Princeton, NJ: Princeton University Press, 1985).

Cave, Terence, *Recognitions: A Study in Poetics* (Oxford: Clarendon Press, 1988).

Chambers, E. K., *The Elizabethan Stage*, 4 vols. (Oxford University Press, 1923). *The Medieval Stage*, 2 vols. (Oxford University Press, 1903).

Chew, Samuel, *The Pilgrimage of Life* (New Haven, CT and London: Yale University Press, 1962).

Cox, Nancy and Clare Walsh, "'Their Shops Are Dens, the Buyer Is Their Prey': Shop Design and Sale Techniques" in *The Complete Tradesman: A Study of Retailing, 1550–1820*, ed. Nancy Cox (Aldershot, Hants: Ashgate, 2000).

Crandall, Coryl, *"Swetnam the Woman-hater": The Controversy and the Play* (West Lafayette, IN: Purdue University Studies, 1969).

Cressy, David and Lori Anne Ferrell, *Religion and Society in Early Modern England: A Sourcebook* (London and New York, NY: Routledge, 1996), doi.org/10 .4324/9780203221808.

Danson, Lawrence and Ivo Camps, ed., *The Phoenix* in *Thomas Middleton, The Collected Works*, ed. Gary Taylor, John Lavagnino and John Jowett (Oxford University Press, 2007).

Davis, Lloyd, *Guise and Disguise: Rhetoric and Characterization in the English Renaissance* (University of Toronto Press, 1993).

Dessen, Alan C., "Editing and Staging *The Revenger's Tragedy*: Three Problems" in *Early Modern Drama in Performance: Essays in Honor of Lois Potter*, ed. Bradley Ryner, Darlene Farabee and Mark Netzloff (University of Delaware Press, 2013).

Elizabethan Stage Conventions and Modern Interpreters (Cambridge University Press, 1984).

Recovering Shakespeare's Theatrical Vocabulary (Cambridge University Press, 1995).

"Stage Directions as Evidence: The Question of Provenance" in *Shakespeare: Text and Theater*, ed. Lois Potter and Arthur F. Kinney (Newark, DE: Associated University Presses, 1999), 229–47.

Dessen, Alan C. and Leslie Thomson, *A Dictionary of Stage Directions in English Drama, 1580–1642* (Cambridge University Press, 1999).

Dillon, Janette, "From Scaffold to Discovery-Space: Change and Continuity" in *Medieval Shakespeare*, ed. Ruth Morse, Helen Cooper and Peter Holland (Cambridge University Press, 2013).

Duffy Eamon, *The Stripping of the Altars* (New Haven, CT: Yale University Press, 1992).

Egan, Gabriel, "Reconstructions of the Globe: A Retrospective," *Shakespeare Survey*, 52 (1999), 1–16.

Ewbank, Inga-Stina, "The Triumph of Time in *The Winter's Tale*," *Review of English Literature*, 5 (1964), 83–100.

Fabiny, Tibor, "'Veritas Filia Temporis': The Iconography of Time and Truth and Shakespeare," *Acta Litteraria Academiae Scientiarum Hungaricae*, 26 (1984), 61–98.

Fitzpatrick, Tim, *Playwright, Space and Place in Early Modern Performance* (Farnham, Surrey; Burlington, VT: Ashgate, 2011).

Fitzpatrick, Tim and Wendy Millyard, "Hangings, Doors and Discoveries: Conflicting Evidence or Problematic Assumptions?" *Theatre Notebook*, 54 (2000), 2–23.

Foakes, R. A., "Henslowe's Rose/Shakespeare's Globe" in *From Script to Stage in Early Modern England*, ed. Peter Holland and Stephen Orgel (Basingstoke: Palgrave Macmillan, 2004).

Illustrations of the English Stage 1580–1642 (London: Scolar Press, 1985).

Foakes, R. A., ed., *The Revenger's Tragedy* (Manchester University Press, 1966).

Foakes, R. A. and R. T. Rickert, eds., *Henslowe's Diary* (Cambridge University Press, 1961).

Freeburg, Victor Oscar, *Disguise Plots in Elizabethan Drama* (New York, NY: Columbia University Press, 1915; reissued, Benjamin Blom, 1965).

Frye, Northrop, *The Great Code* (Middlesex: Penguin, 1990).

Gleason, John. B., "The Dutch Humanist Origins of The De Witt Drawing of the Swan Theatre," *Shakespeare Quarterly*, 32 (1981), 324–38, doi.org/10.2307/2870249.

Gordon, Donald, "'Veritas Filia Temporis': Hadrianus Junius and Geoffrey Whitney," *Journal of the Warburg and Courtauld Institutes*, 3 (1940), 228–40, doi.org/10.2307/750275.

Graham-Dixon, Andrew, "In the Picture," *The Sunday Telegraph*, 2 March 2003; Andrew Graham-Dixon Archive (andrewgrahamdixon.com/archive/itp-150-the-fight-between-carnival-and-lent-by-pieter-bruegel-the-elder.html).

Graves, R. B., *Lighting the Shakespearean Stage, 1567–1642* (Carbondale and Edwardsville, IL: Southern Illinois University Press, 1999).

Greg, W. W., *Dramatic Documents from the Elizabethan Playhouses*, 2 vols. (Oxford University Press, 1931).

Greenfield, Jon with assistance from Peter McCurdy, "Practical Evidence for a Reimagined Indoor Jacobean Theatre" in *Moving Shakespeare Indoors*, ed. Andrew Gurr and Farah Karim-Cooper (Cambridge University Press, 2014), doi.org/10.1017/cbo9781139629195.004.

Gurr, Andrew, "The Bare Island," *Shakespeare Survey*, 47 (1994), 29–44, doi.org/10.1017/ccol0521470846.003.

"Doors at the Globe," *Theatre Notebook*, 55 (2001), 59–71.

"The Rose Repertory: What the Plays Might Tell Us about the Stage" in *New Issues in the Reconstruction of Shakespeare's Theatre* (New York, NY: Peter Lang, 1990).

The Shakespearean Stage 1574–1642 (Cambridge University Press, 1970; revised and reprinted 1980, 1991, 2009).

"Staging at the Globe" in *Shakespeare's Globe Rebuilt*, ed. J. R. Mulryne and Margaret Shewring (Cambridge University Press, 1997).

"Why the Globe Is Famous," in *The Oxford Handbook of Early Modern Theatre*, ed. Richard Dutton (Oxford University Press, 2009), doi.org/10.1093/oxfordhb/9780199697861.013.0012.

Gurr, Andrew and Farah Karim-Cooper, eds., *Moving Shakespeare Indoors* (Cambridge University Press, 2014), doi.org/10.1017/cb09781139629195.

Gurr, Andrew and Mariko Ichikawa, *Staging in Shakespeare's Theatres* (Oxford University Press, 2000).

Hamblin, William J. and David Rolph Seely, *Solomon's Temple* (Thames and Hudson, 2007).

Harbage, Alfred, *Annals of English Drama, 975–1700*, revised by S. Schoenbaum, third edition revised by Sylvia Stoler Wagonheim (London and New York, NY: Routledge, 1989).

Hemeldonck, G. van, "Ciborium (ii)," *Grove Art Online, Oxford Art Online* (Oxford University Press).

Higgott, Gordon, "Reassessing the Drawings for the Inigo Jones Theatre: A Restoration Project by John Webb?" Paper based on a lecture given at a conference at Shakespeare's Globe, 13 February 2005, bristol.ac.uk/drama/jacobean/research4.html.

Hodges, C. Walter, *The Globe Restored* (London: Ernest Benn, 1953).

Hodges, Devon, *Renaissance Fictions of Anatomy* (Amherst, MA: University of Massachusetts Press, 1985).

Höfele, Andreas, "John Foxe, *Christus Triumphans*" in *The Oxford Handbook of Tudor Drama*. ed. Thomas Betteridge and Greg Walker (Oxford University Press, 2012), doi.org/10.1093/oxfordhb/9780199566471.013.0008.

Hollander, Martha, *An Entrance for the Eyes: Space and Meaning in Seventeenth-Century Dutch Art* (Berkeley: University of California Press, 2002).

The Holy Bible, Authorized King James Version (London and New York: Collins, nd).

Hosley, Richard, "The Discovery-Space in Shakespeare's Globe," *Shakespeare Survey*, 12 (1959), 35–46, doi.org/10.1017/ccol0521064252.005.

"The Origins of the Shakespearian Playhouse," *Shakespeare Quarterly*, 15 (1964), 29–39, doi.org/10.2307/2867872.

"The Playhouses" in *The Revels History of Drama in English*, vol. 3, 1576–1613, ed. J. Leeds Barroll, Alexander Leggatt, Richard Hosley and Alvin Kernan (London: Methuen, 1975).

"A Reconstruction of the Second Blackfriars" in *Elizabethan Theatre II*, ed. David Galloway (Toronto: Macmillan, 1969).

"The Staging of Desdemona's Bed," *Shakespeare Quarterly*, 14 (1963), 57–65, doi .org/10.2307/2868138.

Howard-Hill, Trevor, ed., *A Game at Chess* (Manchester University Press, 1993).

Howarth, David, *Images of Rule: Art and Politics in the English Renaissance* (Berkeley, CA: University of California Press), 1997.

Hoy, Cyrus, *Introductions, Notes, and Commentaries* to texts in "*The Dramatic Works of Thomas Dekker*," ed. Fredson Bowers, vol. II (Cambridge University Press, 1979).

Humphries, A. R., ed., *Much Ado About Nothing* (London: Methuen, 1984).

Hyde, Mary Crapo, *Playwriting for Elizabethans, 1600–1605* (New York, NY: Columbia University Press, 1949).

Hyland, Peter, *Disguise on the Early Modern English Stage* (Farnham, Surrey and Burlington, VT: Ashgate, 2011), doi.org/10.4324/9781315577562.

Ichikawa, Mariko, *Shakespearean Entrances* (Basingstoke and New York, NY: Palgrave Macmillan, 2002).

Jackson, MacDonald P., ed., *The Revenger's Tragedy* in *Thomas Middleton, The Collected Works*, ed. Gary Taylor, John Lavagnino, and John Jowett (Oxford University Press, 2007).

Jones, Oliver, "Documentary Evidence for an Indoor Jacobean Theatre" in *Moving Shakespeare Indoors*, ed. Andrew Gurr and Farah Karim-Cooper (Cambridge University Press, 2014), doi.org/10.1017/cbo9781139629195.005.

Jupin, Arvin H., ed., *"Mucedorus": A Contextual Study and Modern Spelling Edition* (New York, NY: Garland, 1987).

Kiefer, Frederick, "Curtains on the Shakespearean Stage," *Medieval and Renaissance Drama in England*, 20 (2007), 151–86.

Shakespeare's Visual Theatre: Staging the Personified Characters (Cambridge University Press, 2003).

Kiernan, Pauline, *Staging Shakespeare at the New Globe* (Macmillan, 1999), doi.org/10.1057/9780230380158.

King, T. J., *Shakespearean Staging, 1599–1642* (Cambridge, MA: Harvard University Press, 1971).

"The Stage in the Time of Shakespeare: A Survey of Major Scholarship," *Renaissance Drama*, n.s. IV (1971), 199–235, doi.org/10.1086/rd.4.41917083.

Klausner, David, ed., *Two Moral Interludes,* The Pride of Life *and* Wisdom, Introduction d.lib.rochester.edu/teams/text/klausner-two-moral-interludes-the-pride-of-life#303.

Knowles, James, "Cecil's Shopping Centre: The Rediscovery of a Ben Jonson Masque in Praise of Trade," *Times Literary Supplement* (7 February 1997), 14–15.

"Jonson's *Entertainment at Britain's Burse*" in *Re-presenting Ben Jonson*, ed. Martin Butler (Houndmills, Basingstoke: Macmillan, 1999).

Lane, Barbara G., "'Ecce Panis Angelorum': The Manger as Altar in Hugo's Berlin Nativity," *The Art Bulletin*, 57 (1975), 476–86, doi.org/10.1080/00043079.1975.10787210.

The Altar and the Altarpiece: Sacramental Themes in Early Netherlandish Painting (New York, NY: Harper and Row, 1984).

Lancashire, Anne, ed., *The Second Maiden's Tragedy* (Manchester University Press; Baltimore, MD: Johns Hopkins University Press, 1978).

Long, William B., "'A bed / for woodstock': A Warning for the Unwary," *Medieval and Renaissance Drama in England*, 2 (1985), 91–118.

Lopez, Jeremy, *Theatrical Convention and Audience Response in Early Modern Drama* (Cambridge University Press, 2003), doi.org/10.1017/cbo9780511483714.

Low, Jennifer A., "Behind Closed Doors: Perspective and Painterly Technique on the Early Modern English Stage" in *Shakespeare Expressed*, ed. Kathryn M. Moncrief, Kathryn R. McPherson and Sarah Enloe (Madison, NJ: Fairleigh Dickinson University Press, 2013).

Massey, Dawn, "*Veritas filia Temporis*: Apocalyptic Polemics in the Drama of the English Reformation," *Comparative Drama*, 32 (1998–9), 146–75, doi.org/10.1353/cdr.1998.0033.

Maus, Katharine Eisaman, *Inwardness and Theater in the English Renaissance* (University of Chicago Press, 1995).

McCarthy, Jeanne H., "'The Sanctuarie Is Become a Plaiers Stage': Chapel Stagings and Tudor 'Secular' Drama," *Medieval and Renaissance Drama in England*, 21 (2008), 56–86.

McGavin, John, and Greg Walker, *Imagining Spectatorship* (Oxford University Press, 2016), doi.org/10.1093/acprof:oso/9780198768616.001.0001.

McGee, C. E., ed., *The World Tossed at Tennis* in *Thomas Middleton, The Collected Works*, ed. Gary Taylor, John Lavagnino, and John Jowett (Oxford University Press, 2007).

McMillin, Scott, *The Elizabethan Theatre and "The Book of Sir Thomas More"* (Ithaca, NY and London: Cornell University Press, 1987).

"The Rose and the Swan" in *The Development of Shakespeare's Theater*, ed. John H. Astington (New York, NY: AMS Press, 1992).

McMillin, Scott and Sally-Beth MacLean, *The Queen's Men and Their Plays* (Cambridge University Press, 1998).

Meads, Chris, *Banquets Set Forth* (Manchester University Press, 2001).

Meagher, John C., "The First Progress of Henry VII," *Renaissance Drama*, 1 (1968), 45–73.

Menzer, Paul and Ralph Alan Cohen, "Introduction: Shakespeare Inside and Out" in *Inside Shakespeare*, ed. Paul Menzer (Cranbury, NJ: Associated University Presses, 2006).

Meredith, Peter and John E. Tailby, eds., *The Staging of Religious Drama in Europe in the Later Middle Ages: Texts and Documents in English Translation* (Kalamazoo, MI: Medieval Institute Publications, 1983).

Miles, Rosalind, *The Problem of "Measure for Measure"* (London: Vision Press, 1976).

Montrose, Louis, "Idols of the Queen: Policy, Gender, and the Picturing of Elizabeth I," *Representations*, 68 (1999), 108–61.

Neill, Michael, *Issues of Death: Mortality and Identity in English Renaissance Tragedy* (Oxford: Clarendon Press, 1997), doi.org/10.1093/acprof:oso/9780198183860.001.0001.

Nicoll, Allardyce, *Stuart Masques and the Renaissance Stage* (London: George G. Harrap and Co., 1938).

OED Online (Oxford University Press, September 2016).

Ogden, Dunbar, *The Staging of Drama in the Medieval Church* (Newark, DE: University of Delaware Press; London: Associated University Presses, 2002).

Orgel, Stephen, *Ben Jonson: The Complete Masques* (New Haven, CT: Yale University Press, 1969).

The Jonsonian Masque (Cambridge, MA: Harvard University Press, 1965).

Orlin, Lena Cowen, "Gertrude's Closet," *Shakespeare Jahrbuch*, 134 (1998), 44–67.

Locating Privacy in Tudor London (Oxford University Press, 2007).

Private Matters and Public Culture in Post-Reformation England (Ithaca, NY and London: Cornell University Press, 1994).

Panofsky, Erwin, *Early Netherlandish Painting*, vol. 1 (Cambridge, MA: The President and Fellows of Harvard College, 1953).

Studies in Iconology: Humanistic Themes in the Art of the Renaissance (New York, NY: Harper and Row, 1972).

Pearlman, E., "R. Willis and The Cradle of Security (c. 1572)," *English Literary Renaissance*, 20 (1990), 357–73.

Quarmby, Kevin A., *The Disguised Ruler in Shakespeare and His Contemporaries* (Ashgate, 2012), doi.org/10.4324/9781315615592.

Reynolds, G. F., *On Shakespeare's Stage*, ed. Richard K. Kraub (Boulder, CO: University of Colorado Press, 1967).

The Staging of Elizabethan Plays at the Red Bull Theater, 1605–1625 (New York, NY: MLA, 1940).

Riely, Marianne Gateson, ed., *"The Whore of Babylon" by Thomas Dekker* (New York, NY and London: Garland, 1980).

Roberts, Sasha, "'Let Me the Curtains Draw': The Dramatic and Symbolic Properties of the Bed in Shakespearean Tragedy" in *Staged Properties in Early Modern English Drama*, ed. Jonathan Gil Harris and Natasha Korda (Cambridge University Press, 2002).

Robortellus, Franciscus, "On Comedy" in *Comic Theory in the Sixteenth Century*, trans. Marvin T. Herrick (Urbana, IL: University of Illinois Press, 1964).

Rutter, Carol Chillington, ed., *Documents of the Rose Playhouse*, rev. ed. (Manchester University Press, 1999).

Sargent, Roussel, "Theme and Structure in Middleton's *A Game at Chess*," *Modern Language Review*, 66 (1971), 721–30, doi.org/10.2307/3722976.

Saunders, Claire, "'Dead in His Bed': Shakespeare's Staging of the Death of the Duke of Gloucester in *2 Henry VI*," *Review of English Studies*, n.s. 36 (1985), 19–34, doi.org/10.1093/res/xxxvi.141.19.

Sawday, Jonathan, *The Body Emblazoned* (London and New York, NY: Routledge, 1995), doi.org/10.4324/9781315887753.

Saxl, Fritz, "Veritas Filia Temporis" in *Philosophy and History: Essays Presented to Ernst Cassirer*, ed. Raymond Klibansky and H. J. Paton (Oxford: Clarendon Press, 1936).

Schmidt, Suzanne Karr and Kimberly Nichols, *Altered and Adorned: Using Renaissance Prints in Daily Life* (New Haven, CT: Art Institute of Chicago and London: Yale University Press, 2011).

Schofield, John, ed., *The London Surveys of Ralph Treswell* (London: London Topographical Society, 1987).

Seneca, Lucius Annaeus, *Letters from a Stoic*, Volume II, trans. Richard Mott Gummere (1920) in *Seneca Six Pack 2* (Los Angeles: Enhanced Media, 2016).

Shakespeare, William, *The Norton Facsimile: The First Folio of Shakespeare*, prep. by Charlton Hinman, second edition, with a new introduction by Peter W. M. Blayney (New York, NY: W. W. Norton, 1996).

Shapiro, Michael, *Gender in Play on the Shakespearean Stage* (Ann Arbor, MI: University of Michigan Press, 1994).

Shohet, Lauren, *Reading Masques* (Oxford, 2010), doi.org/10.1093/acprof:oso/97 80199295890.001.0001.

Smith, Bruce R., *The Key of Green: Passion and Perception in Renaissance Culture* (University of Chicago Press, 2009), doi.org/10.7208/chicago/9780226763811 .001.0001.

Smith, Irwin, *Shakespeare's Blackfriars Playhouse* (New York University Press, 1964).

Snyder, Susan and Deborah Curren-Aquino, eds., *The Winter's Tale* (Cambridge University Press, 2007).

Southern, Richard, "On Reconstructing a Practicable Elizabethan Public Playhouse," *Shakespeare Survey*, 12 (1959), 22–34. doi.org/10.1017/cco lo521064252.004.

The Seven Ages of the Theatre (New York, NY: Hill and Wang, 1961).

The Staging of Plays before Shakespeare (London: Faber, 1973).

Stern, Tiffany, "Actors' Parts" in *The Oxford Handbook of Early Modern Theatre*, ed. Richard Dutton (Oxford University Press, 2009), doi.org/10.1093/oxfor dhb/9780199697861.013.0030.

Streitberger, W. R., *Court Revels, 1485–1559* (University of Toronto Press, 1994).

Styan, J. L., *Shakespeare's Stagecraft* (Cambridge University Press, 1967).

Taylor, Gary, ed., *A Game at Chess: A Later Form* in *Thomas Middleton, The Collected Works*, ed. Gary Taylor, John Lavagnino, and John Jowett (Oxford University Press, 2007).

Thomson, Leslie, "'As Proper a Woman as Any in Cheap': Women in Shops on the Early Modern Stage," *Medieval and Renaissance Drama in England*, 16 (2003), 145–61.

"Beds on the Early Modern Stage," *Early Theatre*, 19 (2016), 31–57, doi.org/10 .12745/et.19.2.2923.

"Blackfriars Stage Sitters and the Staging of *The Tempest, The Maid's Tragedy* and *The Two Noble Kinsmen*" in *Shakespeare Embodied*, ed. Kathryn Moncrief, Kathryn McPherson and Sarah Enloe (Madison, NJ: Fairleigh Dickinson University Press, 2013), 175–85.

"Dumb Shows in Performance on the Early Modern Stage," *Medieval and Renaissance Drama in England*, 29 (2016), 17–45.

"Marlowe's Staging of Meaning," *Medieval and Renaissance Drama in England*, 18 (2005), 19–36.

"*Mucedorus:* From Revision to Nostalgia," *Theatre Notebook*, 71 (2017), 140–60.

"Staging on the Road, 1586–1594: A New Look at Some Old Assumptions," *Shakespeare Quarterly*, 61 (2010): 526–50.

Thorndike, Ashley H., "Appendix I: 'A List of Stage Directions Illustrating the Utse of the Curtains and the Inner Stage in Plays Acted 1576–1642'" in *Shakespeare's Theater* (New York, NY: Macmillan, 1916).

Thornton, Peter, *Seventeenth-Century Interior Decoration in England, France, and Holland* (New Haven, CT and London: Yale University Press for the Paul Mellon Centre for Studies in British Art, 1978).

Tilley, Morris Palmer, *A Dictionary of the Proverbs in England in the Sixteenth and Seventeenth Centuries* (Ann Arbor, MI: University of Michigan Press, 1950).

Tribble, Evelyn B., *Cognition in the Globe* (New York, NY: Palgrave Macmillan, 2011).

"Distributing Cognition in the Globe," *Shakespeare Quarterly*, 56 (2005), 135–55, doi.org/10.1353/shq.2005.0065.

Twycross, Meg and Sarah Carpenter, *Masks and Masking in Medieval and Early Tudor England* (Aldershot: Ashgate, 2002).

Tydeman, William, *The Theatre in the Middle Ages: Western European Stage Conditions, c. 800–1576* (Cambridge University Press, 1978).

Warkentin, Germaine, ed., *The Queen's Majesty's Passage and Related Documents* (Toronto: Centre for Reformation and Renaissance Studies, 2004).

Weiner, Albert, "Elizabethan Interior and Aloft Scenes: A Speculative Essay," *Theatre Survey*, 2 (1961), 15–34, doi.org/10.1017/s0040557400006761.

Wickham, Glynne, *Early English Stages 1300 to 1660*, 3 vols. (London: Routledge and Kegan Paul; New York, NY: Columbia University Press, 1963).

"The Stage and Its Surroundings" in *The Third Globe*, ed. C. Walter Hodges, S. Schoenbaum, and Leonard Leone (Detroit, MI: Wayne State University Press, 1981), 136–50.

Wiggins, Martin and Catherine Richardson, *British Drama, 1533–1642: A Catalogue*, vols. I–VII (Oxford University Press, 2012–2016).

Williamson, Elizabeth, *The Materiality of Religion in Early Modern English Drama* (Farnham, Surrey and Burlington, VT: Ashgate, 2006).

Wilson, Jean, *The Archaeology of Shakespeare* (Stroud: Alan Sutton, 1997).

Yamada, Akihiro, ed., *The Widow's Tears* (London: Methuen, 1975).

Young, Karl, "*Officium Pastorum*: A Study of the Dramatic Developments within the Liturgy of Christmas," *Transactions of the Wisconsin Academy of Sciences, Arts and Letters*, 17 (1911), 299–396.

Zuker, David Hard, *Stage and Image in the Plays of Christopher Marlowe* (Salzburg: Salzburg Studies in English Literature, 1972).

Index

For EU product safety concerns, contact us at Calle de José Abascal, 56–1°,
28003 Madrid, Spain or eugpsr@cambridge.org.